Everyday Life During the Civil War

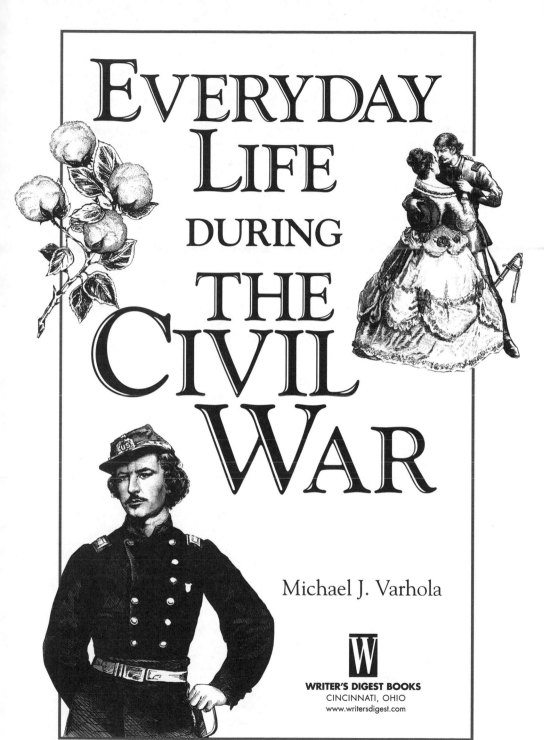

EVERYDAY LIFE
DURING
THE
CIVIL
WAR

Michael J. Varhola

WRITER'S DIGEST BOOKS
CINCINNATI, OHIO
www.writersdigest.com

Other fine Writer's Digest Books are available from your local bookstore or direct from the publisher.

Visit our Web site at www.writersdigest.com for information on more resources for writers.

To receive a free weekly E-mail newsletter delivering tips and updates about writing and about Writer's Digest products, send an E-mail with ''Subscribe Newsletter'' in the body of the message to newsletter-request@writersdigest.com, or register directly at our Web site at www.writersdigest.com.

05   04   03   02   01   6   5   4   3   2

Library of Congress Cataloging-in-Publication Data

Varhola, Michael J.
   Everyday life during the Civil War / by Michael J. Varhola.
     p.   cm.
   Includes bibliographical references and index.
   ISBN 0-89879-922-8 (pbk.: alk. paper)
   1. United States—History—Civil War, 1861-1865—Social aspects. 2. United States—Social life and customs—1783-1865. I. Title.
E468.9 .V37   1999
973.7′1 21—dc21   99-045940
                                                 CIP

Editor: David Borcherding
Production editor: Michelle Howry
Cover designer: Kathy DeZarn
Interior designer: Sandy Conopeotis Kent
Production coordinator: John Peavler
Author photo: Chip Cassano

DEDICATION

To my father, mother and brother, each of whom has contributed to my love of history in his or her own way.

ACKNOWLEDGMENTS

A number of people helped me successfully complete this book. Foremost among them is my wife, Diane, who, despite her protestations to the contrary, really did know what "benign neglect" meant most of the time.

Other people who made valuable contributions include Les Albers, whose background as a teacher and a reenactor allowed him to help me with some of the more esoteric aspects of this work, and some of his students, who offered their comments on parts of the book; Scott O'Connell, who brought his experience as a military historian and publisher to proofing and fact-checking some of the chapters; my University of Maryland University College colleagues, especially writer Chip Cassano, who on more than one occasion covered things at the office so that I could stay home to work on this book when I needed to, and editor Lynn Walter, whose feedback and comments were most appreciated; Writer's Digest editor Dave Borcherding, who helped me stay focused and keep this project on track; Lee Hadden, who demonstrated his prowess as a deadline writer by authoring a foreword for this book with very little notice; writer Larry Cywin, whose articles on nineteenth-century gardening and produce proved very useful to me; expert reader Christopher Anderson, many of whose comments helped ensure the integrity of this work; Scott T. Price of the U.S. Coast Guard Historian's Office, who very graciously provided information and resources for the section on the Revenue Cutter Service; Scott Gutzke, who helped track down information about the numbers of people involved in Civil War reenacting; Sharon Daugherty, who assisted me with the tedious job of indexing; and my daughter, Lindsey, who spent thirty minutes keying in notes for me and insisted she be listed here in return.

If there is anyone I have left out, I sincerely beg their forgiveness and thank them for their help.

ABOUT THE AUTHOR

 Michael J. Varhola is a writer and editor whose interests include international affairs, military history, travel, wargaming, and world cultures. He has written a number of other books, including *Fire and Ice: The Korean War, 1950-1953* (Savas Publishing, 2000), and contributed to *The Writer's Complete Fantasy Reference* (Writer's Digest, 1998).

Varhola has founded or helped run several print publications, notably *Living History* magazine; ran a Middle East newsire based in Washington, D.C.; and has written articles or columns for dozens of publications, including *Renaissance*, *The Unspeakable Oath*, and *Dragon*.

He also runs a number of Web sites, including Living History Online (http://www.LivingHistoryOnline.com), KoreanWar.net (http://www.KoreanWar.net), and Skirmisher Online Gaming Magazine (http://www.skirmisher.com).

Before devoting his life to publishing, Varhola served as a U.S. Army infantryman for eight years. During the Cold War, he was a member of the 1st Infantry Division (Forward) in Stuttgart, Germany, and during Desert Storm he was part of a Civil Affairs team attached to the 3rd Armored Division in Saudi Arabia and Iraq.

After studying psychology at Metropolitan State College in Denver, Colorado, and European Culture at the American University of Paris in France, Varhola earned a B.S. in journalism from the University of Maryland, College Park.

Varhola has lived throughout the United States, in Pennsylvania, California, Colorado, Georgia, Maryland, New Mexico, North Carolina, and Virginia, and finally settled in the Washington, D.C., area in 1991. He has also lived overseas, in Belgium, France, Germany, and Greece.

ILLUSTRATIONS

TABLE OF CONTENTS

FOREWORD

History, whether as formal classroom learning in school or the casual reading by armchair historians, is an intellectual discipline. An understanding of history demonstrates a logical progression in thinking, and requires analysis and interpretation of events, people and trends. The importance of knowing about everyday life during any period of history, therefore, cannot be overemphasized. This is especially true of the Civil War period, an era in which political, economic, social and moral pressures divided a nation.

History without interpretation is simply a sterile listing of facts. Interpretation without facts is merely fantasy. Like an interpreter between two languages, the historian and historical writer must truthfully interpret the meanings of human events and interactions to audiences who do not necessarily have a common basis of experience. More than a translator of facts, the writer as interpreter must also present the tone and implications of the speaker to those who do not understand the language.

The student's connection between information and his insights in to the meaning of that information is one of the greatest intellectual pleasures the world holds. This is what makes history come alive. To help the student make the connections and relate what he has learned to what he understands is the mark of a good interpreter. This is the challenge for the historian, the writer and the teacher.

The history of any people is the sum of their personalities and experiences as shaped by various events and stimuli. Without a knowledge and understanding of how people lived and thought, the interpretation of their times cannot be internalized or comprehended by the reader or student.

Humans are enormously intuitive, and a good historian or writer knows how to blend the everyday life of the individual into the telling of his story. But to accomplish this, the historian needs a solid grounding in the facts of the everyday life of past times. To understand the soldier of the Civil War and to tell his story well, the writer needs to explain the soldier's world to the reader—the economy, life, language and patterns of thought that combined to make him a complex and three-dimensional person. Civil War soldiers did things differently from Americans today, and to understand their actions we need to know how they lived and how they were different from us.

Defining a fence rail and explaining how hard it was to cut, trim and split trees into rails, and how many fence rails were needed each year for even a small farm, does much to explain the popular attraction of Abe Lincoln as the "rail-splitter president." A good historical writer knows the need for this kind of written explanation and interpretation in telling the story of American politics. Rail splitting for fences was an everyday life event known by almost everyone in mid-nineteenth-century America, yet that experience is almost totally unknown to people today. The historian must bridge the gap in knowledge and understanding between the world that was and the world that is.

It is even more important that fiction writers know the everyday life of the world they are writing about. The background and atmosphere of everyday life in a tale give shape and structure to characterization and plot. Without an accurate background in things like clothing or housing, the reader will not have a place to put the characters and events in context, and will soon lose interest in the writer's story.

Many writers from the past are still popular today, in part because they interpret and describe so well the everyday world their characters lived in. Laura Ingalls Wilder and Mark Twain are noted for their abilities to describe life in nineteenth-century America in ways that are easily understood today by both adults and children. Whether it is describing the common summer chore of a boy whitewashing a board fence in Missouri or a little girl breaking the ice in the sink before washing her face and hands during a Wisconsin winter, good writers evoke and interpret an everyday world that any reader can instinctively understand. The background of everyday life is the stimuli characters respond to, and they show their abilities, likability and personality as they interact with others to this stimulus. Even readers who have never taken a cold shower can shiver when reading about washing hands in icy water. The task of the fiction writer is to lead the reader by the hand through a world that does not exist.

Everyday Life During the Civil War is an account of how and why Americans lived the way they did during one of America's greatest conflicts. Writers, historians and students need this sort of background material to understand the thinking and motivations of the individuals touched by the greatest social conflict our nation has ever experienced. Mr. Varhola ably sketches the civilian and military scene in our country during the American Civil War. His book is a prologue to understanding and interpreting the individuals, events and results of the horrendous four years that forever changed the shape of our people's character and molded the direction of our country's future.

R. Lee Hadden, 1999
Author of *Reliving the Civil War: A Reenactor's Handbook*

INTRODUCTION

The Civil War has captivated the interest of people in the United States and beyond more than any other episode in U.S. history. Over the course of four years, this conflict evolved from unpredictable political turmoil into a massive total war that claimed the lives of more than 600,000 Americans (more than all U.S. personnel killed in World War I, World War II, the Korean War and the Vietnam War combined). The Civil War arguably did more to influence the course of our nation than any other single event.

Today, an unprecedented number of people are interested in the American Civil War, fueling the creation of movies, documentaries, history books and novels about the Civil War. Movies like *Gettysburg* and *Glory* gained instant followings; Ken Burns' PBS documentary *The Civil War* is widely considered one of the best documentaries ever made; and novels about the Civil War, such as *The Killer Angels, Gods and Generals* and *Cold Mountain,* are regularly on the best-seller lists. Indeed, since the Civil War ended in 1865, more nonfiction books and novels have been written about it than about any other war involving the United States.

This fascination with the Civil War has persisted for more than 130 years and is not likely to fade any time soon. One reason for this fervent interest is the proximity of the war's events to the everyday lives of so many modern Americans.

Reminders of this are provided by streets still bearing the names that appear in period accounts of the war, by towns contested by the opposing armies and by cities and military posts named for the generals who led the opposing forces. People in Pennsylvania, Maryland, Virginia, North Carolina, South Carolina, Georgia and Washington, DC, drive to work and the store on the same roads massive armies marched along more than 130 years ago. Boaters cruise the same inland waterways, coasts and rivers that U.S. Navy ships guarded, desperate blockade runners plied by night and armored gunboats patrolled. Inhabitants of the Mississippi River Valley live within hours of the savage raids and battles of the war in the West. Citizens of places like Baltimore, Atlanta and New Orleans live in cities that were under military occupation. Indeed, the greatest, most destructive war ever seen in North America was fought on ground many of those citizens walk across every single day.

Everyday Life During the Civil War is intended to be a broad-based introduction to the day-to-day conditions, attitudes and events of the period. For some, this book may be the only tool they need to research the Civil War, or one of just a few, while for others it will serve as one resource among many and a guide toward finding more.

While the war was fought from 1861 to 1865, it is a bit contrived to imagine this period existed in a vacuum. Thus, the years 1859 to 1877 are also covered to some extent, from John Brown's raid on Harpers Ferry, Virginia, through the end of Reconstruction.

Resources provided in this book include an overview of the North and the South before, during and after the war; descriptions of life during the war, including what people ate, what they wore, the sort of work they did, how they entertained themselves and where they got their information; an overview of the opposing armies and the soldiers who fought in them; a time line that describes the major events and battles of the war and its aftermath in chronological order; examples of songs and poems composed during the Civil War; and resources readers can use to do further research into specific aspects of the Civil War.

Depending on the historical depth the reader seeks, additional information may be needed. For example, the time line covers all the major battles of the war, but only briefly. Thus, readers who seek information about specific military actions, such as battles or campaigns, should read more in-depth descriptions of them in history books or memoirs. In any case, this book will be a useful tool for anyone interested in one of the most fascinating episodes in American history.

CHAPTER ONE

NORTH AND SOUTH: ONE NATION, TWO PEOPLES

"Prior to my installation here, it had been inculcated that any State had a lawful right to secede from the national Union, and that it would be expedient to exercise that right whenever the devotees of the doctrine should fail to elect a President to their own liking; and, accordingly, so far as it was legally possible, they had taken seven States out of the Union, had seized many of the United States forts, and had fired upon the United States flag, all before I was inaugurated, and, of course, before I had done any official act whatever. The Rebellion thus begun soon ran into the present Civil War. . . ."
—President Abraham Lincoln, in a June 12, 1863, open letter to prominent Albany, New York, Democrat Erastus Corning.

When the Civil War erupted in early 1861, people in the North and the South had long regarded themselves as separate. Indeed, the customs, economies and philosophies of the two peoples were markedly different. Nonetheless, the two portions of the country had developed alongside each other, and were bound in ways that did not become apparent until they were locked in total war against each other.

During the war, the combined population of the two opposing nations was a bit more than thirty-one million people. From this relatively small population base (the population of the United States today, at the start of the twenty-first century, is nearly 300 million), the North ultimately put two million men into uniform, the South one million. With three million men under arms, the combined Union and Confederate militaries were proportionately about twenty times larger than the active duty U.S. armed forces today, which number about 1.4 million personnel (i.e., nearly 10 percent of the population during the Civil War vs. about half of one percent of the population today).

By May 1861, the country was divided into nineteen states that had declared loyalty to the Union; four slave states that had not seceded but were at risk of trying to leave the Union and were essentially neutral until January 1863; eleven Confederate states; and a number of large, unorganized U.S. government territories—their number varied during the war, as new territories were partitioned from larger ones.

Two more states were admitted to the Union after the war began, West Virginia in 1863 and Nevada in 1864, raising the number of states within the Union to twenty-five.

Union States: California, Connecticut, Illinois, Indiana, Iowa, Kansas, Maine, Massachusetts, Michigan, Minnesota, Nevada (1864), New Hampshire, New Jersey, New York, Ohio, Oregon, Pennsylvania, Rhode Island, Vermont, West Virginia (1863) and Wisconsin.

Border ("neutral" slave) states: Delaware, Maryland, Kentucky and Missouri.

Confederate States (in order of secession): South Carolina, Mississippi, Florida, Alabama, Georgia, Louisiana, Texas, Virginia, Arkansas, North Carolina and Tennessee.

Territories: Arizona Territory, Colorado Territory, Dakota Territory, Indian Territory, Nebraska Territory, New Mexico Territory, Utah Territory and Washington Territory.

THE NORTH

More than twenty-two million of the thirty-one million people living in America when the Civil War broke out lived in states that remained loyal to the Union.

The North was far more industrialized than the South and had within its borders some 100,000 factories, including almost all of the nation's shipyards and means of arms production. More than one million workers were employed in these factories. The Union also controlled most of the components of industry. These components included almost all the country's coal mines, which produced the fuel needed to run factories and steamships, and most of the canals, needed to transport coal and other heavy goods. And naturally, the North also controlled most of the fruits of industrialization, such as 70 percent of the country's railroads (22,385 miles) and about 95 percent of its rolling stock and railway equipment.

Despite the fact that it was so industrialized, the North was also largely self-sufficient in agriculture, and produced more than the South in every agricultural category except for cotton. Thus, it was not dependent upon the seceding states for food to feed its people.

Financially, the Union controlled more than 80 percent of the total U.S. bank deposits, about $189 million, and about 60 percent of the total gold reserves, or about $56 million worth of gold. These factors immeasurably helped the North finance a successful war effort.

Public primary education was fairly widespread in the Northern states, especially in urbanized areas, and many institutions of higher education had existed since Colonial times and continued to be established throughout the nineteenth century. As a result, Northerners enjoyed a relatively high level of education and literacy.

THE SOUTH

Only about nine million of the thirty-one million people living in the United States at the time of the Civil War lived in the South, and a third of them were slaves. This was a relatively small population for a region that, while smaller than the North, was still bigger than all of western Europe, about 750,000 square miles.

Industrially, the South was far behind the North, with only 20,000 factories (as compared to 100,000) employing some 100,000 workers (as opposed to more than one million workers in the North). Only 30 percent, or about 6,700 miles of the nation's railroads lay within the Confederacy, along with a mere 5 percent of its rolling stock and railway equipment.

While the South was not highly industrialized, it was not poor, either, and its major cash crop, cotton, afforded a high standard of living for many of its people. Nonetheless, at the outbreak of war the Confederacy controlled just under 20 percent of the country's total bank deposits, about $47 million, and about 40 percent of the total gold reserves, worth some $37 million.

Lack of industrialization and financing contributed greatly to the ruination of the South and its defeat during the Civil War.

Also, a short-sighted policy early in the war of withholding cotton from European markets in an attempt to make the European states support the Confederacy in exchange for an uninterrupted supply of cotton, backfired and deprived the South of much needed revenue. Some cloth manufacturers in

Great Britain had to shut down mills and fire workers, causing some elements to call for backing of the South to keep the peace among English workers and mill owners. Ultimately, however, Europe looked to other sources for cotton, such as Egypt; by the time the Confederacy reversed its policy, the Federal naval blockade ensured that little cotton could be successfully exported.

While public education had been established to some extent in the South, and while some of the country's oldest colleges were in the South, notably Virginia, such institutions were less widespread than in the North. In consequence, levels of education and literacy were much lower throughout the South than in the North.

UNION AND CONFEDERATE STATES

The following brief descriptions of the territories and the various Union and Confederate states will give writers an idea of prevailing conditions within each state and some taste of its unique flavor. These will point toward areas of further research, and help writers choose settings for stories and homes for characters and military units. Each state's geography and history before or after the war are outside the scope of this work, but are among the things writers might wish to further explore. Writers are encouraged to do more research on states they intend to use as primary settings for their stories. For example, the topography and climate of a state, information not provided here, can add color to a story.

One particularly interesting note is how many of the states on either side were settled or granted statehood only a few years before the war, a reminder that in the 1860s much of the United States was still unsettled frontier and sparsely populated farm country.

America's greatest cities also had distinct characters at the time of the Civil War, and writers can use them as stages for their characters and plots. Information on some of these cities is included in the descriptions of states.

The Union States
Following are brief overviews of the states that remained loyal to the Union during the Civil War. Slave states that remained within the Union are marked with an (S).

California
California was the westernmost state at the time of the Civil War. U.S. forces had invaded the region, then controlled by Mexico, in 1846, and officially acquired California two years later through the **Treaty of Guadalupe Hidalgo**. Although much of southern California was in favor of slavery, the entire state

remained loyal to the Union during the Civil War, which had little direct effect on the state.

While no troops were raised for combat in the East, five hundred California volunteers served with a Massachusetts unit. Volunteer regiments were raised to provide security within the state, fight in Arizona and New Mexico and garrison outposts in Washington and Oregon.

On January 24, 1848, gold was discovered at Sutter's Mill in northern California, sparking a gold rush that brought thousands of "forty-niners" into the state; by 1850, the state's non-Indian population had more than tripled to 93,000 inhabitants, and by 1860 was nearly 380,000, about 4,000 of whom were free blacks.

California was admitted to the Union in 1850 as a free state under the **Compromise of 1850**. Gold production declined in the early 1850s, and in the 1860s fruit, grain and wine making became important components of the state economy. In 1869, the first transcontinental railroad, linking Sacramento with the rest of the country, was completed.

California's 1849 constitution called for free statewide public education. Institutions of higher education included Mills College, the University of the Pacific, the University of San Francisco and Santa Clara University.

Connecticut

Connecticut abolished slavery in 1848, and most of its citizens opposed it at the start of the Civil War. About fifty-five thousand men from Connecticut fought for the Union during the war (eight thousand of them of Irish descent), and the state provided blankets, ammunition, firearms and several ships to the war effort. At the start of the war, the state's total population was around 460,000. About 8,600 of these people were free blacks.

Connecticut's economy grew markedly during the nineteenth century, with industry surpassing agriculture by the 1850s. Commerce, insurance and shipping were important components of the state's economy; Connecticut also manufactured brasswork, clocks, rubber goods and textiles. Industry continued to grow in the postwar years.

(S) Delaware

As one of the Mid-Atlantic states, it is fitting that in 1860 Delaware was a synthesis of the urbanized, industrial North and the more rural, agricultural South. Although a slave state, on the eve of the war Delaware had only about 1,800 slaves and more than ten times as many free blacks, out of a total population of more than 112,000. While its people remained divided over the issue of slavery during the war, most of them were moderates who supported the Union, and many soldiers from Delaware fought in the Union armed forces.

After the war, economic growth continued in Delaware, concentrated in the Wilmington area. Like many Southern states in the postwar years, Delaware vigorously opposed black rights through a variety of corrupt political tactics, including an 1873 poll tax.

Delaware had established public education in 1829, but it was underfunded, uneven in quality and excluded blacks.

Illinois

Illinois, home to U.S. President Abraham Lincoln, was populated by many first-and second-generation Southerners at the time of the Civil War, creating divided loyalties within the state. Like many midwestern states, it was a hotbed of Copperhead sentiment (see chapter six for more information).

Nonetheless, many Illinoisans were proud of their connection with Lincoln, and the state sent some 257,000 soldiers to fight for the Union, out of a total population of about 1,712,000 (it has been estimated that one-seventh of these soldiers died during the war). Illinois was also a major Northern source of iron products, meat and grain.

Indiana

Indiana had supported intensive development of its infrastructure in the decades prior to the Civil War, especially canals and railroads, nearly bankrupting itself in the process. In 1851, the state constitution responded by requiring the government to have a balanced budget at the end of each fiscal year.

Although many Indianans were of Southern origin, the state supported the Union war effort with matériel and more than 208,000 troops, out of a total population of about 1,350,000. Little action took place on Indiana soil, the major event being an 1863 raid led by Confederate Brig. Gen. John Hunt Morgan.

After the Civil War, farming, forestry and mining emerged as mainstays of the state's economy. Industrialization was facilitated by European immigrants who helped launch local glass, furniture, brick, steel and tile manufacturing industries.

America's first free kindergarten, trade school and coeducational teaching system were founded in New Harmony in the first half of the nineteenth century. Butler University, one of the country's first higher education institutions to admit women, was opened in 1855.

Iowa

Iowa entered the Union as a state in 1846, and at the time of the Civil War had a population of about 675,000 (a decade later, it nearly doubled to

1,194,000). All of the state's major communities, such as Cedar Falls and Iowa Falls, were built along rivers, railroads or both.

Initially Democratic, Iowa became staunchly Republican and abolitionist in 1856. In keeping with this tradition, many Iowans participated in the **Underground Railroad**, and the state sent a larger proportion of its men to fight in the Civil War than any other state except Massachusetts—nearly eighty thousand of them. No battles, however, were fought on Iowan soil.

Agriculture and commerce were dual mainstays of Iowa's economy in the mid-nineteenth century, and from its earliest days the state was commercially linked to the rest of the country. A preponderance of the state's citizens were settlers, and many eventually moved westward again. Iowa became fully settled after the war and the railroads improved, moving the state toward commercial rather than subsistence farming. Agrarian activity, such as the **Granger movement**, reacted to widespread distrust of banks and politicians and price gouging by the railroads.

Educational institutions at the time of the Civil War included the University of Iowa and Iowa State University of Science and Technology (a **land-grant** institution). The University of Northern Iowa was founded in 1876.

Kansas

Kansas was largely uninhabited by whites until the mid-1850s, when the local Indians were relocated to Oklahoma and the U.S. government opened it to settlement under the provisions of the 1854 **Kansas-Nebraska Act**. The act stipulated that the question of whether a territory would be admitted as a slave state or a free state would be decided by a popular referendum.

Abolitionist and proslavery organizations each began pushing for immigration by sympathizers to their causes, and by 1855 the proponents of these rival camps had established opposing governments. Violence eventually broke out between the two factions and escalated, giving the territory the nickname "**bleeding Kansas**"; prior to his final battle at Harpers Ferry, Virginia, rabid abolitionist John Brown had been deeply involved in this violence.

Conflict continued both within the territory and in the U.S. Congress until January 29, 1861, when Kansas was finally admitted to the Union as a free state. Savage guerrilla raids characterized the Civil War in Kansas, directed against soldiers and civilians alike along the border with Missouri. About 107,000 people lived in Kansas at the outbreak of the Civil War.

Thousands of immigrants flocked to the state in the 1870s, including many Germans, Swedes and Russians, sparking a major land boom. German-Russian Mennonites brought winter wheat to Kansas, transforming the face of agriculture in the state.

Institutes of higher education included the University of Kansas (1866), Kansas State University (1863) and Emporia State University (1863).

(S) Kentucky

Kentucky, a slave state on the border between the North and South, tried to stay neutral during the Civil War. However, its strategic positioning and the divided loyalties of its citizens made this impossible.

Agriculture was the basis of Kentucky's economy at the start of the Civil War. Farmers, who wanted access to the port of New Orleans via the Mississippi River, opposed secession because they believed commerce would be impeded by it. On the other hand, plantation owners and advocates of states rights favored separation from the Union. As a result, the Civil War really was a "brothers' war" for Kentucky, which sent regiments of troops to fight for both the Union and the Confederacy. From a population of just over 1,155,000, about 75,000 Kentuckians served in the Union forces, while about 35,000 fought for the Confederacy (marking Kentucky as a Rebel state in the eyes of many Northerners).

A Confederate army invaded Kentucky in 1861 but was driven out in October 1862. After that, the Confederacy contested ownership of the state largely through cavalry raids and guerilla warfare.

Kentucky changed both economically and socially after the war ended. Hemp was replaced by tobacco as the major cash crop, expansion of the railroads stimulated coal mining in the eastern part of the state, and major urban areas grew as manufacturing and industry increased in the northern end of the state.

Kentucky's first school opened in 1775, and a public school system was established by the state legislature in 1838. Higher education institutions included Transylvania Seminary, chartered in 1780, the University of Louisville, founded in 1798, and the University of Kentucky, established in 1865.

Maine

Maine was a prosperous shipbuilding and trade center at the time of the Civil War, conducting a brisk seaborne trade in lumber with Asia, Europe and the West Indies.

At the outbreak of the war, Maine had a population of about 628,000. About 73,000 of its men served in the Union military during the Civil War (some 6,700 in the navy and Marine Corps), and nearly one in ten of them was killed. Maine also contributed significant amounts of supplies for the Union cause during the war.

After the Civil War ended, the mainstays of Maine's economy shifted from the coastal regions and agriculture, shipping and lumbering, to manufacturing in the interior. State, local and private interests expanded the state's infrastructure, notably roads and streets, lighting and electricity, libraries and education, and public transportation and communication systems. Population growth slowed during this period, despite the considerable numbers of French Canadians and Irish who came to the state.

Maine's institutions of higher education included Bowdoin College (1794), Colby College (1813) and Bates College (1855).

(S) Maryland

Maryland was a synthesis of the North and South during the Civil War. Like many Southern states, it had a rural economy (based on large tobacco plantations in the east and small farms in the west), but like Northern states it thrived on trade and manufacturing. Baltimore was a vital port, becoming a shipbuilding and industrial center that rivalled Boston, New York and Philadelphia. It had a population of more than 170,000 at the time of the Civil War (overall, the state's population was about 687,000). Equal numbers of free and enslaved blacks lived within the state.

Maryland had strong Southern sympathies and was leaning toward secession in 1861. Maryland in general, and Baltimore in particular, was incredibly important to the Federal war effort because of its role as a major port and rail hub and because of its proximity to Washington, DC. To prevent its loss to the Union, Lincoln garrisoned Baltimore with soldiers throughout the war. Fort McHenry, site of the British siege that inspired Francis Scott Key to compose the national anthem, was occupied by Federal troops and used as a stronghold to control the city. Baltimoreans responded with civil unrest and rioting, and on more than one occasion troops were attacked in the streets, resulting in both civilian and military casualties.

Confederate destruction of Maryland property cooled sympathy for the Southern cause amongst those financially affected by such actions. For example, in June 1861, Confederate Maj. Gen. Joseph Johnston ordered the destruction in the Shenandoah Valley of 42 locomotives and 386 cars owned by the Baltimore and Ohio Railroad, ostensibly to keep them from falling into Union hands. This inflicted total losses of more than $1 million on the company and its stockholders.

Some of the heaviest fighting of the war took place on Maryland soil, including the 1862 battles of South Mountain and Antietam and the Battle of Monocacy in 1864.

Industrialization expanded rapidly after the war and eventually became the mainstay of the state's economy. Thousands of rural blacks and immigrants from Germany, Greece, Italy, Poland and Russia came to Baltimore seeking jobs in the city's factories.

Statewide education was established in Maryland in 1826, but, naturally, excluded blacks. In 1867, a separate school system was established for black students.

Massachusetts

Massachusetts enjoyed a period of prosperity in the decades leading to the Civil War. Agriculture remained important during this period and continued to spread into the state's hilly interior. All of its main cities were connected by toll roads, canals or railroads, and its textile and shoe industries began to grow and dominate the state's economy.

Indeed, many Irish arrived in the state in the 1840s and took jobs in the textile mills, which had originally been operated by people recruited from the state's farms. Many factory towns doubled their populations in less than a decade. As natural water power proved inadequate for the needs of the mills, it was increasingly replaced with coal-powered steam engines. Living and working conditions were often substandard, and unrest began to grow among many workers.

Massachusetts, long a center of abolitionism, entered the Civil War enthusiastically. Many troops from the state fought for the Union cause, including the now-famous Fifty-fourth Massachusetts Infantry Regiment, the first all-black unit (except for officers) sanctioned by the government. Altogether, about 160,000 served in the Union army, plus more in the navy than from any other state except New York. Massachusetts also provided huge numbers of blankets, guns, tents and shoes to the Federal war effort.

Nearly every system of education currently used in the United States originated in Massachusetts before or during the nineteenth century. Boston Latin School, the nation's first public secondary school, opened in 1635; Harvard, the first college, was founded in 1636; laws making education compulsory were passed from 1642 onward; the first vocational school was established in 1821; and the first high school for girls opened in 1826.

Michigan

Michigan sent more than 90,000 military-age men to fight for the Union during the Civil War, and about 14,000 of them were killed during the conflict. The labor shortages this created fostered many labor-saving devices in the state's industries, laying the way for large-scale industrialization.

During and after the war, farming of wheat, potatoes and hops; sheep raising; and lumbering were staples of Michigan's economy. Loggers in Michigan cleared vast tracts of timber in the years following the Civil War, annihilating the state's virgin forests in a few decades.

Public education has been important in Michigan since 1787 when the Northwest Ordinance called for the state to "encourage education." America's first state primary school fund was established in 1837, free primary schooling was made available in 1869, and in 1874 the state supreme court upheld the legality of using local taxes to pay for the establishment of high schools. The *Detroit News* was one of the state's principal newspapers in the mid-nineteenth century.

Minnesota

Minnesota, admitted to the Union as a state in 1858, had a population of about 172,000 at the time of the Civil War and an economy based on lumbering, milling and wheat farming. Altogether, more than twenty thousand Minnesotans fought for the Union.

While no battles against Confederate forces took place on Minnesota soil, the state did suffer from Indian uprisings during the war. During the 1850s, the local Indians were forced to give up claims to their homelands and move onto reservations. In 1862, food and money promised to the reservations was diverted to the Union war effort, leading to an armed uprising. Over a period of several days, the angry Sioux killed more than four hundred white settlers before the rebellion was quashed and the Indians captured. Some 306 of the Sioux were sentenced to death and eighteen to prison before Abraham Lincoln intervened and commuted the death sentences of all but thirty-nine of them, an action resented by most of the white settlers.

In 1849, Minnesota's territorial government established provisions for school districts and declared that common schools were to be open to all people between the ages of four and twenty-one, supported by a general sales tax and part of the proceeds from fines and licenses. However, by the early 1850s only about 250 children were enrolled in three privately operated schools.

(S) Missouri

Missouri had for many years been a jumping-off point for innumerable expeditions to the West because of its central location and access to navigable waterways, notably the Mississippi and Missouri rivers, which had been plied by steamboats from the 1820s onward. Some 1,182,000 people lived in the state when the war began.

Many people in largely agricultural Missouri, particularly in the Ozarks, were subsistence farmers and woodsmen, and the state's plantations tended to be much smaller than those of the Deep South. By the 1850s, slavery was becoming uneconomical, and the demographics began to shift as many German and Irish immigrants came to the state.

Slavery became a controversial issue in the state in the 1850s. *Dred Scott vs.*

Sandford, heard by the U.S. Supreme Court in 1856 and 1857, originated in Missouri, and the moderate abolitionist stance of longtime Missouri Senator Thomas Hart Benton destroyed his political career.

Nonetheless, a Missouri state convention voted in 1861 to remain within the Union rather than secede. While 110,000 Missourians fought under the United States flag, some 40,000 of them served in the Confederate forces. A number of major battles took place in the state during the ensuing Civil War, and conflict in Missouri was characterized by savage guerrilla warfare that led to the destruction of entire towns.

After the war, antiblack extremist groups caused trouble, and many former guerrillas, most notably Jesse James, turned to banditry and continued to plague the state with violence. By the 1870s, however, stability had largely been restored. Railroad building was expanded, and movement toward the American West once again ensued.

Before the Civil War, education in Missouri took place mainly in private institutions. After it ended, however, free public education became available in most parts of the state. Higher education institutions included St. Louis University (1818), the University of Missouri (1839, the first state university west of the Mississippi), Washington University (1853) and Lincoln University (1866).

Nevada

Nevada was part of land granted to the United States by the 1848 **Treaty of Guadalupe Hidalgo** and was initially part of the Utah Territory. The first whites to settle it were Mormons who founded the first permanent settlement at Genoa in the Carson Valley in 1849 and established a mission in the Las Vegas Valley in 1855. Monthly mail service across the northern part of the state began in 1853, and the Pony Express crossed central Nevada from 1860 until it was replaced by telegraphy in September 1861.

Nevada's economy boomed with the discovery of the Comstock Lode in 1858, and between 1860 and 1870 the population grew sixfold, from 7,000 to 42,000. Nevada separated from the Utah Territory in 1861 and was admitted to the Union on October 31, 1864; it is sometimes said to have been "battle born" for becoming a state in the midst of a great national war.

Nevada's major contribution to the Union during the Civil War was gold and silver bullion, used by the U.S. government as collateral for credit. This earned Nevada the nickname the Silver State. The state raised thirteen companies of troops. One served with a California regiment and the others fought against local tribes of hostile Indians; none of them saw action against Confederate troops.

Mining continued to flourish in the postwar years. The first transcontinental railroad was completed across Nevada in 1869, and the Central Pacific Railroad gained the lucrative freight concession from the Comstock mines. Cattle ranching also started in the 1860s, followed by sheep herding in the 1870s. Both activities were pursued by the state's Spanish immigrant population.

New Hampshire

New Hampshire, with a population of about 326,000, was a highly industrialized manufacturing state by the time the Civil War began. A great number of textile mills had been established from the 1810s onward, and by the 1830s railroad lines stretching into the breadbasket of the midwestern states eroded the role of agriculture in the local economy. Farmland was reclaimed by forest, and stone walls that once marked fields and pastures crumbled. New Hampshire sent eighteen regiments of troops to fight for the United States, and about thirty-nine thousand men from the state served in the Union forces during the war. After the war, large-scale shoe factories joined the textile mills as important industries.

Many colleges and universities existed in New Hampshire in the mid-nineteenth century, including Dartmouth College (1769) and the University of New Hampshire (1866, a **land-grant institution**). America's first free public library, the Juvenile Library, was established in 1822 in Dublin, and the first free public library supported by public funds was opened in Peterborough in 1833.

New Jersey

New Jersey was divided during the Civil War, with many of its citizens having Southern sympathies. A largely Democratic state, New Jersey did not support Abraham Lincoln for reelection in 1864, casting its votes instead for former U.S. Gen. George B. McClellan, a Democrat and a son of the state who campaigned on a platform of peace at the price of the Union. Nonetheless, about 88,000 men from New Jersey fought under the Federal flag during the war.

New Jersey's wartime population of 672,000 people was predominantly of northern European extraction until after the Civil War, when many blacks migrated from the South in search of unskilled factory work, along with overseas immigrants from southern and eastern Europe.

During the nineteenth century, New Jersey gained a reputation as the home of several important inventors. In the early 1800s, John Stevens built the world's first steam ferry line and America's first steam locomotive, and later in the century Thomas Alva Edison set up shop at Menlo Park.

In 1871, statewide public education was established in New Jersey, and an

1875 amendment to the state constitution required free public schooling be provided for all children between ages five and eighteen.

New York

New York has been known as the Empire State since its earliest years. At the time of the Civil War, it had the largest population of any state in the Union, swelled in part by immigrants to more than 3,880,000, and led the way in industry and manufacturing.

New York society had become more liberalized through the 1840s, abolishing slavery and seeking reform in the areas of women's rights, temperance and education. A strong abolitionist movement had developed in New York during this period. Some 500,000 New Yorkers fought for the Union during the war, and one in ten of them was killed. Support for the war was not universal throughout the state, however, and dissent against the war effort was demonstrated most dramatically by the 1863 draft riots.

After the war, New York's economy developed rapidly, as did the state's urban areas, inflated by the vast waves of European immigrants flowing into the state. Political corruption, unjust labor practices and inadequate social services attended these expansions.

Since 1784, education in New York has been the responsibility of the sixteen regents of the University of the State of New York. Institutions of higher learning included Fordham University, founded by Jesuits in 1841; New York University, established in 1831; and the U.S. Army Military Academy at West Point, founded in 1802 at the site of a military fortification overlooking the Hudson River.

Ohio

Ohio was strongly identified with abolitionist sentiment before and during the Civil War. The **Underground Railroad** was active on Lake Erie and along the Ohio River, and by 1848 the state had repealed its black laws. Nearly 320,000 men from the state fought for the Union.

During the war, Confederate Brig. Gen. John Hunt Morgan led a cavalry raid-in-force into Ohio on July 13, 1863. Two weeks later, on July 26, Morgan and his men were captured and imprisoned as horse thieves, rather than soldiers.

At the time of the Civil War, Ohio was well-known nationally as a prosperous agricultural and industrial state, and it was home to about 2,400,000 people. An efficient railroad network had been growing since 1850 when the Dayton-Sandusky line opened, which had increased farm income and land values in the northern and western farming areas and encouraged development of the Ohio coal industry.

Ohio was home to U.S. General and President Ulysses S. Grant (as well as six other future U.S. presidents) and became influential on a national level in the decades following the Civil War.

An 1825 state law required counties to fund public education.

Oregon

Oregon entered the Union as a state in 1859, less than two years before the Civil War began. At that time it had a white population of only about 52,000 and was almost completely unaffected by the hostilities. A half dozen companies of troops were raised for local security duties but did not see action outside of the region.

Most settlers to the region came with the intention of pursuing agriculture, including bee farming. In 1849, however, some of them were drawn to California by the discovery of gold, and others by the discovery of gold in southwestern Oregon a year later; another rush ensued in 1860, when gold was discovered in eastern Oregon. Farming and ranching were stimulated by the role of gold in the economy, and Oregon eventually began to export wheat and beef. After the war, railroad building allowed Oregon's timber and fruit to be exported across the country to the East.

Educational institutions included Oregon State University, a **land-grant** school founded in 1868, and the University of Oregon, founded in 1872.

Pennsylvania

Pennsylvania contributed heavily to the Union cause during the Civil War in terms of troops and materiel. Out of a total population of around 2,906,000, some 338,000 men served in the U.S. Army and about 14,000 in the U.S. Navy.

Key routes led into Pennsylvania from the South, enticing Gen. Robert E. Lee to lead his Army of Northern Virginia into the state in 1863. His army encountered Union forces at Gettysburg, leading to a major Confederate defeat and one of the bloodiest battles of the war. Nearly a third of the Federal troops who fought in the Battle of Gettysburg were native Pennsylvanians.

Pennsylvania's steel production expanded dramatically after the war ended, and by 1870 Pittsburgh had become the primary center of the U.S. steel industry, producing more than 65 percent of the national total.

Public education had existed in Pennsylvania since 1790, developing slowly but being well established by the time of the Civil War. At this time there were also more than a dozen institutions of higher education throughout the state, including the University of Pittsburgh (1787) and Pennsylvania State University (1855). Pennsylvania newspapers included the *American Weekly Mercury* and the *Pennsylvania Gazette.*

Rhode Island

Rhode Island was one of America's most industrialized states by the time of the Civil War, following a trend established by the construction of the first factory in America in 1790—a textile mill in the Blackstone Valley. Nearly 24,000 Rhode Island men, out of a population of about 175,000, fought for the Union during the Civil War, and more than one in ten of them was killed or injured.

Jewelry and silverware manufacturing, whaling and overseas trade were also important to Rhode Island. However, foreign trade began to decline in the 1840s and demand for whale oil declined after the discovery of oil in America. In the postwar years, mills producing woolen goods began to proliferate, and the area soon became the nation's largest source of them.

Public higher education in Rhode Island began with the founding of the Henry Barnard School of Law in 1845. Other institutions included Brown University (1764), Rhode Island Normal School (1854), Bryant College (1863) and Rhode Island School of Design (1877).

Vermont

Vermont, the only New England state without a seacoast, was the region's most productive agricultural state at the time of the Civil War and had a population of about 315,000. In 1823, the Champlain Canal connected Lake Champlain with the Hudson River, allowing Vermont farmers to ship goods to New York City. This stimulated agriculture, wool production and, in the 1860s, dairy farming, which eventually dominated the local economy.

About thirty-five thousand men from Vermont served in the U.S. forces during the war, and more than one in seven of them died during the hostilities. In 1864, the northernmost Confederate raid into the United States occurred at St. Albans, during which twenty-two Confederate soldiers ventured across the border from Quebec, robbed several banks, then fled back into Canada.

Educational institutions at the time of the war included the University of Vermont at Burlington, founded in 1791, and Middlebury College, founded in 1800. Vermont newspapers included the weekly *Rutland Herald*, founded in 1794.

West Virginia

West Virginia entered the Union as a new state in 1863 after a preponderance of the citizens of western Virginia opposed secession from the Union and counterseceded from the mother state in 1861. Its population was about 423,000.

During the Civil War, many rural West Virginians from both the lowest and highest levels of society fought for the Confederacy (about ten thousand), while the more urbanized middle classes (generally of Scotch-Irish descent) tended to be typical of those who fought for the Union (about thirty-two thousand).

During the war, Union sympathizers (supported by the Republican party) had pushed for statehood and made the northern panhandle city of Wheeling the capital. After the war, pro-Southerners gained political control of the state and made Charleston the capital in 1870. Power shifted again in 1875, and Wheeling became the capital again, until 1885, when Charleston regained the status permanently.

Wisconsin

Wisconsin at the time of the Civil War had a population of about 775,000, about 300,000 of whom were recent immigrants, more than 100,000 of them from Germany. Many of these immigrants balked at volunteering to fight for their new country, and Wisconsin resorted to a draft to fill its troop quotas. Wisconsin itself was fairly new to the Union at the beginning of the war, having become the thirtieth state on May 29, 1848.

Nonetheless, some of the most stalwart units of the war came from Wisconsin, including three regiments (the Second, Sixth and Seventh) of the legendary Iron Brigade. Altogether the state sent more than ninety-one thousand men to fight for the Union.

War also interrupted the state's economic growth, and Wisconsin did not change or develop much from 1860 to 1870. In the following decade, however, farming expanded northward, helped by the replacement of oxen with horses for draft animals, and technological innovations like the reaper. A local dairy industry also began to grow in the mid-1870s.

Wisconsin's 1848 state constitution provided for free public education. Institutions of higher education at the time of the war included the University of Wisconsin (a **land-grant institution** originally founded in 1848), Beloit College (1846) and Roman Catholic Marquette University (1864).

The Confederate States

A general overview is provided for each of the Confederate states, presented in the order of their secession from the Union.

South Carolina

South Carolina had strong tendencies toward independence from the U.S. government for decades, and in 1832 a special state convention had nullified the Federal Tariff Act. President Andrew Jackson responded with the Force Act and although the crisis was resolved through compromise, a state's rights movement began to grow in South Carolina.

On December 20, 1860, South Carolina became the first Southern state to secede from the Union. On April 12, 1861, South Carolinian forces fired on Union-held Fort Sumter, sparking the Civil War. At that time, the state was home to more than 703,000 people.

Beyond the effects of the Union blockade, some relatively minor land actions and the capture by Federal forces of Beaufort and Port Royal on November 7, 1861, the impact of war was not heavily felt in South Carolina until Union Maj. Gen. William Tecumseh Sherman invaded the state in early 1865. Throughout the course of the war, some sixty-three thousand South Carolinians fought for the Confederacy, about a quarter of whom were killed.

Reconstruction was long and hard in South Carolina, which suffered from state debt created by corrupt officials. In 1876, Reconstruction in the state ended with the election of Governor Wade Hampton (a former Confederate general) and the departure of Federal troops.

Prior to the Civil War, education was provided in South Carolina by private academies. In 1868, a new state constitution called for public education for all children, but this did not actually occur in South Carolina until the 1890s. One of the main state newspapers was the *Charleston Post and Courier,* started in 1803.

Mississippi

Mississippi left the Union on January 9, 1861, the second Southern state to do so. Mississippi politician Jefferson Davis—a West Point graduate, member of Congress and former secretary of war—became the first and only president of the Confederacy.

Several Civil War actions took place in Mississippi, including much of the crucial Vicksburg campaign, which ended in Confederate defeat in December 1863, ending control over the Mississippi River Valley. Over the course of the war, about 80,000 Mississippians fought for the Confederacy, out of a population of about 791,000.

After the war, Reconstruction and Federal government rule lasted until 1870, when Mississippi was readmitted to the Union.

Like other Deep South states, Mississippi's economy was based on cotton plantations. Mississippi did not change much in the years following cessation of hostilities, and on the eve of the twentieth century was much the same as it had been before the Civil War. Freed blacks became sharecroppers, but their status and treatment remained much the same as it had been under slavery.

Education in antebellum Mississippi was provided by private academies, nine of which had been established by 1817. In 1830, Oakland College was started by Presbyterians, and in 1844 the University of Mississippi was founded. A prominent state newspaper was the *Mississippi Gazette,* begun in 1799.

Revered by some in the South as a hero, but by even more in the North as a villain, C.S. President Jefferson Davis led the confederacy of Southern states during its four long, hard years.

Florida

Florida seceded from the Union on January 10, 1861, after entering it as a slave state on March 3, 1845. In 1861, Florida's population was around 140,000, about 63,000 of whom were black.

Union forces captured most of the state's coastal towns early in the war, but not Tallahassee, which the Confederacy never lost during the war. Fort Jefferson, a massive fortification on the Dry Tortugas islands, served as a Union military prison during and after the war. One of the Confederacy's last victories, the Battle of Olustee, was fought in Florida on February 20, 1864. About fifteen thousand Floridians served in the Confederate forces.

In 1868, Florida adopted a new constitution authorizing voting rights for blacks and a statewide system of public education. The state was readmitted to the Union. As with many Southern states during Reconstruction, Republicans held political power until 1876, when the Democrats once again took power.

Florida did not experience much economic growth until the 1880s, when phosphate deposits were discovered, citrus groves were planted, swampland was drained for farmland and railroads were built.

Florida's first newspaper, the *East Florida Gazette*, was founded in 1783 in St. Augustine.

Alabama

Alabama on the eve of the Civil War was a predominantly rural state, and Mobile, a growing seaport, was its only sizable city. Like other Deep South states, Alabama's economy was dominated by large cotton plantations, and of its 964,000 inhabitants, 435,000 were slaves. Most of its citizens viewed slavery as an integral part of Alabama's economic and social systems. It became the fourth state to secede from the Union on January 11, 1861.

In February 1861, the Confederate States of America was established at Montgomery, which was subsequently named capital of the Confederacy (it had been the state capital since 1847); it served in that capacity until May, when Virginia seceded and the capital was moved to Richmond. Some 100,000 troops from Alabama fought for the Confederacy during the Civil War, about a quarter of whom were killed during the conflict.

A handful of land battles were fought in Alabama throughout the war. Union forces captured the Tennessee Valley in 1862 and occupied Montgomery in 1865. One of the most dramatic actions took place in August 1864, however, when Union Flag Officer David G. Farragut led his warships into Mobile Bay—reputedly proclaiming ''Damn the torpedoes, full speed ahead!''—and won a major naval victory.

Reconstruction was a difficult period for Alabama, which refused to ratify the Fourteenth Amendment and was placed under military rule in 1867. Alabama was readmitted to the Union in 1868 after it ratified the constitutional amendment and guaranteed citizenship for blacks. Black and white Republicans wielded considerable power in the state until 1874, when white Democrats, who included among their ranks many former secessionists, regained control of the state. In the decades following the end of Reconstruction, legislators in Alabama wrote racial segregation into many state and local laws.

Prior to and during the Civil War, waterways were the primary means of transportation in Alabama; the state also had about 683 miles of railroad. One of Alabama's main newspapers during the war was the *Mobile Register*, founded in 1813.

Georgia

Georgia was a state whose social, economic and political structures at the time of the Civil War were based largely on the needs of large-scale rice and cotton farming. Out of a total population of about 1,057,000, more than 462,000 were slaves.

Increased demand for cotton had spurred settlement and plantation building in Georgia through about 1840, creating a demand for land, slaves and removal of the local Indian population. From 1832 to 1838, the U.S. government removed Cherokees to lands in the western territories, the final segment of which became known as the Trail of Tears. As a result, much of southern Georgia was sparsely populated until well after the end of the war.

Georgia, which seceded on January 19, 1861, suffered severely during the Civil War. Its heaviest blow came when the sixty-thousand-man army of Union Maj. Gen. William Tecumseh Sherman crossed the state in 1864. Sherman's troops burned Atlanta in November and moved toward Savannah, reaching it a month later and leaving across the state a swath of destruction sixty miles wide. About seventy-five thousand Georgians fought for the Confederacy.

During Reconstruction, Georgia's state legislature refused to ratify the Fourteenth Amendment, and the Federal government placed the state under military rule until 1870, when it was readmitted to the Union.

Although slavery had been abolished, Georgia's planters, like those in several other Southern states, adopted a tenancy system that kept many blacks and whites alike in servile poverty. Georgia was largely untouched by the waves of immigrants that came to America in the decades following the war, leaving its demographics and social status quo largely unchanged.

Louisiana

Louisiana, which seceded on January 26, 1861, occupied a strategic position on the Mississippi, making it a Union target early in the war. On April 25, 1862, a Federal naval assault smashed through Confederate defenses on the Mississippi and captured the critical port of New Orleans. Ironically, Union control of New Orleans allowed for trade directly with the North, making it an even more important economic zone than it otherwise would have been.

Louisiana had been under French control until 1803, when it was acquired by the United States as part of the Louisiana Purchase. In 1861, the state was home to about 708,000 people, more than 331,000 of whom were slaves. Its economy was largely agricultural, with large plantations run by slave labor on one end of the scale and subsistence farming by Scotch-Irish in the hills and Cajuns in the south on the other end. Waterways were the traditional transportation routes in the state since it was settled. By 1860 travel by steamboat peaked, and many communities in the state could be reached by such vessels.

Union occupation and Reconstruction took a heavy toll on Louisiana, which, along with slow moves toward industrialization, hampered the economic recovery of the state. Railroads began to improve after the war, causing the importance of the traditional steamboats to decline.

Louisiana's first school is thought to have been the Ursuline Convent for girls in New Orleans, founded in 1728. There was little in the way of public education until 1841, when New Orleans established free public schools and supported them with **poll taxes** and property taxes.

Texas

Texas entered the Union in 1845, with the former independent republic claiming all the territory from the mouth of the Rio Grande River to its source in Colorado. This claim was vigorously opposed by those who wanted to exclude slavery from the territories recently acquired from Mexico. In 1850, Texas relinquished its claim to parts of Colorado, Wyoming, Oklahoma, Kansas and half of what is now New Mexico in exchange for $10 million, as part of the **Compromise of 1850**.

On February 23, 1861, Texas withdrew from the Union and joined the Confederacy. While the state raised ten regiments of troops for the Confederacy, some two thousand Texans volunteered for service with the Union. Little fighting took place on Texas soil. The capture and subsequent recapture of Galveston, a major supply port for the Confederacy, were the most important actions, and the Battle of Palmito Ranch, fought after the Rebel surrender at Appomattox, was the last land battle of the war.

When the Civil War ended, Texas was subjected to military rule and flooded with carpetbaggers. However, it was readmitted to the Union on March 30, 1870, after ratifying the Thirteenth, Fourteenth, and Fifteenth Amendments to the Constitution. Cattle ranching became increasingly important to the state's economy in the postwar years, and huge herds were driven over the Chisholm Trail to the railhead in Kansas.

Moves toward public education began in 1839 when Texas set aside land for a state university and designated land in each county for public schools. The state's oldest English-language newspaper, the *Galveston Daily News*, was started in 1842.

Virginia

Virginia played a critical role during the Civil War, serving as the capital of the Confederacy and having more major battles fought on its soil than any other state. At the beginning of the war, it had a population of about 1,596,000; after its western portion became the new state of West Virginia, its population was reduced to about 1,173,000.

Virginia seceded from the Union on April 17, 1861, after Confederate forces attacked Fort Sumter and Abraham Lincoln called for mobilization of state

Richmond, capital of the Confederacy and a constant target of Union invasions, was almost completely destroyed in the last months of the war.

militia forces. Soon after joining the Confederacy, Richmond became the new capital of the Confederacy, replacing Montgomery, Alabama.

Major actions on Virginia soil included the battles of First and Second Bull Run; Union Gen. George B. McClellan's Peninsular Campaign; the battles of Fredericksburg, Chancellorsville, the Wilderness and Spotsylvania; the siege of Petersburg; and constant combat in the Shenandoah Valley. Virginia was utterly ravaged by the end of the war, and unlike other states, actually lost a large part of its territory as a result of the Civil War. The western part of the state had not cooperated with secession from the start and entered the Union as the state of West Virginia in 1863.

As in many other Southern states, radical Republicans ran the state government during Reconstruction but were replaced by more conservative politicians as soon as possible. In 1870, Virginia was readmitted to the Union.

In the nineteenth century, as today, the state was sometimes referred to as the Old Dominion (because of the decision of Charles II to make Virginia a fourth dominion of his realm, after England, Scotland and Ireland). Virginia had a long tradition of educational institutions, the Syms Free School being founded in 1634 and the College of William and Mary in 1693. However, the state made no provisions for public education until 1810, when the Literary Fund was established to assist poor children. The state constitution first provided for schools in 1869. Thomas Jefferson founded the University of Virginia in 1819. Some of the oldest newspapers in the country were published in Virginia, including *The Virginia Gazette*, begun in 1736, and the *Alexandria Gazette*, begun in 1784.

Arkansas

Arkansas was acquired by the United States in 1803 as part of the Louisiana Purchase and became the twenty-fifth state in 1836.

When the Civil War began, Arkansas had a population of about 435,000, of whom 111,000 were slaves. Eastern and southern Arkansas had an economy based on cotton plantations, farmed by the labor of black slaves, while northern and western Arkansas had an economy based on subsistence farming. These two halves were divided in their loyalty to the Union—the plantation owners opting for secession and the small farmers opposing it. In March 1861, the state legislature voted to remain within the Union, but this decision was reversed amidst much dissension on May 6, 1861, when the legislature voted to secede. Over the course of the ensuing war, more than fifty thousand Arkansans served in the Confederate forces, while some thirteen thousand, many black, served in the Union forces.

On March 7-8, 1862, Union forces defeated Confederate troops in an especially bloody battle at Pea Ridge, Arkansas. The Federal government took over Little Rock in 1863 and used it as a base to control the rest of the state. A new Rebel capital was established in Washington, in southern Arkansas, and by early 1864 Confederate forces were confined to this part of the state.

From 1866 to 1867, Southern sympathizers in control of the Arkansas legislature passed a number of measures restricting the rights of freed blacks, which led to the state being placed under Federal military rule. In mid-1868, Arkansas ratified a new state constitution and was readmitted to the Union. Republicans controlled the state government from 1867 until 1874, when the Democrats once again took power, for nearly a century.

Arkansas's first school was the Dwight Mission, founded in 1822 for Cherokee Indians. In 1843, Arkansas established a statewide system of public schools, but private academies dominated education until a decade after the end of the Civil War. The state's oldest newspaper, and the first west of the Mississippi, was the *Arkansas Gazette,* founded in 1819.

North Carolina

North Carolina was a relatively progressive Southern state with an economy based largely on agriculture and tobacco plantations on the eve of the Civil War. It had a population of more than 992,000.

From 1815 to 1835, the state had stagnated politically and economically, the reform-minded western portion of the state controlled by the more conservative east. In 1835, however, a reapportionment allowed the western part of the state to gain control of the state house of representatives, while the eastern part retained control of the senate. As a result, progress in education, tax reform, transportation and women's rights, as well as agricultural expansion and greater prosperity, continued until 1860, reversing a downward economic and political spiral and discouraging a trend toward emigration to the west and south.

War brought these improvements to an end. Pro-Union sentiment stalled secession, and on May 20, 1861, North Carolina became the next-to-last state to secede. Nonetheless, 125,000 North Carolinians, more than the number of registered voters, fought for the Confederacy, and about 40,000 of them died during the course of the war. Notable Civil War events in North Carolina include the battles of Fort Hatteras, Plymouth, Fort Fisher and Bentonville; Union Major General Sherman's 1865 invasion; and Confederate Gen. Joseph Johnston's surrender to Sherman near Durham on April 26, 1865.

Reconstruction exacerbated the wartime political and social disruptions that had existed in the state. In 1870, the Democratic party regained legislative control, and in 1876 reelected wartime Gov. Zebulon B. Vance, ending the Reconstruction period in North Carolina.

North Carolina's first public schools began in 1840. The state's oldest newspaper, the *North Carolina Gazette*, was begun in 1751.

Tennessee

Tennessee, torn by almost unanimous support of the Confederacy in its slave-holding middle and west, and equally fervent support for the Union in its east, was the last Southern state to secede, on June 8, 1861. Because of its position as a border state, Tennessee was ravaged by the Civil War. More battles were fought on its soil than any other state but Virginia, the most devastating being the Battle of Shiloh. From its population of about 1,110,000, Tennessee sent 186,652 men to fight for the Confederacy and 31,092 to fight for the Union.

After the Union victory at Fort Donelson, Tennessee was placed under military rule, with Andrew Johnson as military governor.

When the war ended, Tennessee was the first Confederate state to be readmitted to the Union, but Reconstruction still proved to be difficult. Agriculture made a slow revival as the mainstay of Tennessee's economy in the postwar years, coupled with moves toward industrialization.

In 1870, Democrat John C. Brown was elected governor, ending Reconstruction in the state and beginning nearly a century of Democratic domination of state politics. In 1878, while losses from the war could still be felt, a yellow-fever epidemic nearly wiped out the entire population of Memphis.

Education in Tennessee was provided largely by private schools and churches until well after the Civil War. Tennessee established a statewide public school system funded by taxes in 1873, but it was underfunded and largely ineffective until the early twentieth century.

UNITED STATES TERRITORIES

In addition to the states that had been admitted to the Union, the country owned several vast territories. These were administered loosely, if at all, and inhabited largely by Indians, pioneers, soldiers, prospectors, explorers, adventurers, outlaws and escaped slaves.

Arizona Territory

Northern Arizona was acquired from Mexico in 1848 under the provisions of the **Treaty of Guadalupe Hidalgo**, and in 1853 the **Gadsden Purchase** acquired southern Arizona. Both were part of what was then the New Mexico Territory.

Much of southern Arizona had been settled by Southerners, particularly Texans, and when the Civil War broke out most Arizonans supported the Confederacy. Rebel troops occupied Tucson in February 1862, making southern Arizona a Confederate territory. Two months later, in April 1862, the one battle of the war fought on Arizona soil took place at Picacho Peak. In May 1862, U.S. Army Col. James Carlson led his California Column into Arizona, recapturing it for the United States. In 1864, the white population of the territory was only about 4,500.

President Abraham Lincoln was certain that Arizona gold and silver could be used to finance the Union war effort, and on February 24, 1863, Arizona was proclaimed a separate U.S. territory. In the postwar years, violence broke out between settlers in the territory and the local Apaches, led by Geronimo, Cochise and Mangas Coloradas, and continued throughout the mid-1880s.

Arizona opened its first public school in 1871, and in 1879 the territory's legislature founded the office of the state superintendent of public instruction.

Colorado Territory

In 1858, gold was discovered in the northern part of the Kansas Territory. A year later, on August 1, 1858, the local settlers met and established the Territory of Jefferson, roughly corresponding to what is now Colorado. Embroiled in the controversy over slavery, Congress refused to consider a partition of the Kansas Territory. Nonetheless, the local convention proceeded to adopt a constitution for the Jefferson Territory on October 24.

In February 1861, Congress formed the Territory of Colorado, superseding the illegal local government, which had been unable to effectively govern the region.

Colorado raised eleven companies of U.S. troops during the war, but nearly as many men from the territory fought for the Confederacy.

Dakota Territory

In 1803, the United States acquired the Dakota Territory from France as part of the Louisiana Purchase. Trading posts like Fort Pierre, established in 1817, thrived with the fur trade. In 1859, the first permanent white settlement was founded at Yankton, made possible by a treaty with the Yanktonai Sioux. When the Civil War broke out, the territory was home to only about 2,400 whites, and in 1862, Yankton was made its capital. A number of settlements were established along the Missouri River and its tributaries over the following decade, multiplying rapidly with the arrival of the railroad in the 1870s.

In 1874, Lt. Col. George Armstrong Custer led an expedition into the Black Hills and discovered gold, which spurred settlement of territory and the foundation of towns like Deadwood. Conflicts with the Sioux intensified as settlers increasingly encroached on land granted to the Indians by treaty. In 1876, Custer led his troops against the Sioux and was killed at the Battle of the Little Bighorn.

Indian Territory

Prior to the 1830s, the term "Indian Territory" was loosely applied to vast areas of the western United States occupied by Indians. In the 1830s, however, a number of laws were passed, including the 1830 Indian Removal Act and the 1834 Indian Intercourse Act, which defined Indian Territory as the area of what is now Oklahoma, Kansas, Nebraska and the Dakotas—areas into which Indians were being moved by force.

In 1854, the **Kansas-Nebraska Act** further curtailed Indian Territory, reducing it to the area of what is now Oklahoma, an area occupied by the Five Civilized Tribes.

Justifiably unhappy with their treatment at the hands of the Federal government, these tribes allied themselves with the Confederacy during the Civil War. After the war ended, the tribes were forced by a series of 1866 treaties to give up the western half of their land, which became part of the new Oklahoma Territory.

Nebraska Territory

In 1803, the United States acquired the Nebraska Territory as part of the Louisiana Purchase. It was a vast area that encompassed what is now Montana, North Dakota, South Dakota, Wyoming and Nebraska. It was considered part of various territories from 1803 until 1854, when the **Kansas-Nebraska Act** defined it as the Nebraska Territory. A territorial legislature first met on January 16, 1855.

Part of the territory was admitted to the Union as the state of Nebraska in

1867. In the 1820s, expeditions through the area led by Stephen H. Long had described Nebraska (as well as Colorado and other parts of the region) as unfit for agriculture and dismissed it as a part of the "Great American Desert." Because of this, the territory was largely ignored in favor of settlement further west. Nonetheless, enough settlers remained that Nebraska's population exploded after the Civil War, from a mere 2,732 in 1854 to more than 122,000 in 1870.

New Mexico Territory

U.S. Army Gen. Stephen Kearny captured Santa Fe and acquired New Mexico for the United States in 1846 during the Mexican War. In 1850, the Territory of New Mexico was organized. It was expanded in 1853 when the Gadsden Purchase added a strip of land in its south. In 1863, the territory was divided to create the Arizona Territory, reducing New Mexico to its present boundaries.

At the start of the Civil War, Confederate forces seized much of the territory. In March 1862, however, Union troops decisively defeated the Confederates at Glorieta Pass, near Santa Fe, and the rebel forces soon withdrew from New Mexico.

When the war ended, cattle ranching became an important industry in New Mexico, leading to conflicts between cattle ranchers and sheep herders.

Utah Territory/State of Deseret

Utah was first settled in 1847 by Mormons fleeing persecution in Illinois. When they arrived, the area was still owned by Mexico. It became part of the United States in 1848, at which time the Mormons declared the State of Deseret (which encompassed an area from Oregon to Mexico) and requested admission to the Union.

Congress refused to recognize Deseret or its boundaries, however, and created the Territory of Utah instead, roughly corresponding the current states of Utah and Nevada, with Mormon leader Brigham Young as governor. Violence broke out between the Mormons and the local Indians, notably the Ute, and continued until 1867, when the Ute were settled on a reservation.

In 1857, the Utah War broke out between the Mormons and the U.S. government, which was opposed to the Mormon practice of polygamy, and continued until 1858, when U.S. President James Buchanan sent soldiers and a new governor to Utah. The territory was partitioned in 1861 and Nevada was granted statehood in 1864.

A wave of new settlers, many of them non-Mormons, followed the linking of the transcontinental railroad in 1869, sparking agriculture, industrialization, and the mining of gold, silver and lead.

Public education began in 1850, when the Mormon settlers founded the University of Deseret, the first public university west of the Mississippi River.

Washington Territory

White settlements were established in what is now Washington in the 1840s and 1850s, a period marked by constant warfare with the indigenous Indian population. In 1853, Washington was made a U.S. territory, narrowly missing being named the Columbia Territory.

Peace treaties were signed with the local Indian tribes in the following years, most notably the 1855 Treaty of Point Elliott. Settlers had been allowed by the Donation Act since before 1850 to file claims up to 320 acres for single people or 640 acres for married couples. By the early 1860s most of the territory's accessible land was owned and occupied. When the Civil War began, the local white population was about twelve thousand.

Lumbering, mining and salmon fishing emerged as state industries during and after the Civil War, and an area dubbed the "Inland Empire" was established for these purposes and was increasingly serviced with railroad lines.

Primary and secondary education existed in Washington since its earliest days as a territory. It was admitted to the Union as a state in 1889.

TERMS

black laws, black codes: State and local laws regulating the behavior and status of free blacks, before, during and after the Civil War (laws governing slaves were called slave codes). Under such laws, blacks were generally prevented from bearing arms, meeting in unsupervised groups or testifying in court unless party to a legal proceeding. Such laws also specified harsher legal penalties for blacks than for whites, criminal rather than civil liability for some actions (such as breaking labor contracts), discriminatory vagrancy laws and forced "apprenticeships" for black children, which were little better than slavery.

Bleeding Kansas: Term applied to Kansas during the period 1854 to 1861, where a savage war was fought between pro and antislavery factions. This border war was sparked by the Kansas-Nebraska Act of 1854, which left the question of whether Kansas or Nebraska should be slave states a matter of popular choice.

Compromise of 1850: Five laws enacted by the U.S. Congress that provided for the admission of California to the Union as a free state; organization of New Mexico and Utah as territories that could enter the Union with or without slavery; the settlement of the Texas boundary claims with the federal government assuming $10 million in debts contracted by the Republic of Texas; the prohibition of the slave trade—though not slavery—in the District of Columbia; and a more stringent Fugitive Slave Law. These laws were aimed at ending sectional disputes seen as threats to the Union.

Gadsden Purchase: Name given to a strip of land in southern Arizona and New Mexico purchased by the U.S. government from Mexico in 1853 as an adjustment to the Treaty of Guadalupe Hidalgo. On December 30, 1853, U.S. diplomat James Gadsden signed a treaty that called for Mexico to cede a rectangular strip of about thirty thousand square miles to the United States in exchange for $10 million. One practical effect of the treaty would have been a railroad route to the Pacific for the South, plans that were interrupted by the Civil War.

Granger movement: A movement of the 1860s and 1870s in which farmers in Minnesota, Iowa, Illinois and Wisconsin organized to have laws passed limiting the power of railroad and warehouse monopolies.

Kansas-Nebraska Act: A May 30, 1854, act of the U.S. Congress that established the territories of Kansas and Nebraska and repealed the 1820 Missouri Compromise. However, passage of the act reopened controversy over the expansion of slavery in the western territories. Sectional differences between North and South were eventually aggravated to the point that reconciliation was virtually impossible, driving the country closer to the Civil War.

land-grant institutions: State colleges and universities founded or expanded with the help of Federal land grants (under the provisions of the 1862 Land Grant Act), in exchange for establishing programs in agricultural, scientific, industrial and military studies.

poll tax: A uniform tax that had to be paid by all adults in the taxed area. Poll taxes were used after the Civil War to prevent free blacks, who often could not afford to pay them, from voting.

Treaty of Guadalupe Hidalgo: Treaty signed February 2, 1848, ending the Mexican War. It recognized U.S. dominion over Texas (with the Rio Grand River as its southern border) and called for Mexico to cede to the United States what is now California, New Mexico and Arizona. In return, the United States agreed to pay Mexico $15 million, grant citizenship to any Mexicans living in the area, assume any claims of U.S. citizens against Mexico, and recognize previous land grants in the region. Some parts of the negotiated boundary between the United States and Mexico were unsurveyable and had to be adjusted by the 1853 Gadsden Purchase.

Underground Railroad: A secret network that helped slaves escape from the South and work their way north to Canada, where the Fugitive Slave Law and other legislation could not affect them.

CHAPTER TWO

WAGES, CURRENCY, CLOTHING AND DRY GOODS

A

s during any period of national strife, the economies of both the North and the South suffered from inflation and price increases. For a variety of reasons, including the lack of industrialization in the South and the Union blockade of its ports, these effects were more profound in the Confederacy than in the Union.

Costs of clothing and other dry goods, examples of salaries, and the values and appearance of United States and Confederate currency are all covered here.

WAGES

While it is difficult to characterize an average American's wages during the Civil War era—with factors like age, race, geographic location, occupation, inflation, demand and gender all playing a role—it is nonetheless possible to get an idea of what many people earned by looking at a number of specific examples.

Once the war began, inflation caused wages to increase more in the Confederacy than in the Union states, but Southerners actually tended to have less buying power than people in the North (e.g., in 1863, a Federal dollar was worth about seven Confederate dollars). Local conditions in some areas, such as labor shortages, also affected salaries.

Pay for soldiers, sailors and other military personnel remained fairly static throughout the course of the war (e.g., U.S. Army infantry, artillery and cavalry privates earned $13 per month in 1861 and still earned $13 per month in 1864). From their pay, Union privates had $2 per month withheld until expiration of their terms of enlistment, and another 12.5¢ per month withdrawn for support of the Soldiers' Home, a home for old or invalid retirees.

All Union enlisted men, both privates and noncommissioned officers, earned an additional $2 per month for reenlisting, provided that they reenlisted within a month of the expiration of their term, and an additional $1 per month for each five-year period after the first. States also offered reenlistment bonuses for veteran soldiers that could be quite substantial, typically $100 to $400 per reenlistment (other incentives were also offered, such as thirty days leave in between enlistments). Such bonuses were sometimes contingent upon many or most of the soldiers in the regiment reenlisting together.

Military rates of pay were often theoretical, however, as soldiers on both sides were frequently paid late; contemporary diarists wrote of being paid in lump sum up to six months late. And, because of rampant inflation in the South, Confederate soldiers' pay in the latter part of the war was worth little, whether it was on time or not.

Following are examples of what some jobs paid in both the North and South. Wages for many unskilled civilian jobs in the period 1866–1877 are probably comparable to what they would have been in the North prior to the war; in the South, slaves would have performed much of this work.

Although salaries increased dramatically in the South during the war, sometimes they were still not enough to provide for the needs of a family. In many cases, men who were not in military service had to take second jobs, and women had to leave their homes and seek employment. In almost all cases, women were paid considerably less than men for comparable work, usually about half as much, a trend that continued after the war.

1860
Streetcar driver in Washington, DC: $1.50 per day.

Carpenter: $1.60 per ten-hour day.

Clerk in U.S. Government Printing Office: $16 per week for a ten-hour day.

Southern workman: $3 per day.

Teacher: $2 per student per month (i.e., by subscription), plus room and board with local families.

1861

U.S. Army infantry, cavalry or artillery private: $13 per month.

Confederate army private: $11 per month.

Confederate marine private: c. $8 per month.

Southern workman: $4 per day.

Pressman in U.S. Government Treasury Department: $5 per week.

Clerk in War Department in Richmond, Virginia: $1,200 per year.

1863

Clerk in U.S. Government Printing Office: $18 per week for an eight-hour day.

Confederate post office clerk: $700 to $800 per year.

Female worker in U.S. Government Treasury Department: $50 per month.

Female clerk in U.S. Patent Office in Washington, DC: $1,400 per year.

Streetcar driver in Washington, DC: $2 per day.

Southern clerk: $125 per month.

Southern workman: $30 per day (in area with labor shortages).

Nurse, North or South: $12 per month (from which she was expected to buy small items to help care for the soldiers in her charge).

Pressman in U.S. Government Treasury Department: $6 per week for a six-day week.

Female spindle or loom operator in the South: $8 to $10 per week.

1864

U.S. Navy seaman: $14 to $18 per month.

U.S. Navy rear admiral: $3,000 to $5,000 per year.

Female U.S. Army nurse: 40¢ per day, plus one ration.

U.S. Army general: $209.50 to $720 per month.

Confederate army private: $18 per month ($20 by midyear).

Confederate marine private: c. $15 per month.

Married woman working for Confederate States Laboratory, in Richmond, Virginia: $7 per day.

Single woman working for Confederate States Laboratory: $5 per day.

Clerk in War Department in Richmond, Virginia: $3,000 per year.

1865

U.S. Army infantry, cavalry or artillery private: $16 per month.

Blacksmith, carpenter or machinist in a Confederate government workshop: $10 per day.

1866–1877

Street vendor (e.g., matches, pencils, shoelaces, newspapers): a few cents a day.

Scullery maid in a home: $1 to $2 per week, plus room and board.

Domestic worker/maid in a home: $2 per week, plus room and board.
  Cook in a home: $2 to $10 per week, plus room and board.

U.S. Army infantry, cavalry or artillery private: $13 per month (reverted from $16 per month in 1871).

Laborer, unskilled: $1.50 per twelve-hour day.

Teamster: $2 per day.

Boilermaker: $2.50 per day.

Blacksmith: $2.50 to $3 per day.

Laborer, skilled (e.g., carpenter, mason, plumber): $2.80 to $3.80 per day.

Iron worker, skilled: c. $4.50 to $6 per ten-hour day (highest rate in any industry during this period).

Teacher: $2 per student per month (i.e., by subscription), plus room and board, or $25 to $30 per month in state-supported schools.

Fireman: $1,000 per year.

Police officer: $1,200 per year.

Clerk, bookkeeper, etc.: $1,000 to $2,000 per year if male, $500 to $1,000 per year if female.

U.S. $1 and $2 bills.

CURRENCY

Both the Union and the Confederacy helped finance their war efforts through the issuance of paper currency, which led to inflation in both North and South. However, inflation was always far worse in the South and ultimately reached crisis level, which it never did in the North. In the North, the cost of most goods and services increased by 80 percent from 1861 to 1865; in the South, goods cost sixty to seventy times as much in 1865 as they had at the start of the war.

The main types of currency used during the Civil War and their general appearances are described next. These images can be drawn upon by writers when describing card games, purchases or any situation in which a character has to contemplate or handle money.

Currency in the North

In the North, Congress took advantage of the war to establish a stronger centralized banking system. In February 1862 it authorized the first legal tender paper banknotes and throughout the course of the war issued nearly $500 million worth of them. By the end of the war, inflation reduced the value of such bills to 39 percent of face value (i.e., a $1 bill was worth 39¢ in gold). Currency issues were not the only means of financing the war, however; they were used in conjunction with taxes, loans and bond issues.

Union Notes and Coins

Some of the most common Union coins and notes in use during the Civil War are described next, along with the years they were issued. U.S. banknotes were green in color and, naturally, immediately acquired the nickname "greenbacks."

2-Cent Pieces (bronze, 1864–1865, although actually issued through 1873). These coins, the first to be minted bearing the motto "In God We Trust," depict images of a shield, an eagle and a laurel sprig.

3-Cent Pieces (silver, 1860–1873, minted in a different form starting in 1851). Depict images of a star and shield.

Half Dimes (silver, 1860–1873). Depict an image of Liberty seated on the obverse and the words "United States of America" and a wreath on the reverse. Originally minted in a different form in 1794.

Dimes (silver, 1860–1891). Depict an image of Liberty seated and the words "United States of America" on the obverse and a wreath on the reverse.

Quarters (silver, 1838–1865). Depict an image of Liberty seated on the obverse and of an eagle on the reverse.

Half-Dollars (silver, 1839–1866). Depict an image of Liberty seated on the obverse and an eagle on the reverse.

Dollars (silver, 1840–1865). Depict an image of Liberty seated on the obverse and an eagle on the reverse. Minted both before 1840 and after 1865 in different forms.

Dollars (gold, 1856–1889). Depict a large Liberty head wearing a feathered headdress on the obverse. A mint mark appeared below a laurel wreath on the reverse. Originally minted in a different form in 1849.

$2.50 "Quarter Eagles" (gold, 1840–1907). Depict a Liberty head wearing a coronet on the obverse and a mint mark beneath an eagle on the reverse. Minted both before 1840 and after 1907 in different forms.

$3 Gold Pieces (gold, 1854–1889). Depict a Liberty head wearing a feathered headdress on the obverse. A mint mark appeared below a wreath on the reverse.

Because coins were in such short supply, the U.S. postal service issued un-gummed stamps that could be used as change.

$5 "Half Eagles" (gold, 1839–1908). Depict a Liberty head wearing a coronet on the obverse and an eagle (with no motto) on the reverse.

$10 Eagles (gold, 1838–1907). Depict a Liberty head wearing a coronet and no motto on the obverse and an eagle with a mint mark below it on the reverse.

$20 Double Eagles (gold, 1838–1907). Depict a Liberty head on the obverse and an eagle on the reverse.

Union Fractional and Postal Currency

Faced with early battlefield defeats and the prospect of funding a long, expensive war, and reluctant to levy new taxes, the Federal government, along with Northern banks, stopped issuing coinage soon after the Civil War began. This action shook public confidence in the government, prompting people to hoard coinage. Before long, coins had virtually disappeared from circulation.

Merchants responded to this dearth of coinage by issuing due bills, tickets and other forms of private obligation in lieu of change, and soon after, the U.S. Congress authorized the use of postage stamps as change. Such glue-coated money proved very unpopular and inconvenient, however, and Congress finally approved glueless stamps that were referred to as postal currency.

This stop-gap measure was supplanted in October 1863, when the government began issuing fractional paper currency in 3, 5, 10, 15, 25 and 50 cent denominations. Such fractional currency was flimsy, easily became torn and

A wide variety of banknotes were issued by the Confederate states, including fractional currency. $10 notes were the most common in the Confederacy.

dirty, and was widely considered unattractive, gaining the derisive nickname "shinplasters."

Public outcry resulted when the 5-cent note was issued bearing the image of a Bureau of Engraving and Printing division chief (the image of U.S. Treasurer Francis E. Spinner appeared on the 50-cent note, something which apparently did not upset people). This public protest induced Congress to pass a law prohibiting the likeness of any living person from being used on U.S. Treasury notes.

Despite the problems with shinplasters, people eventually accepted them in place of metal coinage. By the time the government stopped issuing fractional currency in February 1876, more than $368 million worth of it had been put into circulation.

Confederate Currency

The Confederacy did not widely employ measures like taxes and loans to finance its war effort, and did so almost entirely through seven different issues of paper currency between 1861 and 1864.

These issues had a total face value of more than $1 billion and as much as $1.5 billion, a total uncertain in part because of counterfeiting (see page 44). In any case, none of this currency was backed by gold or silver, which, coupled with increasing shortages of consumer goods, led to some of the worst inflation ever seen in America.

Over the course of the war, the Confederate States Treasury Department issued seventy different notes with imagery that included day-to-day themes, such as laboring blacks, and classical themes, like Roman deities. Coins were far more rare in the Confederacy, the only ones struck by the Confederate States of America being experimental pennies and half-dollars.

Confederate currency always exchanged at a lower rate than did Federal money, and depreciated steadily throughout the course of the war, even as shortages caused prices to increase. When Confederate currency was first issued in 1861, it was valued at 95 U.S. cents on the dollar.

By 1863, the notes were worth about one-third this amount and were trading at 33 U.S. cents to the dollar, prompting one resident of Richmond, Virginia, to remark in a letter that "Confederate money is not worth keeping."

Indeed, Southerners had almost no confidence at all in Confederate currency in the last year or so of the war. Goods and services could be purchased only through barter or with U.S. greenbacks obtained on the black market; Union currency was even used to some extent for paying Rebel soldiers.

After April 9, 1865, when Lee surrendered his army to the Union, the value of the notes dropped to 1.6¢ against the Union dollar. Less than a month later, on May 1, 1865, on the last known day that Confederate currency was actively traded, it was sold in bales of 1,200 notes for $1.

C.S. paper currency, as well as the banknotes issued by many Southern states, was printed in all the denominations found in the United States, including fractional currency, which was needed as much in the South as the North.

Counterfeit Confederate Currency

Confederate currency was easy to counterfeit, and large amounts of it were printed in the North and circulated in the Confederacy in an attempt to debase its value, something that has contributed to uncertainty as to how much was legitimately issued.

One of the best known of the Civil War counterfeiters was Samuel C. Upham, who printed fake Confederate currency and claimed to be selling it for novelty purposes, each note supposedly being labeled in its margin with the words "Fac-Simile Confederate notes sold, wholesale or retail, by S. C. Upham, 403 Chestnut Street, Phila." How much this impeded their circulation in the South is not clear; the words may not have been noticeable at a glance, might have been deliberately obscured by those who wished to spend the notes, and would have been meaningless to the illiterate.

"I sold the notes as curiosities—mementos of the rebellion—and advertised them as such in several of the most widely circulated papers in the Union," he said. "During the publication of those facsimile notes I was the 'best abused man' in the Union (by the Confederacy). Senator Foote, in a speech before the Rebel Congress, at Richmond, in 1862, said I had done more to injure the Confederate cause than Gen. McClellan and his army.''

Confederate Notes and Coins

Some of the various banknotes issued by the Confederacy over the course of the war, along with the two Confederate coins, are described next, including years of issue. Most Confederate banknotes were blue-gray in color and as a result acquired the nicknames "graybacks" and "bluebacks.''

1-Cent Pieces/Pennies (copper or silver, 1861). Depict a Liberty head on the obverse and a laurel wreath on the reverse.

Half-Dollars (silver, 1861). Depict Liberty seated on obverse, Liberty cap, stalk of sugar cane, cotton and the words "Confederate States of America Half Dol.'' on reverse.

$2 Notes (1861). Show a personification of the South striking down the Union.

$5 Notes (1861). Depict the legend "Confederate States of America'' in blue on the reverse.

$10 Notes (1861). Printed in black and red ink on red fiber paper, showing a pair of Indians in the center, **Thetis** at left and a maiden with the numeral "X'' at right.

$10 Notes (1864). Show horses pulling cannon. More than nine million such notes were issued, more than any other denomination.

$20 Notes (1861). Show **Ceres** seated between Commerce and Navigation in the center and Liberty on the left.

$50 Notes (1861). Depict a bust of C.S. President Jefferson Davis.

$50 Notes (1864). Depict a bust of C.S. President Jefferson Davis.

$100 Notes (1861). Depict **Moneta** seated next to treasure chests in the center and a sailor in the lower left.

CLOTHING AND OTHER DRY GOODS

Clothing

During the mid-nineteenth century, Americans scrupulously imitated European fashions, which they modified little or not at all. This was in keeping with a trend established in Colonial times and adhered to until the 1910s. This rigidity of style was always greatest in the East, especially in urban areas, and became more and more diluted the farther West one went. During this period, most clothing was still hand-sewn, regardless of whether it was made at home or purchased from a tailor.

While styles were rigid and conventional, they were not always austere, and men and women in the big cities, such as New York, Charleston or New Orleans, were more likely to be concerned with elegance and ostentation. Writers should research the mores of the areas they are writing about to gauge how fashions would be affected. For example, the Puritan heritage of Boston's upper crust or the Quaker underpinnings of Philadelphia society would have made sobriety more acceptable than caprice, at least in the most conservative circles.

Once shortages began to take their toll on the Confederacy, many Southern women who could not afford to buy cloth or clothing, or simply balked at the inflated prices, learned to make their own cloth, thread and yarn. Just as we consider such activities a thing of the past, so did many Civil War-era women, who had to pull old spinning wheels and looms from attics or storerooms and learn how to use them from people of their parents' or grandparents' generations.

Men's Clothing

During the era of the Civil War and the years following it, the prevailing image in men's clothing was that of the lawyer-statesman, as exemplified by Abraham Lincoln himself. Men wanted to present a distinguished appearance, impress their peers and appear substantial. An austere black suit, white linen shirt, black bow tie and low-cut boots was the quintessential outfit for the middle- or upper-class man.

An elegant appearance was important to men in certain circles, especially those in major urban centers like New York or New Orleans. While a certain sobriety accompanied the appearance of professional men in the smaller cities and towns, more ostentation (e.g., fur-trimmed cuffs and collars) could be found in the garb of big city dwellers.

Work clothing was less formal but not much less conventional, and typically included trousers, boots and a double-breasted wool pullover shirt that buttoned up only from the waist to the collar; depending on the sort of work they did, men's garb also frequently included a jacket or sack coat. Nonetheless, many farmers, clerks and other lower-middle-class or working-class men were sensitive to their image and attempted to appear prosperous or ambitious through their apparel.

Foremost among men's accessories were hats, amongst which top hats and derbies predominated. Top hats, generally worn for business and formal occasions, came in a variety of shapes, brim widths and crown heights, and included bell crowns and stovepipes. Derbies, including bowlers, were hard, round-

The frock coat was the quintessential item of formal and business apparel for American men during the mid-nineteenth century.

crowned hats that originated in the 1850s. Such hats were less formal than top hats and popular with all classes of men. The most expensive men's hats were made from beaver fur felt (which contributed to the expansive North American fur trade). Other popular accessories included canes and suspenders.

Writers can use clothing and accessories to say a lot about how their male characters see themselves, what they are trying to project and how their environments react to them as a result.

A man of the mid-nineteenth century wearing casual walking clothes.

Women's Clothing

Women had very little flexibility of dress in the years leading up to and including the Civil War, and slavishly imitated European fashions, drawing many of their rules of attire from the popular *Godey's Lady's Book.*

Formal ball gowns and hoopskirts, of the sort worn by Vivien Leigh in *Gone With the Wind* or Deborah Kerr in *The King and I,* are the women's clothing most associated with this era. Many different variations came into style, and women would have been judged, or sensitive to judgment, for their fashion

Garibaldi shirts and dresses, with puffed sleeves, and military-style shoulders and collars, were popular with women during the Civil War.

sense as much as anybody today. Generally, such dresses had a tightly fitting bodice that rode low on the shoulder and had a V-shaped neckline. Gowns were cinched tight around the waist, and then mushroomed out to several feet wide at the floor, stiffened, pushed outward, and given their characteristic shape by hoops and specialized undergarments called **crinolines**.

Other female undergarments, many worn for day-to-day use, included **petticoats**, **camisoles**, **chemises**, **corsets**, **corset covers**, pantaloonlike drawers and

Elaborate floor-length gowns supported by hoops and stays were worn by women for formal occasions at the time of the Civil War.

stockings. Such garments could be made of cotton, wool or silk, and were often patterned, in keeping with prevailing fashions.

Naturally, working-class women and those whose activities took them near battlefields, did not wear cumbersome hoop dresses and lace on a daily basis, if at all. Plain, long skirts, blouses, bonnets and completely hidden petticoats were standard garb. Aprons were also typical and appeared in many styles, from those that simply tied around the waist to ones worn like smocks.

Garibaldi shirts, reminiscent of the shirts worn by the followers of Italian revolutionary Giuseppe Garibaldi, were another popular style of women's garb, and featured dropped shoulders, a bloused bodice and puffed sleeves. A variation on this theme was the Garibaldi dress, which featured a bodice similar to the Garibaldi shirt.

Once the war began, military-style dresses came into fashion for informal or day-to-day wear.

Women's Accessories

Parasols were probably the most important women's accessory during the Civil War. Such small umbrellas came in all appearances and materials, and were imported from as far away as Europe or China.

Practically, the main function of a **parasol** was to help protect the delicate female complexion from the sun—a pale-to-fair skin being considered attractive and a sign of social standing (i.e., upper-class women did not have to spend time in the sun working).

Other popular accessories included bonnets, fans, **snoods**, reticules and cloaks, often with hoods large enough to accommodate a bonnet.

In all classes of society, a certain modesty was expected of women. The limits of such strictures could be, and were, however, tastefully stretched. While the **parasol** did have a practical function, it was also used in rather elaborate flirting rituals. And, while the **petticoat** was an undergarment that was generally hidden, at times it was also fashionable to wear a decorative **petticoat** that was meant to be glimpsed.

Women also frequently carried fans in hot weather for cooling themselves. Like **parasols**, the use of fans went beyond their practical applications, however, and they too played an important role in flirting.

Hard times forced many women, especially in the South, to sell their jewelry or to donate in support of the war effort. Nonetheless, women still wanted things with which to adorn themselves and made new jewelry from available items. In the absence of precious metals, broaches, bracelets, necklaces and rings were fashioned from bone, wood, brightly colored scraps of yarn and fabric, seeds, fruit pits, palmetto, **gutta-percha** and even shiny fish scales.

Combs were another accessory that could be expensive to replace if lost or broken, and replacements were made from wood, horn and bone. Hairpins could also be made from these materials, and even from large thorns.

Hair switches, pieces of hair used to augment women's own hair, were generally manufactured in Europe and became harder to obtain as a result of the blockade, forcing women to either make substitutes or make do without them.

As with men's clothing, writers can say a lot about characters with what they wear and how people react to them. For example, a young woman from a Unionist family in New Orleans who is sent to live with relatives in Boston might be embarrassed rather than pleased with the reactions her ornamental petticoats receive at a party.

Children's Clothing

Children's clothing was not quite so conventional as adult clothing, and imitated military uniforms increasingly after the onset of hostilities. Indeed, little soldier and sailor outfits were especially popular for both boys and girls during the Civil War. Photographs and other media exist depicting boys wearing military-style shirts, coats and jackets, and girls wearing Garibaldi shirts and Zouave-style outfits.

Cloth

Cotton, being a plentiful prewar crop, was a primary component in many clothes. Wool and silk were other important clothing materials, especially for imported goods.

Shortages for cloth and clothing seem to have been nearly as acute as for food and other commodities. In the South, some cloth was produced at a handful of textile mills, but the rest of it had to be imported. This made cloth and clothing more difficult to obtain for those with means, and out of the reach of the less affluent. "There seemed to be no scarcity of dry-goods of ordinary kinds," Judith McGuire, a Southern woman, wrote in late November, 1863. "**Bombazines**, silks, etc., are scarce and very high. Carpets are not to be found, since they are too large to run the blockade from Baltimore." Relative costs of cloth and typical items of clothing as the war progressed are shown on pages 57-59.

Although many women turned to carding fibers, spinning thread and yarn, and weaving cloth themselves, these activities were impeded by many obstacles. For one, many farmers had stopped growing cotton in lieu of food (something many large plantations were not forced to do), and there were fewer sheep than before the war, so the raw materials needed for thread and cloth were often hard to obtain. Hair from cows, dogs, horses, rabbits and raccoons was mixed with cotton or wool to make it go further, and fibers from nettles were used instead of flax to make a fabric akin to linen.

Buttons

Buttons were made from a wide variety of materials, especially brass, pewter, tin, bone, wood and mother-of-pearl.

Brass buttons predominated for military uniform jackets and generally bore some national or state symbol, such as a Federal eagle, Texas star or North

Carolina sunburst. Confederate buttons might also bear a branch marking, such as an "E" or "M," as worn by the Confederate Army Engineers or the Confederate Marines, respectively. And, in ethnic units, such as an Irish regiment, they might bear a foreign phrase or slogan, such as the Gaellic "*Erin Go Bragh*" ("Ireland Forever"). Brass buttons were also used on some military equipment.

Pewter buttons were used on heavier garb, such as great coats, as well as other heavy-duty gear. As with brass buttons, they were also often emblazoned with characteristic symbols, such as a Louisiana pelican or Scottish thistle.

Wood, bone and mother-of-pearl were typically used for shirt, frock, trouser or blouse buttons. Tin buttons were used for men's trousers or military equipment like shelter halves.

After the war began, machine-made buttons were no longer available in the South, and buttons had to be recycled from old garments or made by hand. Wood, bone, horn, peach pits and other large seeds, bark, pasteboard, balls made from stuffed squares of fabric, and pieces of dried gourd covered with cloth were all used for homemade buttons. Some of these would be ruined by immersion in water and had to be removed before laundering the garment they were attached to.

Thread

Because yarn and thread became increasingly scarce during the war, Southern women often had to make their own. Such thread was adequate for hand-sewing, but was too coarse for sewing machines, which required much finer, machine-spun thread. Thus, Southern women who owned sewing machines were often unable to use them for want of proper thread.

SHORTAGES AND SUBSTITUTIONS

Shortages and inflation forced people in both the North and South, but especially the latter, to devise substitutes for many common items and the components of which they were comprised, including clothing, dye, cloth and thread; fans, jewelry and other accessories; and toiletry items and medicines.

People also wanted to maintain the illusion or pretense that they were able to look as nice or live as well as they always had, despite the effects of the war (remember the scene in *Gone With the Wind* where Scarlet O'Hara has a dress made from draperies?). Often, however, conditions conspired to make this impossible.

As it became more difficult in some parts of the country to obtain new clothing and accessories, people made much more of an effort than they had before to take care of the things they had and make them last as long as possible; even the affluent in the South were considerably less likely or able to discard items from previous years for the latest fashions from London or Paris.

In addition to the ways people dealt with clothing shortages, they devised substitutes and replacements for most other types of dry goods that became difficult or expensive to obtain. Some examples follow.

Toiletries

Hygiene remained as important during the war as it ever had been (even more so, as cleanliness helped impede the diseases that claimed so many, although most people in the mid-nineteenth century, even physicians, did not understand this).

Soap in its simplest form could be produced from water, lye and grease (rosin and salt were other possible components) and had long been made at home by women in the country. When lye became hard to obtain, it could be produced at home by filtering water through a tray filled with wood ash. As meat became less common, so did grease, and chinaberry and cottonseed oil could be used instead. Soap root and yucca root could also be used as satisfactory substitutes for soap itself.

Tooth powder (rather than paste) was made from mixtures of many different items, including arrowroot, chalk, charcoal, cuttlefish bone, honey, myrrh, orris root, salt and soda. Toothbrushes could be made from hog bristles or from twigs or licorice roots whose ends had been frayed like brushes by chewing them.

Substitutes for many sorts of cosmetics were devised. These included face powder, which could be replaced with rice flour, and hair oil, which was made from lard that had been left to melt in the sun and scented with rose petals.

Furnishings and Housewares

Refugees and other people who had been driven from their homes or had them destroyed often had trouble replacing their furniture, tableware and other items. Soldiers in winter quarters might also have employed many of the following to make their lives more comfortable.

Bed frames were fitted with poles or ropes pulled taut. When down or feathers were unavailable for pillows and mattresses, they were instead stuffed with things like corn shucks, leaves, moss, palmetto and cotton (which was considered the best substitute). Blankets were replaced with rugs and carpeting. Bed linens, cannibalized for bandages and clothing, often could not be replaced in the South, and many families had none at all by the end of the war.

China and glassware were replaced with clayware, which was cheaper and sturdier. Tin cups were often unavailable so emptied tin cans were used instead, and tumblers were made from bottles that had been cut off at the necks. Broken, lost or stolen silverware was replaced with knives, forks and spoons made of wood. Bowls, cups, dippers and ladles were made from gourds. Boxes and other containers were replaced with handwoven baskets.

Heat and Lighting

Sources of lighting like whale oil, kerosene and candles were in short supply in the Confederacy, all of them having been imported from the North. Firelight was one substitute, but was not always practical or available, especially as coal and wood became more expensive, notably in urban areas, necessitating fuel substitutes like "**fireballs**."

Candles were made at home, ideally from beeswax, but more often from **tallow** (which produced more smoke than other candle components) or a combination of both. Wax could also be extracted from myrtle berries, blackberries and prickly pear leaves by boiling them, although very large quantities were needed to obtain a reasonable quantity of wax.

"Confederate candles" were one method of stretching limited quantities of wax. They were made by impregnating a strand of twine with a mixture of **tallow** and beeswax or beeswax and rosin or fresh turpentine. The strand would then be wrapped tightly around a bottle and a few inches of it pulled above the mouth of the bottle, which could be lit and pulled upward as it burned down (six inches could burn for up to twenty minutes).

Kerosene for lamps was replaced with a mixture of cottonseed oil, peanut oil and melted lard. Other means of producing light included burning knots from pine branches and stalks of candlewick plants that had been soaked in grease or tallow, and "**fairy lights**," makeshift lamps made by floating sweet, burning balls of gum in saucers of melted lard.

Pen, Paper and the Like

Paper, ink, pens and pencils were often unavailable, especially in the South.

Once the war began, much of the paper produced in both the North and South tended to be lower in quality than people were accustomed to using for correspondence or journals. It was often brown, coarse or very soft. Old business forms, wallpaper and other scrap paper were folded into envelopes. Blackboards or slates and chalk were used for temporary work.

Letter writers conserved paper by turning a page 90 degrees once it was covered with words and then writing across them until it was full again, a method called "cross-hatching." This technique made letters a bit harder to read, but they were still legible and allowed someone to get twice the words onto a single sheet of paper. People also wrote letters in pencil so the recipient could erase the writing and use the paper again. However, subsequent writing was harder to read, the paper eventually wore out and this method did not allow letters to be kept.

Ink could be made from logwood extract or berry juice, especially from elderberries. Pencils could be made using coal or even lead rather than graphite, although the latter did not leave much more than a faint gray streak on paper.

Newspapers dealt with shortages by printing smaller issues or by using paper other than newsprint (e.g., some wartime newspapers were printed on wallpaper). Nonetheless, many Southern newspapers went out of business during the Civil War.

Glue was made from cherry, peach or plum tree gum, or from egg whites mixed with lime. Paste was made from a mixture of water and flour, and a type of putty was made by mixing flour with a warm, mashed Spanish potato.

Other Items

People had to devise substitutes for many other items, especially in the unindustrialized South. Metal goods especially, including pins, needles, fishhooks, screws, nails and locks, could not be replaced easily or at all.

Wooden pegs and joints were used whenever possible instead of screws or nails. Thorns or splinters of wood were sometimes used instead of pins.

Starch was made by soaking grated green corn, potatoes or wheat bran until it fermented, skimming the surface and straining the remaining solution. It could then be used to starch clothes or other cloth items.

Tobacco pipes, ideally made from briarwood or meerschaum, could instead be made from clay or carved by hand from other woods, such as dogwood, hickory, mahogany or walnut.

COSTS OF GOODS AND SERVICES

As with food, the cost of other goods and services also increased dramatically during the course of the war. As the value of goods increased and the value of money decreased, many people, especially women, tried to sell or trade their homemade items, like soap, for food and other necessities. Soldiers often acquired items that were in short supply in some areas (such as pins and needles from housewives or buttons from uniforms) and then used them to trade with the locals (whether friendly or enemy) for food, money or other items.

Prices were affected throughout the country. In the North, this was due to the costs of supporting the war effort, and, in the case of some goods, because of shortages of goods that had normally come from the South (e.g., cotton and indigo). In the South, however, which produced almost nothing other than cash crops that it had previously been able to export, such price increases were worst.

Following are examples of costs of goods and services in the South year to year during the war. Prices in the North for most items would not have changed much after the start of the war, probably not even quite doubling over a four-year period, with the exception of cotton goods, which would have been even more expensive or completely unavailable.

1861

beeswax: 21¢ to 26¢ per pound.

cotton fabric, bleached: 12.5¢ per yard.

dresses: $9 to $30 each.

firewood: $2.50 per **cord**.

handkerchiefs: 50¢ each.

soap, common: 3.5¢ to 10¢ per pound.

tallow: 4¢ per pound.

wool: 23¢ to 33¢ per pound.

1862

boots: $30 per pair.

calico: 75¢ to $2 per yard.

firewood: $20 per **cord**.

homespun, plain: $1 per yard.

laundry: $3 per dozen pieces.

muslin dress fabric: $6 to $8 per yard.

quinine: $60 per ounce.

soap: $1.25 per cake.

shoes, men's: $18 per pair.

shoes, women's: $15 per pair.

1863

boots: $50 per pair.

bonnets: $25 to $60 each.

calico: $2.50 to $4 per yard.

cloth: $2.25 to $5.50 per yard.

cotton fabric, bleached: $3.50 per yard.

cotton stockings, fine: $6 per pair.

cotton thread: 50¢ per spool.

dental services: gold filling, $120 each; upper set of dentures on a gold or vulcanite base, $1,800 to $4,000 per set.

dresses: $50 to $195 each.

firewood: $40 per **cord**.

gingham, black-and-white: $4.50 per yard.

handkerchiefs: $5 each.

merino dress: $150 each.

resole shoes: $10 per pair.

shoes: $25 to $50 per pair.

soap, common: $1 to $1.10 per pound.

toothbrushes: $2.50 each.

toweling: $1.25 per yard.

Cost of living for a family of five in a major Union city: $1,333 per month.

1864

boots, women's Morocco: $110 per pair.

cloth: $15 to $45 per yard.

coal: $1.75 per bushel.

cotton thread: $5 to $10 per spool.

dresses: $150 or more each.

firewood: $100 per **cord**.

hats, men's: $75 each.

linen: $22 per yard.

sewing pins: $5 per packet.

resole shoes: $50 per pair.

shoes: $125 to $800 per pair.

uniforms, officers': $2,000 each.

1865

alpaca dress fabric: $60 per yard.

bonnet, new: $200 each.

bonnet, used: $70 each.

boots, Balmoral: $250 per pair.

calico: $25 to $35 per yard.

cloaks: $1,000 to $1,500 each.

cloth, cotton: $15 to $50 per yard.

dresses, fine wool: $800 each.

firewood: $100 to $150 per **cord.**

gloves, French kid: $125 to $175 per pair.

hats, women's: $600 to $1,500 each.

linen, Irish: $50 to $100 per yard.

ribbon: $25 per yard.

TERMS

barege: A sheer, woven fabric made from cotton (as well as silk or wool) used for women's clothing.

bombazine: A fine, twilled fabric made of silk and cotton or wool that was often dyed black and used for women's mourning clothes.

calico: A coarse cotton cloth often printed with bright designs.

camisole: A women's undershirt, typically sleeveless and made of cotton or silk.

Ceres: A classical goddess of agriculture and abundance.

chemise: A women's undergarment that typically rode low on the shoulders and fell to just below the knee.

cord: A unit used for measuring cut fuel wood equivalent to 128 cubic feet (i.e., a stack four feet wide by eight feet long by four feet high).

corset, corset cover: Undergarments that emphasized the feminine form by constricting the waist and accentuating the bust. Corsets, which were often noted for their discomfort, were typically worn over a chemise, fastened in the front with a clasp and then tightened with laces in back or one of the sides.

crinoline: A women's undergarment, cinched around the waist and extending to just a few inches above the floor, that was worn under a dress to give it body. Such devices could be made simply of padded material, such as cotton, but more often consisted of about two-dozen connected hoops, held together like a beehive-shaped cage.

ebonite: See **vulcanite**.

fairy light: A lamp made by floating sweet, burning balls of gum in a saucer of melted lard. Used mostly in the South.

fireball: A substitute for coal and wood used in the South. Made from a mixture of sawdust, small pieces of coal, water, clay and sand, which was rolled into small balls and allowed to dry and harden.

flounce: A strip of gathered or pleated material attached to the hem of a dress, gown or **crinoline** to help protect it from contact with the ground.

gutta-percha: A rubbery material derived from raw latex and used to make containers waterproof (e.g., collar boxes) or to fashion other small items.

housewife: A sewing kit often owned by soldiers, containing needles, thread, pins, buttons and other items for repairing clothing and uniforms.

merino: The fine wool taken from merino sheep, used especially for knitting hosiery, undergarments and other items of clothing.

Moneta: In Roman mythology, a name applied to Juno, wife of Jupiter and queen of heaven, that emphasized her role as an advisor.

obverse: The primary ("front" or "head") side of a coin, as opposed to its reverse.

parasol: A small umbrella carried by women made of cloth or paper and with a frame of cane or wire. Such accessories could be plain or decorated with ruffles or fringe, and varieties for many different occasions existed (e.g., the plain paper parasol used for a stroll in the country would be replaced by a more frilly cloth one for a more formal occasion).

petticoat: A women's underskirt.

reticule: A drawstring purse or handbag, often of netlike fabric.

reverse: The back ("tail") side of a coin.

snood: A cloth net covering for women's hair.

tallow: The tasteless, solid white fat rendered from cattle, horses or sheep and used as a component in food, candles, leather dressings, lubricants and soap.

Thetis: In classical mythology, a minor goddess who was the mother of the hero Achilles.

toweling: A cotton fabric used for making towels.

vulcanite: A period term for hard rubber, which was used for items like buttons, pocket combs, cups, denture bases, flasks, pipes, soap boxes and syringes.

CHAPTER THREE

LIFE IN CITY, TOWN AND COUNTRY

merica was not a widely urbanized country at the time of the Civil War, but as a result of the **Industrial Revolution** its cities were multiplying and expanding. In the decades after the war, technology advanced rapidly, allowing farms to be tended by fewer people and creating more factory jobs in urban areas. These factors caused the nation to move toward becoming an urban, rather than a rural, society.

Having an idea of the physical environment people lived in can be useful to writers when setting scenes and when describing their characters' actions and motivations.

WHERE PEOPLE LIVED IN THE NORTH

Northern society was more urbanized than the South in the middle of the nineteenth century. Virtually all of the nation's largest cities were located in the North, including the three largest, Chicago, New York and Philadelphia, as well as Boston, Cincinnati, Baltimore and St. Louis (although the latter two were in "border states" that vacillated in their loyalty to the Union).

Some 5.5 million Northerners were city dwellers, about a quarter of the 22 million living in the Northern states. The balance, about 16.5 million people, lived in towns, villages or on farms.

WHERE PEOPLE LIVED IN THE SOUTH

Southern society was far less urbanized than in the North, and only about 10 percent of the population, less than a million people, lived in cities, while the balance, just over eight million, lived in small towns, villages, plantations and farms.

Southern cities, such as Charleston, New Orleans and Richmond, tended to be less large, industrialized or congested than urban areas in the North.

COUNTRY LIFE

At the onset of the Civil War, rural people lived on farms and in small communities such as communes, plantations and villages.

In 1860, the average American farm was about sixty acres in size and about a half mile away from a neighboring farm. This varied widely by region; farms in the West tended to be farther away from each other than farms in the East, and in newly settled states or the territories it was often possible to go many miles without encountering any sort of homestead.

People settled in the new states and territories for a wide variety of reasons, many because land was cheap and plentiful. While many settlers embraced the isolation of rural life, many others suffered from loneliness, and periodic social events with their neighbors became very important. Another way people tried to offset the loneliness and isolation of rural life in the nineteenth century, especially in the decades after the Civil War, was through the foundation of small villages, sometimes referred to as "rural neighborhoods."

Far too many regional and economic differences allow for a brief description of a "typical" nineteenth-century farmhouse. However, the most prosperous of such dwellings (e.g., those with two stories) generally included a ground level bedroom that functioned as a "birthing room" when necessary but was otherwise rented to travellers for the night. Such rooms tended to be far more popular than village inns, which were often much less clean or hospitable.

Communes

In the latter part of the eighteenth century and into the nineteenth century, various religious groups and intellectual movements in America had established and lived in communal villages, where they practiced farming and sometimes other industries. Most of the early communes were founded by conservative Christian sects, such as Mennonites, Moravians and Shakers.

One of the most notable examples was the Amana Society, a conservative, pacifistic religious community that held all property in common. In 1842, some eight hundred members of the Amana group migrated to the United States from Germany. They settled initially in Ebenezer, New York, but eventually moved on to Iowa (they still exist today and are known for making kitchen appliances).

Another good example are the Shakers, who established a small community at Watervliet, New York, in 1776. By 1830, some six thousand Shakers lived in communities in eight states. Shaker communes were marked by industry and became noted for manufacturing high quality furniture. Unlike many other contemporary religious communes, the Shakers did not shun technology, and were noted for their technological innovations.

After the first quarter of the century and into the decades following the Civil War, various other groups founded communes throughout the country, including socialists, anarchists, Hutterites, Bohemians, Christian socialists, Theosophists and Jews. A notable example is Robert Owen's utopian New Harmony commune in Indiana, which he founded in 1825.

Most communes lasted only a few years and then dissolved, especially in the years following the Civil War, when revivalism declined. Those based on conservative religious principles seem to have had the most longevity.

Plantations

Plantations, one of the most characteristic institutions of the antebellum South, were large-scale agricultural ventures overseen by an owner or manager who used a large slave labor force to produce cash crops for export. Plantations in America originated in Virginia and soon spread elsewhere, mainly to the South and West.

Plantations shared many aspects of a village, the main differences being that they were generally owned by a single individual, family or organization and that the land around it was worked not by free white farmers, but instead by black slaves. Many plantations even looked like villages. Besides the main house plantations included buildings like slave quarters, barns, stables, storage buildings, mills, workshops and anything else it required. A plantation's occupants included the master and his family, overseers (who were sometimes cousins or other relatives) and a labor force of black slaves, anywhere from several hundred on the largest plantations, but fewer than fifty on most.

Many Southern plantations specialized in a single crop, usually cotton, rice, sugarcane, corn and tobacco, as dictated by regional conditions (e.g., cotton and sugarcane were primary crops along the lower Mississippi River, while South Carolina was the country's leading rice producer in the nineteenth century).

"During the summer months, rice crops waved over fields of thousands of acres in extent, and upon a surface so level and unbroken, that in casting one's eye up and down the [Santee] river, there was not for miles, an intervening object to obstruct the sight," one visitor wrote in *The American Monthly Magazine* in 1836, revealing the intense level of agriculture that the plantation system allowed.

Plantation owners reaped the rewards of this system and were often able to use their wealth to build large houses, lead extravagant lifestyles and dominate the economic, social and political life of the antebellum South. This wealth and power was acquired, of course, at the expense of others, and about half of all enslaved Southern blacks were "plantation negroes."

In addition to planting and harvesting crops, plantation slaves were required to do many other activities. These included clearing land, cutting and hauling wood, digging ditches, slaughtering livestock and repairing tools and buildings. Some slaves were taught other trades or skills needed on the plantation and served as carpenters, blacksmiths, machinists, drivers and in other capacities. Inside the plantation house, slaves served as maids, butlers, cooks, nannies, wet nurses and in all the other roles needed to run a large household.

America's plantation system was dealt a mortal blow by the Civil War, which ended slavery. In the aftermath of the war, plantation owners tried to maintain their way of life by using the sharecropping and tenancy systems to exploit free but impoverished blacks and whites alike. Eventually, however, machinery replaced mass labor.

Villages and Towns

American towns were as diverse as the people who lived in them, and ranged from neat, orderly, prosperous communities in the farm country of the West, to raw, vital boomtowns in frontier areas, to sleepy, decaying former state capitals like Williamsburg, Virginia. The number of people living in a town ranged from several hundred to a few thousand. Such communities often served as a focus for outlying farms and smaller communities.

Town streets and sidewalks were generally not paved, nor were there streetlights. Buildings visitors were likely to find included residences, inns, taverns, general stores, churches, cemeteries, tradesmen's workshops, doctors' and lawyers' offices, or pharmacists' shops, as well as public areas where people could meet, such as town greens or commons and market squares. Other possible features included militia armories, warehouses (especially in port or rail towns), theaters (not cinemas), hospitals or sanitariums and town, county or district courthouses. Also, most towns had some sort of school or educational center, and some had several (e.g., Williamsburg had nine private schools and colleges). While there were not likely to be any public parks, there tended to be considerably more shade trees than in contemporary cities.

Facilities not likely to be present in many towns during or immediately after the Civil War included banks, telegraph offices and railway stations (unless the town had deliberately been built along a rail line).

Leading citizens of the town generally included gentleman farmers, doctors, lawyers and the most prosperous merchants. Other inhabitants included laborers, slaves, servants, lesser merchants, tavern owners, tradesmen and inn keepers.

In areas heavily contested during the war, many towns changed hands several times over the course of the hostilities, having a profound effect upon the lives of the residents of those communities. When soldiers of the same side took control of the town, the inhabitants cheered them, opened their houses to the soldiers and provided them with food and other amenities, or even returned if they had previously fled. When enemy soldiers took control, people sometimes fled, shut up their houses, hid their food or valuables, and generally avoided the invaders as much as possible.

CITY LIFE

In the years leading up to the Civil War, increasing numbers of Americans and immigrants were being drawn to the large cities for the financial and social benefits they offered.

In the North, drafts were one of the war's most profound effects upon city dwellers. Industry, however, flourished, providing jobs for increasing numbers of immigrants.

In the South and border regions, where several cities were occupied by Federal troops (including Baltimore, New Orleans and Charleston) or almost completely destroyed (as were Atlanta and Richmond), the war was felt much more directly. Destruction and occupation created a refugee problem, making it difficult to find adequate living space in many Southern cities. In one case, six Southern families shared an eight-room house for two and one-half years.

Characteristics of Cities
American cities were generally divided up by function, into areas for industry and manufacturing; shopping, business and entertainment; worship; education; and living.

With very few exceptions, American cities did not have any central organization. They were laid out on a rigid "gridiron" of city blocks, which generally did not take the natural geography in to account. These squares were further divided into lots that were owned by businesses, individuals and other interests.

This lack of central planning was in striking contrast to most major European cities. However, Europe was a land of kings, emperors, strong central governments and limited personal freedoms. While there were limitations,

American landowners had an amazing amount of freedom in what they could do with their land. And, for the most part, the government was not empowered to direct the development of urban areas. According to Gunther Barth, author of *City People*, Americans "recognized neither prince, priest, nor planner as guide" even though many were subsequently "dismayed by the chaotic scenes that the free use of space produced."

A few American cities, built for specific purposes, did come into being as the result of central planning. These included Washington, DC, selected by George Washington as the site of the nation's capital in 1790 and the seat of the Federal government since 1800; Salt Lake City, Utah, founded in 1847 by Brigham Young and the Mormon church as the seat of their religion; and Savannah, Georgia, founded in 1733 by James Oglethorpe as a mercantile and shipping center.

Prior to the invention of the elevator, buildings could not practically be more than five or six stories tall, and as a result the skylines of American cities were much lower than they were by the end of the century. In 1857, Elisha Graves Otis introduced the first passenger elevator, and by the late 1870s his sons had developed a hydraulic elevator with a speed of eight hundred feet per minute (a working electric elevator was introduced in 1889). Such devices encouraged the construction of much taller buildings than ever before.

The first skyscrapers were built in the years following the Civil War and included the New York Tribune Building in New York City, completed in 1875 and designed by architect Richard Morris Hunt. It was Chicago, however, that became most closely associated with skyscrapers in the decades following the Civil War.

By 1870, Chicago had a population of nearly 300,000 and had become a major American center of commerce. In October 1871, a fire broke out in a barn and quickly spread out of control, destroying a third of the city in two days. Because of elevators, architects no longer faced the same height limitations on the building designs, and a new "Chicago school of architecture" was created as designers moved toward rebuilding the city with structures that reached toward the sky. By 1890, the city was full of nine- and ten-story buildings.

Transportation

In the middle of the nineteenth century, the disparate areas of the city, along with its suburbs, were increasingly linked with various forms of transportation. Streetcars and horse-drawn omnibuses were among the most common forms of public transportation prevalent along major downtown streets. Horsecars were an important means of linking the cities with the middle-class suburbs, particularly in the decades immediately following the Civil War.

Areas of the city often developed in response to the sort of transportation accessible from it. For example, warehouse districts grew up near railway terminals, and factories were built in the corridors along railway lines.

Living Areas

Living areas, or neighborhoods, were divided up like everything else in the city, in their case along class lines. Living conditions between upper-, middle-, and lower- and working-class peoples were much more striking in cities than in small towns or the country, and the various classes of society reacted to the expansion of urban areas in different ways.

Wealthy families either lived in affluent enclaves in or near the city center, or moved out of the city altogether to estates accessible by the main rail lines. Middle-class people became unable to afford houses within the city and increasingly left to live in small houses in the growing suburbs accessible by streetcars or railroads, or, less often in the mid-nineteenth century, rented apartments. And the poor, who could neither afford property within the city nor afford to commute from the suburbs for their menial jobs in workshops, factories and industrial areas, lived increasingly in subdivided tenant houses and tenements.

Upper-Class Neighborhoods

The richest people lived in large houses or mansions, often built in the newest architectural styles, such as Gothic Revival and Greek Revival (see Architectural Styles on pages 73-76), and surrounded by sweeping lawns, gardens and outbuildings like carriage houses. Their exclusive neighborhoods were characterized by broad, well-lit streets, Parisian-style parks and features like art museums.

Such neighborhoods, however, represented a distinct minority and were vastly outnumbered by lower-class living areas.

Middle-Class Neighborhoods

Middle-class families tended to live in rowhouses, freestanding wood-frame houses, or, less often in the 1860s, in apartments (known in mid-nineteenth-century America as "French Flats"). The size and stylishness of such homes varied widely depending on the incomes of the family; the families of prosperous merchants might live in attractive brownstone rowhouses, while those of clerks tended to live on long streets of small, identical homes with tiny front yards.

Young and single middle- and working-class people did not live alone as frequently during the 1860s as they do today. If their families did not live nearby, they tended to rent rooms from families who had extra space. Likewise, in an era of extended families, maiden aunts, grandparents and orphaned nieces and nephews were far more likely to live with relatives, if possible, than on their own or as wards of the state. And in contemporary cities, a majority of homeowners with a spare room would rent it out to a single boarder, often in conjunction with board or an arrangement to share common areas, such as a kitchen or parlor.

Lower- and Working-Class Neighborhoods

The poorest strata of society, which comprised about half the people in many cities, lived either in small, shabby wood-frame houses, or, increasingly, tenant houses and tenements.

"The first tenement New York knew bore the mark of Cain from its birth," wrote journalist Jacob August Riis in 1890 of the once-fashionable houses along the East River that were subdivided into tenant rooms in the first decades of the century. The large rooms of these dwellings were divided into numerous smaller rooms, the rate of rent being determined by the size of the partitioned space. The higher it was above the street, the lower the rent.

Specially built tenant buildings, even worse than subdivided houses, were wooden structures two to four stories high built behind houses in spaces once used for gardens. Such rear tenant houses were often unsound and subject to collapse or fire. Often, more rental space was realized by the upward expansion of the front houses, although, in the words of a contemporary observer, adding such levels "often carried [the building] up to a great height without regard to the strength of the foundation walls."

Tenements were the worst of the dwellings available to the poor. Distinct from any other sort of housing, tenements were often a warren of tiny spaces partitioned from some huge abandoned hulk, such as a church or warehouse, or from an entire city block.

A description of the tenement from a nineteenth-century court case cited by Riis in *How the Other Half Lives* captures its spirit all too well. "It is generally a brick building from four to six stories high on the street, frequently with a store on the first floor, which, when used for the sale of liquor, has a side opening for the benefits of the inmates and to evade the Sunday law," the brief states. "Four families occupy each floor, and a set of rooms consists of one or two dark closets, used as bedrooms, with a living room twelve feet by ten. The staircase is too often a dark well in the center of the house, and no direct through ventilation is possible, each family being separated from the other by partitions. Frequently the rear of the lot is occupied by another building of three stories high with two families on a floor."

Death was a daily fact for people in the worst tenement districts. Infant mortality rates were as high as one in ten in some areas (i.e., considerably worse than Third World countries today). Suicide was also not uncommon. One sad episode involved a young immigrant couple who occupied a room less than ten feet by ten feet; they drank poison together rather than continue their dreary existence. And disease, which often left upper-class districts of the city untouched, could kill nearly 20 percent of the people in the most congested areas. In New York City, the general mortality rate for the city as a whole was 1 in 41.83 in 1815. With the rise of the tenement, this general rate rose to 1 in 27.33 in 1855, a year with a particularly mild epidemic.

At the time of the Civil War, more than half a million people lived in tenements in New York City alone, reaching a population density of 290,000 to the square mile in some areas. According to city health department officials, there are numerous examples of tenement houses in which are lodged several hundred people that have a pro rata allotment of ground area scarcely equal to two square yards upon the city lot, courtyards and all included.

Pigs, the most common urban scavengers, were among the hazards people had to deal with in the worst parts of the city. Such beasts could be aggressive and dangerous, especially to women or children, and their presence persisted on New York City streets until the winter of 1867, when city ordinances were passed prohibiting them from being allowed to roam in built-up areas.

Most of the people who lived under such squalid conditions were recent immigrants, largely Irish, Italians, Scandinavians, Germans and Dutch. Most of them were industrious people who lived in tenement conditions because of their desire to work, which they could do only if they lived in the city; in the absence of automobiles or public transportation outside of the city, people were unable to live outside of the city and commute for work, as so many do today.

Rent for tenements was usually paid a month in advance. Ironically, the cost of renting such miserable rooms was often 30 or 40 percent higher than it would be to rent a small, clean country cottage. However, jobs for the masses were available only in the cities, so people were forced to pay extortionate rates to live under miserable conditions. De facto slavery, then, was a fact of life in the North as well as the South. In light of this, it is less shocking, while no less tragic, that Irish laborers rioting in the summer of 1863 took out their anger against blacks, whom they saw as beneficiaries of the war against the South.

Working-class people in planned industrial communities, such as Lowell, Massachusetts, also lived in company-owned boarding houses, dormitories and rowhouses.

Urban Recreation Areas

As urban areas expanded in the early and mid-nineteenth century, and as property values increased, green spaces within cities diminished and disappeared. As a result of this, city dwellers began to crave areas reminiscent of the country. This, in conjunction with a variety of other factors, led to the rise of public parks.

Unfortunately, people's use of public parks for leisure activities took a toll upon the grass, trees and other plants. This led to officials spending an inordinate amount of time and energy in preventing people from actually using, and thus damaging, public parks. To a great extent, this diminished the value of parks to many city dwellers.

In the absence of parks, cemeteries became popular places for people to meet and walk.

Venues for spectator sports that included green areas, such as racetracks and baseball parks, were also very popular with city dwellers, certainly to some extent because of their appearance, as well as for what they were used for. Racing was America's most popular spectator sport prior to the rise of professional baseball, and tracks had existed since before the Civil War. While baseball had been growing in popularity since the 1840s, it was usually played in parks, fields and empty lots until after the Civil War, when specialized parks began to be built for the sport.

City Water and Sewage Systems

Indoor plumbing depended on municipal water systems, something that had only come into existence in America a few decades before the Civil War and was still not widespread by 1861.

Crowding in urban areas, however, spurred by the Industrial Revolution, had necessitated development of city water and sewage systems. Most urban areas were equipped with storm drains, but disposal of human waste into them had generally been prohibited. As city populations swelled, however, it became more and more difficult to prevent the drains being abused in this way. In the absence of adequate means for providing fresh water and carrying away filth, sewage flowed into lakes, rivers and tidal estuaries. The bodies of water and shallow wells from which people drew their drinking water became heavily contaminated with disease-bearing organisms.

Waterborne diseases like cholera spread unchecked in some cities. In the years following the Civil War, one particularly savage outbreak in Chicago, caused by sewage accidentally flowing into the water system, killed a quarter of the population, some 75,000 people. Chicago responded by developing one of the most advanced water systems in the country, and the threat of such outbreaks prompted administrators in other cities to create adequate water supply systems.

Urban Water Works

In the early 1800s, the invention of the steam engine meant that pumps could be used for maintaining water pressure in city water supply systems. In

1820, Philadelphia was the first American city to finish building municipal water works, and in 1823 Boston completed the first American sewer system.

New York City provides an excellent example of an early water supply and transmission system. Begun in 1830 with the construction of the Croton Reservoir, an impoundment of the Croton River that was completed in 1842, the system conveyed water to the city through a massive system of gravity tunnels (which were long considered one of America's greatest engineering feats).

Water filtration systems were first installed in America in Poughkeepsie, New York, in the 1870s (although even by 1900, only ten filtration plants were in operation throughout the entire country).

Toilets and the Like

Prior to the existence of plumbing, people had generally used outhouses. An outhouse was known as such in the mid-nineteenth century, and might also be called a "privy," "privy house," "**jake**," "**joe**" or "**john**" by rural or lower-class people, and as a "house of office," "necessary house" or "necessary" in more polite society. When separate outhouses were available for men and women, the door to the men's was marked with a sun and the women's with a crescent moon.

Chamber pots were also kept indoors, usually under the bed, for use at night, by the sick or in case of emergencies. Other common names for these implements included "piss pot," and "potty" (for a small chamber pot, as for one used by a child). In the homes of affluent people, a chamber pot was sometimes embellished to look like something else and was referred to as a "commode" or a "*chaise perce.*"

In the mid-1700s, privies began to appear inside of upper-class homes. Initially, these were little more than small rooms containing a chair with a hole in the seat and a chamber pot beneath it (which still had to be emptied, of course). Such a privy was referred to as a "water closet," "closet stool" or "close stool." Actual toilets, sometimes called "**Quinces**," did not come into use until the 1820s, and only then in areas where municipal sewage existed. Toilet covers followed by the late 1830s. By the 1850s, urinals were being used by men in urban areas.

Toilet paper did not become available until the 1880s. Prior to that people used materials like leaves, corn shuckings and old newspapers.

Bathing

By the 1830s, many Americans were bathing on a weekly basis, generally on Saturday night, so they would be clean for Sunday services. This was a radical departure from even a generation earlier, when it was only the wealthy or the eccentric who bathed regularly. A generation before that, bathing had been

Many lower-middle class Americans lived in small wood-frame houses or cottages.

considered immodest, uncomfortable and unnecessary, and many people went their entire lives without ever bathing.

In the 1830s, people generally bathed in large wood or tin tubs in front of a fireplace or kitchen stove where water could easily be heated. During this period, the term "bathroom" was used to refer to a room used only for bathing and which did not contain a toilet, as today.

By the mid-1850s, the homes of some affluent people included bathrooms in the modern sense, with both a bathtub and a toilet (one of the first was installed in 1855 in the New York City mansion of George Vanderbilt).

The trend toward bathing more frequently continued after the end of the Civil War. In 1865, Vassar College made it mandatory for girls to bathe twice a week. By the 1880s, an estimated 15 percent of all American city folk had indoor bathrooms of some sort.

ARCHITECTURAL STYLES

Several distinct styles of architecture predominated in America during the 1860s and could be found in the country's homes, churches, governmental buildings, memorials and other structures. Naturally, some of these styles persisted from earlier decades (e.g., Georgian), as homes and public buildings were not torn down and replaced just because new styles developed. As a loose rule, the styles that predominated in the eighteenth century had their origins in England and those that developed during the nineteenth century were characterized by Romantic revivals and eclecticism.

In the years leading up to, during and following the Civil War, the Georgian, Neoclassic, Greek Revival, Corporate, Egyptian Revival, Italianate, Second Empire Baroque, High Victorian Gothic and Richardsonian Romanesque were all major influences on American architecture. These styles are further described next, along with a few examples of each (mostly public buildings, with which people are more likely to be familiar).

Georgian Architecture

Georgian (1714–1776) was an English-inspired style of architecture that predominated in America until the Revolution. Named for England's King George I, who ascended the throne in 1714, this style of architecture showed a greater concern for style and higher standards of comfort than earlier styles. Georgian architecture, however, carried the taint of British imperialism and colonialism, and it was abandoned after independence was achieved. Georgian-style buildings proliferated throughout the New England and the Southern colonies, and good examples include the Old North Church (1723) and the Old State House (1712), both in Boston.

Neoclassicism

Neoclassicism (1750-1850), influenced heavily by Thomas Jefferson, supplanted Georgian architecture in America and came to represent the political and social identity of the new nation. It included several variations, including Federalist, Idealist, Rationalist and Greek Revival.

FEDERALIST architecture, heavily influenced by English models, was especially prevalent in New England and was used for many official structures. A good example is the State House in Boston (1795–1798), designed by architect Charles Bulfinch.

IDEALIST architecture was an intellectual and moral approach to classicism that was at first inspired by Roman models. Symbolism played an important role in this style, an excellent example of which is Thomas Jefferson's Monticello (1770–1809) in Charlottesville, Virginia.

RATIONALIST architecture emphasized classical structure and building techniques, such as stone vaulting and domes.

GREEK REVIVAL became the first truly national American style of architecture and, being very adaptable, appeared in all sorts of buildings, public and private, throughout every part of the country. One reason this style became so popular was that it was strongly associated with classical traditions and democracy, making it ideal for the buildings of a young republic. Examples include the Ohio State Capitol, Columbus, Ohio (1838–1861), designed predominantly by painter Thomas Cole; and the Treasury Building, in Washington, DC (1839–1869), designed by architect Robert Mills. This style was also used for many mansions and Southern plantation houses.

Corporate

Corporate (1800–1900) architecture was a practical style used for commercial and industrial structures, especially factories, and in its time was considered to be a "style-less style."

Egyptian Revival

Egyptian Revival (1820–1850) was used primarily for memorials, cemeteries, prisons and later, warehouses. The most famous American example of this architectural style is the Washington Monument, an Egyptian-style obelisk.

Gothic Revival

Gothic Revival (1820–1860) architecture, based on English and French styles of the twelfth to fifteenth centuries, was strongly associated with religion and nature and was used for both ecclesiastical and residential structures, from urban churches to rural cottages. Good examples include St. Patrick's Cathedral (1858–1879) in New York City, designed by architect James Renwick, and the "wedding cake" house, built around 1850 in Kennebunkport, Maine.

Italianate

Italianate or Italian Villa Mode (1840–1860) was an architectural style inspired by Renaissance models that was used for domestic structures, notably country houses and villas.

Second Empire Baroque

Second Empire Baroque (1860–1880) originated in France and was largely influenced by the additions to the Louvre in the 1850s and the construction of the Paris Opera. In America, this style was used for both public and residential structures. Good examples include State, Navy and War Building in Washington, DC, designed by architect Alfred B. Mullet, and City Hall in Philadelphia (1868–1901), designed by architect John MacArthur.

High Victorian Gothic

High Victorian Gothic (1860–1880), which originated in England and was named for Queen Victoria I, was used for public, religious and residential buildings. Good examples include the Pennsylvania Academy of Art (1876), in

Italianate-style villas were popular as both country and city residences for well-to-do families.

Philadelphia, designed by architect Frank Furness, and the First Church (1868) in Boston, designed by architects William Ware and Henry Van Brunt.

Richardsonian Romanesque

Richardsonian Romanesque (1870–1895), named for designer Henry Hobson Richardson, was a revival style based on French and Spanish Romanesque styles of the eleventh century. Structures built in this style are somber and dignified and characterized by massive stone walls, dramatic semicircular arches and a dynamism of interior space that was new at the time. Richardsonian Romanesque was the last major style to influence American architecture in the years immediately after the Civil War, and eclipsed all others for a time. Good surviving examples are Grace Church (1867–1869) in Medford, Massachusetts, and Trinity Church in Boston (1872–1877), both designed by Richardson himself.

COSTS OF HOMES AND HOUSING

What it cost to buy a home or rent living space varied widely from city to country and from North to South during the Civil War. Following, however,

Large, well-built farmhouses were evidence of the prosperity of many American farmers both before and after the Civil War.

are some examples of what it cost to buy or rent a home. Some of the costs for homes are from contemporary catalogs and publications, and editorials of the day sometimes derided them as being overpriced.

Price for a prairie-style farmhouse: $800 to $1,000 (1840s).

Price for a large but modest farmhouse: $2,000 to $3,000 (1850s).

Price for a larger, nicer farmhouse: $3,000 to $6,000 (1850s).

Price for a large, extravagant country house: $3,000 to $14,000 (1850s).

Rent for a house: $500 per year (in areas affected by wartime housing shortages, this price was at least doubled).

Rent for a room and board in a boarding house: $30 to $40 per month (1862).

Rent for a furnished house: $80 per month (1863).

Rent for a third-story front room, without carpeting or gas for heat or light: $60 per month (1863).

Rent for a sleeping/dining room, plus use of parlor: $60 per month plus one-half the gas bill (1863).

Room and board in a rooming house: $50 or more per month (1863).

Rent for furnished rooms: $25 to $110 per room, per month (1864).

Rooms in a tenement for a family (in a rear building divided up for ten families, worth $800 altogether): $5 per month.

Stable, rented as a dwelling (one of twenty on a fifty foot by sixty foot lot, worth $600 altogether): $15 per year.

TERMS

Industrial Revolution: the shift from an agrarian into an industrial society that began in America at the end of the eighteenth century and continued throughout the nineteenth century. A central aspect of the revolution was a radical increase in per capita production, facilitated by the mechanization of manufacturing.

Jake, Joe, John: slang terms used primarily by men to refer to either outhouses or chamber pots.

Quincy: a slang term for a toilet that originated in 1825, when a toilet was first installed in the White House during the presidency of John Quincy Adams, an event that prompted much debate and many jokes.

CHAPTER FOUR

FOOD AND DIET

A s with people in any time and place, food for people during the Civil War was important as a source of both life and pleasure. Many contemporary accounts and records describe the diets of soldiers and civilians, the impact of the war upon their eating habits and the financial and health effects of shortages.

Terms used to describe food quantities in the following section are given in a variety of measurement, including larger ones like **bushels** and **barrels**. However, people would have been able to buy smaller amounts of food. Also, terms like "barrel" sometimes reflected merely a measurement of amount, not a type of packaging, as barrels were often completely unavailable later in the war.

FOOD IN THE NORTH

Food and recipes in the North were influenced greatly by the North's prevailing ethnic groups, predominantly the English, Irish and Germans. Diet and the availability of food in the United States was rarely affected by the war, except in areas subject to enemy invasion or raids. In such areas, most items would have been more expensive or even unavailable if the local inhabitants were hoarding or enemy troops had been pillaging.

Ironically, many people in the industrialized North went hungry or were malnourished as a matter of course, and their suffering was neither intensified nor alleviated by the Civil War. These were the inhabitants of the great urban slums who accounted for half the population of some cities. Most of them continued to suffer from the effects of a poor diet, even as the owners of the factories many of them labored in grew rich from wartime contracts.

FOOD IN THE SOUTH

As in the North, Southerners' diets were based on the traditional fare of their English, Irish and German predecessors, and influenced by the large African-American population and crops that flourished in the region, such as rice and okra.

Largely because of the Union blockade and eventually because U.S. troops were marching through the Confederacy and occupying parts of it, food shortages began to affect Southerners early in the war, and grew acute as it progressed. A reduced ability to produce food because so many men and animals had been sent to the armies, along with wastage caused by raids and invasion, exacerbated these shortages.

Shortages tended to be the very worst in urban areas, which produced little food on their own and had relatively large, concentrated populations (populations that were often swelled by the influx of refugees from areas directly affected by the war). As the Confederacy's infrastructure deteriorated, the ability to transport food into the cities eroded. In rural areas, shortages were also felt, especially in areas touched directly by the war. However, shortages tended to be less devastating to people already accustomed to foraging, hunting and growing their own food.

Southern blacks had a traditional diet rather different from their masters, and had long become accustomed to making the most of lesser cuts of meat and second-rate produce. As shortages took their toll on the Confederacy, the diet of whites shifted more and more toward the sorts of dishes blacks had traditionally eaten (for example, Hopping John, a recipe for which is given at the end of this chapter).

CIVILIAN DIET

Wartime conditions led to shortages of food more acutely in the South than in the North, and far more Southerners suffered the effects of malnutrition and starvation than did their Northern counterparts.

People did not have modern chemical preservatives or refrigeration, and foods were either eaten fresh or preserved through canning, pickling, smoking, salting, drying or storing in cool areas like root cellars. Alcohol, salt, sugar and vinegar were all important elements in preserving and canning foods. Some manufactured foods familiar to people today were also eaten by people during the Civil War era, including Underwood Deviled Ham (since 1822), Lea and Perrins Worcestershire Sauce (since 1835), Borden's Condensed Milk (since 1856), Van Camp's Pork and Beans (since 1861) and McIlhenny Company's Tabasco Sauce (since 1868).

Typical food items of the day included a wide variety of soups and stews, many types of fried meats and vegetables, many sorts of breads and biscuits, and fruit pies. People also ate many sorts of regional specialties, such as seafood in coastal areas. Southern specialties included fried ham with **red-eye gravy** and biscuits, and Hopping John, a stew made from bacon, peas or beans, and red pepper. These were favorites of slaves before the war and with just about everyone after it.

Beverages included milk, hot coffee and tea, cold tea, water (which people drank a lot more frequently than they do today) and some commercially produced soft drinks, most notably sarsaparilla, which was similar to ginger ale. People also made a variety of refreshing homemade soft drinks, including lemonade, shrubs, switchels and capillaire (a recipe for the latter appears at the end of this chapter).

Fruits and Vegetables

Many of the varieties of fruits and vegetables eaten by people during the Civil War are today very rare or no longer exist at all (or are available only from dealers of heirloom plant seeds). This is not due to any inferiority amongst such produce; indeed, many varieties of vintage produce are better tasting or have a unique flavor, are more versatile, or better adapted to local conditions than those available today. However, considerations of shelf life and resilience for transportation are more important for people today than they were during the Civil War, when many people grew fruits and vegetables for their own consumption and many others bought what they needed from local markets.

In an age that predated supermarkets, many people had gardens and fruit bearing trees and grew their own fruits and vegetables. This was much more common in the country than in the city, but even urban people might have small garden plots. As the South was more rural than the North, and because food shortages there were much more acute, people in the Confederacy depended much more upon their personal gardens. In both areas, especially the South, women supplemented their family incomes by selling fresh or canned produce from their gardens.

Following are descriptions of many of the sorts of produce people were likely to grow themselves or purchase at the market or from farmers during the Civil War.

Tomatoes were probably the most common home garden produce, but did not become widely popular until just a generation or so before the Civil War. New England Puritans considered tomatoes to be an aphrodisiac and shunned them, the French introduced it into their cooking in New Orleans, Thomas Jefferson grew them as ornamental plants at his Monticello estate, and various gardeners praised their virtues. It was not until 1820, however, when a Col. Robert Johnson publicly ate an entire basketful of tomatoes in front of a crowd on the steps of the courthouse in Salem, New Jersey, that the tomato became an element in the evolving American cuisine (Johnson's personal physician predicted frothing at the mouth and appendicitis, a prophecy that was not fulfilled). Within a few decades, recipes containing tomatoes became commonplace.

Prior to the Civil War, tomato varieties tended to have fairly generic names, like Large Round Red and Yellow Pear-Shaped. By the time of the Civil War, however, more than a thousand varieties had been introduced. Names became more inventive and included varieties like Abraham Lincoln, Brandywine, Mortgage Lifter, Great White Beefsteak, Cherokee Purple and Ruffled Yellow. As these names suggest, a variety of colors besides the familiar red, such as pink, purple, yellow and white, also existed. Some of these can still be found today.

Most Civil War-era tomatoes were not as smooth and round as modern varieties. For example, many were beefsteak varieties, which tend to be flattened; others, like the Ruffled Yellow, had a pleated texture.

Lettuce, including head, leaf and romaine types, was also a familiar item in Civil War-era gardens (although there were not nearly as many varieties as tomatoes). Leaf varieties included Early Curly Simpson, introduced in 1864, and Grandpa Admire's, which had green leaves tinged with bronze and was developed by Civil War veteran George Admire. Head varieties included Tennis Ball, a Boston type (meaning that the heads are loose) that Jefferson also grew at Monticello. It was developed in Kentucky in the early 1800s and is still popular today.

Beans were another common garden item during the Civil War, and many different types were grown throughout the country. Bean varieties included Navy, Great Northern, Yellow Eye, Jacob's Cattle and Cranberry, all of which were used primarily for baking and in soups. Varieties of snap beans included Yellow Pencil Pod, Hickman's Snap and Cherokee.

Sweet corn, intended to be eaten by humans rather than used as fodder, was introduced in the late 1820s but did not really catch on until the 1850s. Corn varieties available during the Civil War included Black Aztec (also called

Mexican), Hooker's and Luther Hill. Black Aztec is unusual in that during the milk stage the kernels are white, but as the corn matures and dries the kernels become black and can be ground to make blue-purple cornmeal. Two yellow varieties especially well suited for making cornmeal included Northstine Dent and Garland Flint, the former reputed to make some of the sweetest cornmeal.

Cabbage was a popular item, especially among people of German and Irish descent. Two common varieties included Early Jersey Wakefield and Winnigstadt, the latter a German variety that had yellowish green leaves and firm, pointed heads.

Several sorts of potato were also grown in areas suited to them (such as Texas and Idaho), including the Early Rose, a variety described as having "light pink skin with deep-set eyes and white flesh, and **Irish potatoes**."

Other plants likely to appear in Civil War gardens included cucumbers, pumpkins, melons and beets.

Houseplants were very popular during the Civil War, especially among middle-class families. Some of these plants could also provide edibles, given bright daylight, moderate water and cool evenings. Fruit-bearing citrus trees were among the most prevalent of such plants, and one of the most popular was the Ponderosa lemon. This sturdy four- to five-foot tree bore huge lemons that could weigh up to five pounds each, and which had thick rinds that allowed them to hang for months without spoiling. For this reason, the fruit was usually left on the tree as a decoration, but could also be eaten if needed.

Produce prices stayed fairly steady in the North during the Civil War. In the South, like everything else, they rose and varied widely from region to region, and from city to country. A few examples include dried apples for 4.5¢ a pound, plums for 7¢ a pound and walnuts for 12¢ a pound in 1861; corn for $15 per **barrel** and wheat for $4.50 per **barrel** in 1862; cabbage for $1 per head, onions for $3 a dozen, sweet potatoes for $21 to $250 per **bushel**, watermelons for $10 each, cornmeal for $16 to $300 per bushel and wheat for $20 per **barrel** in 1863; cherries for $1.50 a quart, peas for $48 per **bushel**, squash for 50¢ each, cornmeal for $104 per **bushel** and turnip greens for $16 per **bushel** in 1864; and beans for $15 per quart, peas for $80 per **bushel** and cornmeal for $400 per bushel in 1865.

Meat

People in the nineteenth century ate most of the same sorts of meat we do today, including beef and veal, pork and bacon, chicken, turkey and lamb. Civil War-era Americans also tended to eat much more game than is common today, along with less familiar fowl, such as pigeon and partridge.

Shortages in the South made meat very expensive and difficult to find as the war progressed. Beef, for example, could be purchased for 12¢ a pound in 1862, $1 or more in 1863, at least $2 in 1864 and $8 per pound in 1865, if it

Meat prices rose everywhere during the war, but mostly in the South, which was hardest hit by the conflict. By 1864, dressed rats hung in the butcher shops of many Confederate cities and many Southerners were reduced to supplementing their diets with vermin.

could be found at all. Fowl was similarly expensive. In 1862, a chicken cost 20¢; in 1863, a partridge 75¢; in 1864, a single turkey from $50 to $100; and in 1865, a simple hen cost $50. Other examples include hams, which were being sold in 1864 for $350; veal, which cost $6 per pound in 1864; and fish, which cost $25 each in 1865.

By 1864, people in cities hardest hit by the war (e.g., by siege) were sometimes reduced to eating animals that a few years earlier would have been considered little better than vermin, including cats and dogs, crows, frogs, locusts, rats, snails, snakes and worms. In some cities, including Richmond, Virginia, and Vicksburg, Mississippi, dressed rats were sold in butcher shops for $2.50 apiece and dog was passed off as lamb. According to Mary Elizabeth Massey, author of *Ersatz in the Confederacy*, conditions like this presaged the South's defeat more than any loss on the battlefield.

Beverages

Coffee was by far the most popular hot beverage in either the North or the South. In the North, coffee rarely ran short for civilians, and the U.S. Army went to great efforts to ensure soldiers always had coffee beans. In the South, however, coffee became nearly nonexistent early into the war.

Southerners experimented with a wide variety of coffee substitutes, none of which was widely satisfactory. Chicory, acorns, beans, beets, bran, corn, corn-meal, cotton seeds, dandelion root, okra seeds, peanuts, peas, sugarcane seeds and wheat berries were variously parched, dried, browned or roasted and used to make ersatz coffee. Other versions used tubers like carrots or yams, which were cut into small pieces, dried, toasted and ground up.

Tea was another popular drink, but was also imported. Tea prices in the South rose dramatically year after year, from an inflated 1862 low of $10 per pound to an 1864 high of $40 per pound, prices that applied only if it was available at all, which near the end of the war it often was not. Decent substitutes for tea were much easier to devise than for coffee, however, as many domesti-cated and wild herbs, as well as leaves from fruit-bearing plants, could be made into an infusion. Leaves of blackberry, dittany, holly, huckleberry, spice berry and the many varieties of mint could all be used to make "tea," as could saw palmetto berries, sassafras roots, sumac berries and yapon shrub twigs.

When the weather was hot, beverages like cider and lemonade were popu-lar, as were **shrubs** and **switchels**, drinks made from cool water, juice, vinegar and a sweetner like **loaf sugar**, **moist sugar** or **treacle**.

Wine, champagne and distilled spirits were generally import items and be-came almost completely unavailable in the South as a result of the Federal blockade of Confederate ports. Simpler, domestic beverages like apple cider and beer had always been popular among people in the lower classes and, because of shortages, frequently had to suffice for the affluent as well. At times, however, even they were not available, and substitutes had to be devised. One type of homemade alcoholic beverage used as a substitute for champagne that became popular in the South was made by mixing one part corn syrup and/ or molasses with three parts water and then fermenting it in a barrel.

Food Preservation

Salt was used widely for preserving meat in the nineteenth century, but was often in short supply or completely unavailable in the South during the Civil War. There were centers of salt production in the South, notably in Louisiana and Virginia, but transporting it to where it was needed became impossible as the war dragged on, the Confederate infrastructure collapsed, and hoarding and speculation increased. Such shortages limited the amount of food that could be preserved for the C.S. Army, not to mention civilians, and contributed to the failure of the Southern war effort.

Small quantities of salt, as for household use, could be extracted from the dirt in smokehouses. When this dirt was mixed with water and boiled, a scum would rise to the top that could be skimmed off and dropped into cold water, the salt sinking to the bottom. Salt could also be obtained in coastal areas by evaporating seawater. When salt was unavailable to use as a seasoning, things with a salty flavor could be used, such as a pinch of wood ashes or a wild plant called coltsfoot, and soldiers sometimes used a dash of gunpowder. Such substitutes did not really help much with food preservation, however.

Meat was sometimes preserved by cutting it into very thin pieces and smoking it without the benefit of salt, and fish was preserved by pounding it flat and drying it in the sun, but these expedients were, presumably, not completely satisfactory. Meat could also be preserved in a briny solution of salt, water, sugar or another sweetener, and a small amount of potassium nitrate (saltpeter), an expedient that used less salt than usual.

Other Food Substitutes

People in the areas hardest hit by the war, especially in the Confederacy, learned how to make substitute food items beyond those mentioned previously. An excellent source of information about how the rigors of war affected the Southern diet was *The Confederate Receipt Book*, published in 1863. It contained many suggestions for substitutes that could be employed in place of traditional food items or recipe ingredients. Such information was also spread via word of mouth, correspondence and newspaper articles.

Cider vinegar was unavailable when apples were in short supply in the country or when it could not be bought in the city. Vinegar substitutes were instead made from beets, figs, honey, **Indian apples**, molasses, **persimmons** and sorghum.

Leavening for baking was often unavailable, and an ersatz version could be made by slowly burning red corncobs in a pan over a bed of coals until they were reduced to a fine white ash. Sometimes this ash was subsequently added to water, left to stand until clear, then strained; the remaining liquid was mixed with sour milk in a one to two ratio.

Traditional jellies, jams and syrups were often impossible to make because sugar was unavailable. Cider, however, could be boiled until thick and when cooled would gel. Also, water would thicken if boiled with red corncobs and could be used as a type of syrup.

Wild fruits like **persimmons** or **pawpaws**, not as popular as dates or figs, made decent substitutes when a preferred item was not available, and often became more palatable when dried, which concentrated their natural sugar and made them taste sweeter.

SHORTAGES AND INFLATION

Shortages made food items more expensive throughout the country. In the South, however, shortages caused prices to soar out of control, inflicting untold hardships on the Confederate home front. For example, a typical Southern family's food bill was $6.65 per month at the time of secession, $68 per month in 1863 and $400 per month in 1864. Indeed, by the spring of 1863, prices for food and dry goods were going up about 10 percent a month in the Confederacy. Ultimately, Confederate currency was so devalued that it quite often could not be used to buy food at all, necessitating barter.

Part of the supply crisis in the South could be attributed to the Union blockade. Beyond that, however, prices for civilians were also affected by the fact that so much food was diverted to the military. For example, according to Southerner Judith McGuire, "butter and milk are scarce because cattle had to go to the armies."

Following is a year-to-year comparison of price increases for basic food items in the South, drawn from a variety of contemporary sources including diaries, letters and publications. Prices would not have been uniform throughout the Confederacy and would have been subject to local conditions and availability, but writers can get some idea of the kinds of price changes. Ranges reflect prices earlier in the year vs. those later in the year. Quality of goods might be a fact as well. For example, in 1863 tea was running $32 a pound in some parts of the Confederacy, and only $7 a pound in others; however, the more expensive was imported green tea, while the less expensive may have been made from local herbs, rather than true tea.

Food prices were often higher in densely populated areas, where resources were spread more thinly. For example, prices in urban Richmond, among the very highest, were considerably greater than rural Halifax County, North Carolina (e.g., sugar cost $1.25 per pound in Halifax in March 1863 and $10 per pound in Richmond in September 1863; even accounting for the six-month gap between these figures, the Richmond prices are much higher). In some cases, certain items were not to be had at any price. For example, by 1865 coffee, tea, milk and sugar were completely unavailable in many Confederate communities.

Finally, items that did not need to be imported were likely to have less dramatic price increases.

Prices were also driven upward by speculators (in the North as well as the South), who were increasingly hated for growing rich upon other people's suffering. For example, in December 1864 a Baptist preacher in Richmond was attacked for selling flour and meal at inflated prices.

Goods were also much more scarce, or altogether unavailable, in areas invaded or occupied by Union troops, with prices consequently much higher.

1861

bacon: 12.5¢ per pound.

butter: 20¢ per pound.

coffee: 35¢ per pound.

flour: $6 per barrel.

potatoes: 75¢ cents per bushel.

1862
bacon: 75¢ per pound.

beef: 12.5¢ per pound.

butter: 75¢ to $2 per pound.

coffee: $1.50 to $4 per pound.

cornmeal: $3.50 per bushel.

flour: $16 to $40 per barrel.

tea: $10 to $20 per pound.

1863
bacon: $1.25 to $6 per pound.

beef: $1 to $3.33 per pound.

butter: $2 to $4 per pound.

coffee: $5 to $30 per pound.

cornmeal: $16 to $300 per bushel.

flour: $30 to $75 per barrel.

potatoes: $12 to $15 per bushel.

tea: $7 to $32 per pound.

1864
bacon: $8 to $9 per pound.

beef: $2 per pound.

butter: $15 to $25 per pound.

coffee: $12 to $60 per pound.

cornmeal: $20 to $104 per bushel.

flour: $125 to $500 per barrel.

Civil War armies were supported by long lines of wagons, which were used to carry food, ammunition, and other supplies toward the front, and, sometimes, wounded troops toward the rear.

potatoes: $25 per bushel.

tea: $22 to $40 per pound.

1865

bacon: $11 to $13 per pound.

beef: $8 per pound.

butter: $15 to $20 per pound.

cornmeal: $400 per bushel.

flour: $325 to $1,000 per barrel.

MILITARY DIET

Soldiers were not very well fed during the Civil War, and malnutrition contributed greatly to illness, disease and death. Officers tended to eat better than their men, as they could generally afford to purchase better rations from sutlers (subject to availability, of course). The most fortunate soldiers were also able to supplement their diets with the contents of packages from home, which could go a long ways toward making up for the deficiencies of a military diet.

Southern soldiers in particular suffered the effects of malnutrition and even starvation, especially toward the end of the war, when food shortages became acute as a combined result of the tightening Union blockade, the loss or destruction of agricultural land and the disruption of Southern rail and supply lines.

In the field, Union soldiers subsisted mostly on hardtack, a thick, hard cracker three and one-half inches square made from flour, water and salt that had been a staple army food item since the Mexican War (1846–1848). Such "**teeth dullers**" were typically issued to soldiers in one-pound packages.

Hardtack was designed for longevity rather than palatability. The high salt content of hardtack made it unattractive to mice and cockroaches but attracted weevils, who lived and laid their larvae in the crackers, inspiring descriptive nicknames like "worm castles," making this staple item even more unappealing to soldiers. While it could be eaten with no preparation, soldiers found ways to make this dreary staple slightly more palatable, including dunking, soaking or crumbling it into coffee, or soaking it in water until soft and then frying it in pork or bacon fat. **Bully soup**, **hellfire stew**, **lobcourse** and **skillygalee** were among the names soldiers gave to the various dishes they made from hardtack.

Confederate soldiers were much less likely to be issued hardtack, unless some of it had been taken in captured or raided Union stores. They were generally provided with coarse, unsifted cornmeal that they baked into corn bread (which attracted vermin as well as, or better than, the Union hardtack).

Other staple food items included coffee, salt pork, bacon and coffee. Fruits, vegetables and fresh meat were considerably more rare.

Coffee was an important beverage for troops on both sides, and the Union army in particular went out of its way to ensure that coffee was one thing soldiers would not be deprived of. In the South, the Union blockade meant that coffee was perpetually in short supply, and soldiers and civilians alike had to make substitute hot beverages brewed from chicory, roasted corn, peanuts, peas, potatoes and rye.

In the absence of modern preservation techniques, meat was preserved by smoking, drying or salting. Despite the best efforts, however, meat frequently went rancid, and the meat provided to soldiers has been described as "black as a shoe" on the outside and "yellow with putrefaction" on the inside. Soldiers preferred salt pork, or **sowbelly**, to bacon, which in hot weather would sweat, saturating their haversacks with grease and possibly ruining other contents or staining uniforms. Pork was usually in short supply, although when it was available soldiers often had so much of it to eat for a time that they became sick of it.

The lack of fresh fruits and vegetables contributed to all sorts of health problems, especially scurvy. To reduce the chance of malnutrition and its effects, the Union army provided troops with what it described as "desiccated and compressed mixed vegetables," dehydrated cakes of beans, beets, carrots,

Soldiers in many units pooled their rations and had them prepared by hired cooks or troops tasked with this responsibility.

onions, turnips and other vegetables. True to form, troops referred to these items as "baled hay." In the Confederate military, some soldiers (notably Gen. Stonewall Jackson) sucked on lemons, a good antidote for scurvy. Of course, these were not always available, especially during the later years of the war, and commissary officers advised soldiers to forage for wild onions.

When fresh vegetables were available for the soldiery, potatoes and onions were the most common. Union soldiers were served a thin soup fortified with sliced potatoes in the mistaken belief that it would help ward off scurvy. It was described in one account as looking like "a dirty brook with leaves floating around" in it. When cooking for themselves, soldiers were more likely to quarter or thinly slice the potatoes, then fry them in bacon grease, a delicacy sometimes referred to as "camp potatoes."

Military Food Preparation

Fresh food, typically beef or vegetables, were provided much less often, and when such fare was provided, soldiers had to prepare it themselves the best they could. This as much as anything contributed to poor diet and malnutrition, as many soldiers simply had no idea how to turn raw components (e.g., bags of meal) into edible food.

Indeed, the concept of a mess hall was unknown during the Civil War, and soldiers generally cooked all their own meals in the field. In camp, companies frequently designated cooks to prepare their rations and would often take up a collection of money so fresh ingredients could be purchased from sutlers. Quite often, these cooks had no particular culinary skill, and, far from adding any quality during preparation, often produced food that was largely unpalatable.

Officers, particularly affluent ones, were sometimes accompanied by servants who cooked for them and thus avoid the difficulties of preparing their own food.

Because they had to cook their own food, soldiers carried with them a variety of cooking implements and utensils. Utensils included traditional implements like knives, forks (usually three- but sometimes four-tined), and spoons, many all of metal or bone- or wood-handled. Some officers, or even common soldiers in well-to-do volunteer regiments, may have also had silver-plated utensils, at least early in the war.

Larger implements were constructed of tin or cast iron and included plates (which could double as pans), cooking pots in a wide variety of sizes, skillets, coffeepots and cups (some with wire handles as well as regular mug handles). Many sorts of makeshift items would have been used as well (e.g., bayonets, which could be used as skewers for roasting meat, or tin cans fitted with wire handles and used for campfire cooking).

In addition to cooking over open fires and coals, soldiers sometimes used manufactured camp stoves, many patents for which were filed after the war broke out. Some of these were quite elaborate and typically included a central firebox, as well as any or all of a double boiler, a baking oven, a broiler, and a flat surface for coffeepots, skillets or pots. One stove inventor, George A. Higgins of New York City, said of his 1861 patent camp stove that "the object of this invention is to obtain a stove of the simplest construction, which, with its necessary fixtures . . . may, when not required for use, be packed within a small compass, and the several parts when in use be capable of being so arranged that a large amount of cooking may be done." Such fancy implements aside, however, as the war progressed most soldiers simply did their cooking over coals or campfires.

RECIPES

Each of the following recipes will give writers some idea of the food and beverages eaten by civilians and soldiers during the Civil War era. They are also simple enough to try out.

Camp Potatoes

"Cut the vegetable into thin slices and throw them into cold water for half an hour; then put them into fat hissing hot and fry them until they acquire a golden hue. Some persons cut them only into quarters, but they are not near so crisp and nice."

—*Camp Fires and Camp Cooking, or Culinary Hints for the Soldier,*
Capt. James M. Sanderson, 1862

Capillaire

"Take one pound of loaf sugar, quarter of a pound of moist sugar, one egg well beaten, one pint of water. Simmer it one hour, skim it while boiling, let it get cold, then boil again and skim, add one ounce of orange-flower water and two tablespoonfuls of brandy. Strain through a jelly-bag, and bottle for use. A spoonful in a tumbler of water makes a pleasant beverage."

—*Godey's Lady's Book,* 1866

Hopping John

    1 lb. dried black-eyed peas
    3 pints cold water
    ½ lb. sliced salt pork or bacon
    1 tsp. Tabasco sauce
    ½ tsp. salt
    2 tbsp. bacon fat or lard
    2 medium onions, chopped
    1 cup uncooked long-grain rice
    1½ cups boiling water

Cover the peas with cold water in a large kettle. Soak overnight. Add salt pork, Tabasco sauce, and salt. Cover and cook over low heat about 30 minutes. Meanwhile, cook onions in bacon fat until yellow, then add to peas along with rice and boiling water. Cook this mixture until rice is tender and water is absorbed, about 20 to 25 minutes, stirring occasionally. Yield: About eight servings.

—McIlhenny Company, 1868

Instant Coffee

"To every ¼ pound of ground coffee, add one teaspoonful of powdered chicory and one pint of water. Freshly roast and grind the coffee; put into a percolator or filter with the chicory and pour slowly over it the above amount of boiling water. When it has all filtered through, warm the coffee to bring it to the simmering point, but do not allow it to boil; then filter it a second time, put it into a clean, dry bottle, cork it well, and it will remain fresh for several days.

Two tablespoons of this essence are quite sufficient for a breakfast-cupful of hot milk.''
—*Book of Household Management*, Isabella Beeton, 1861

TERMS

bully soup, panada: A cooked mixture of crushed hardtack, cornmeal, ginger and wine.

barrel: Used as a unit of measurement, from thirty-one to forty-two gallons.

bushel: A unit of dry measurement equivalent to four pecks (i.e., thirty-two quarts or eight gallons).

Confederate beef: In the first years of the war, a term used by Union soldiers to refer to the Confederate cows and horses that they took for food. After the summer 1863 Siege of Vicksburg, however, this term was more often used to refer to the mules eaten by the Southern defenders of the city.

creeper: A term used by New England soldiers for a small iron skillet.

hellfire stew: Hardtack crushed into pieces, soaked in water to make softer, then fried in bacon fat.

Indian apple: A perennial American herb and its yellowish, egg-shaped fruit. Also called May apple.

Irish potato: The white potato brought to the United States by Irish immigrants.

junk: A slang term used by sailors for salt beef.

loaf sugar: Granulated sugar.

lobcourse: A soup made from hardtack, salt pork and whatever else was on hand.

moist sugar: Brown sugar.

mucket: A large tin mug or kettle with a hinged top that soldiers used for cooking and eating their food. Such implements either had a handle like a traditional mug, a wire handle like a bucket or both.

mud lark: Humorous term used by soldiers to refer to domestic pigs they killed and ate. Presumably, the farmers who owned these pigs were not as amused as the soldiers.

papaw, pawpaw: A bush or small tree and its compact, fleshy fruit, found in temperate regions of North America.

peck: A unit of dry measurement equal to eight quarts. Also used colloquially to mean "a lot."

persimmon: An astringent, plumlike fruit found in the South that is sweet and edible when ripe.

receipt: A period term for a recipe.

red-eye gravy: A reddish gravy made from ham drippings and hot water, typically served with ham and biscuits.

shrub: A drink made from vinegar and fruit juice that was given to sick people as a remedy but widely enjoyed during hot weather.

skillygalee: An informal name for hardtack softened by soaking in water then frying in bacon grease.

slow bear: One of the many lighthearted terms used by foraging troops to refer to the farmers' pigs that they killed and ate.

sowbelly: A term used by soldiers for pork.

switchel: A type of drink popular in hot weather that was made from a mixture of vinegar, a sweetener and chilled water.

teeth dullers: A slang term for hardtack crackers.

treacle: A largely Southern term for molasses.

CHAPTER FIVE

FUN AND GAMES: HOW PEOPLE ENTERTAINED THEMSELVES

D uring the nineteenth century, people were less accustomed than modern Americans to constant sensory bombardment, and were not exposed to television, radio, movie theaters, the World Wide Web, and the huge variety of other media. Nonetheless, civilians and soldiers alike enjoyed games, music, spectator and participant sports, and other recreations as diversions from the problems and tedium of everyday life, or a mental escape from the specter of combat and death.

ENTERTAINMENT IN THE NORTH

Society in the North was becoming increasingly urbanized and diverse, and many forms of entertainment evolved to that were both tailored to large crowds and likely to suit a wide variety of tastes and backgrounds. Spectator sports like horse racing and boxing were popular. Ultimately, however, in the years following the Civil War, baseball trumped all other activities as America's favorite spectator sport of the nineteenth century.

Gambling was also popular, both on spectator sports and at the gaming table, and casual card or board games were played by many friends and families.

Theater, another largely urban form of entertainment, evolved during the nineteenth century, and vaudeville and burlesque emerged as unique forms of staged entertainment for the masses. Circuses, in both cities and the country, also came into their own as a distinct form of entertainment, especially in the years following the Civil War.

ENTERTAINMENT IN THE SOUTH

Being less urbanized than the North, people tended toward smaller-scale kinds of entertainment, especially prior to the war. Balls held by the upper crust, activities shared by farm families and festivals celebrated in towns, villages or plantations predominated. Venues for spectator activities, such as baseball parks or race tracks, were much less widespread than in the North. Participant sports, however, such as horse racing amongst the members of a club or village, were much more likely. Travelling circuses and carnivals, especially in conjunction with county or state fairs, were popular, and broke up the day-to-day routines of rural life.

Shortages imposed by the war changed the nature of many social activities, of course, but Southerners still enjoyed them. "Biscuit parties" were thrown by those able to obtain some wheat flour or by friends who might each bring what they had available. Later in the war, when for many there was not flour or anything else, people held "starvation parties," where the only refreshment served was water.

GAMES

Card, board and dice games were popular among civilians and soldiers alike. Because of the tedium of camp life, many soldiers in particular spent as much time as they could absorbed in games when other duties did not call.

Dice were generally small, a bit crude and made out of wood (although some might be made from flattened musket balls, like those of the Revolutionary War, amongst troops still using muskets). Craps was the dice game played most often, but others included one known variously as birdcage or sweet cloth, in which players placed bets on the numbers that would appear on dice rolled from a cup. Skewed results or even cheating were facilitated by the fact that so many dice were imperfect, or even designed to produce certain results more often than others.

Board games included checkers, chess, cribbage and backgammon, more or less in order of popularity. Checkers, in particular, were popular throughout the armies and navies of both sides. Boards used by soldiers in the field might be handmade and would be small so as not to be an encumbrance. Checkerboard patterns in red and green or red and yellow were as common as today's more familiar red and black. Chess was played much less frequently, but was not unknown.

Many sorts of card games were played by soldiers, enlisted men and officers alike, including draw poker, chuck-a-luck, cribbage, euchre, faro, keno, seven-up and twenty-one. Regiments tended to have games that they favored, poker being the most common. Such games were usually played for stakes, which among less-than-friendly groups could lead to sore feelings or even charges of cheating.

While dice and board game components were frequently crude or home-made, many sorts of manufactured playing cards were available. During the Civil War, many varieties of decks were produced that replaced traditional playing card symbols with military and patriotic imagery. For example, the Union Playing Card Company replaced the traditional suits of spades, clubs, hearts and diamonds with eagles, shields, stars and flags. Similarly, a deck manufactured in the South depicted a different Confederate general or cabinet member on each card.

Although soldiers enjoyed gambling, a preponderance of men considered gambling, "**throwing the papers**," to be a mortal sin. As a result, soldiers would play cards or dice right up until marching off to battle, then destroy or discard their gaming implements so they would not be upon their person if they were slain. After the battle, survivors eager for a game would search the former campsite for their cards or dice or purchase new ones from **sutlers**.

Other games, such as jackstraws, were also played by some civilians and soldiers, and games like **prisoner's base** were also popular with children.

MUSIC

Singing as a group activity was a common activity in the nineteenth century, whether hymns amongst the devout or bawdy drinking songs among comrades, and soldiers in the field often sang around the proverbial campfire. Lyrics to popular songs tended to be widely known, especially in the armies, where they could be disseminated rapidly.

Many people also owned and knew how to play a wide variety of instruments, banjos being among the most popular. While the banjo is today associated with Appalachia and the South, it was as likely to be played in the camps of either army. Piano might be found in middle-class or wealthy homes or saloons, while portable instruments, like harmonicas and mouth harps, were more likely to be found in the hands of the less affluent or those who had to carry their possessions or had less room to store them, like soldiers or sailors.

READING

Many sorts of reading materials were available to people during the Civil War, among them publications like *Harper's Bazaar* and *Godey's Lady's Book*, classic

Soldiers had little of their time occupied by battle, and found many ways to fill the lonely hours of camp life.

and popular literature and a wide variety of daily and weekly newspapers (newspapers are further discussed under Communications in chapter nine). Many families entertained themselves by listening to one member read aloud from a novel or periodical.

Popular novelists of the day included Louisa May Alcott and Augusta Jane Evans, and, in the years following the war, Mark Twain, whose *Innocents Abroad* was published in 1869, and former Gen. Lew Wallace, whose *Ben Hur: A Tale of the Christ* was published in 1880. Popular among many readers were dime novels, which detailed the often exaggerated adventures of people like Buffalo Bill and other heroes of the far West.

Many sorts of magazines and newspapers were also readily available and covered a wide variety of themes, including agriculture, art, children's literature, education, etiquette, fashion, fiction, finance, gardening, home architecture, humor, labor reform, medicine, music, politics, religion, sports and women's issues. And, with subscription rates as low as $2 to $4 per year, such publications could easily be obtained by most of those interested in them. After the war ended, numbers of such publications increased markedly, and by 1870 almost six thousand different periodicals were being published in the United States.

SPORTS

Sports, both as participant and spectator events, were popular with people during the mid-nineteenth century. Prior to the Civil War, horse racing and boxing were among the most popular spectator sports with many Americans, especially in the North. And after the war, baseball entered the scene as America's most popular pastime, a role it has continued to play to a lesser or greater extent. Other popular sports included football, cricket, heel-toe walking races and horse trotting.

THEATER

Prior to and during the nineteenth century, American theater was heavily influenced by trends in Europe.

In Europe as well as America, the Industrial Revolution created a need for entertainments geared toward the tastes of working-class people, such as pantomimes, spectacles, melodrama and the previously mentioned vaudeville. And, on a somewhat higher plane, were romantic dramas and revivals of classic plays and operas, including Shakespeare.

Several different sorts of variety shows arose during the nineteenth century as forms of entertainment for the great masses of working people, many of them immigrants living in the rapidly growing urban areas. Music halls in England and minstrel shows and burlesque in America often employed coarse humor and were generally considered appropriate fare for saloons or male-only audiences. More wholesome variety shows and vaudeville arose in the years following the Civil War as a response to the growing demand for family entertainment.

To a large extent, because the North was more urbanized, such forms of entertainment were better known and more popular there than in the South. In its cities, however, such as New Orleans, minstrel and burlesque shows would have been at home.

Music Halls
At the time of the Civil War, music halls were the most popular form of mass entertainment in England. These were theaters or taverns with stages where people could drink, hear and sing popular songs, and see dance routines, comedy, magic and other acts, all presided over by a master of ceremonies. Many of the professional music hall entertainers became famous throughout England and some of them even toured the United States.

Minstrel Shows

While music halls were, largely, a phenomena peculiar to England, minstrel shows were indigenous to the United States. Together, they helped to influence the rise of the burlesque and vaudeville variety show in America.

Also called blackface shows, minstrel shows had existed in America since Colonial times, mainly as short acts with travelling carnivals. In the 1820s, troupes like the Virginia Minstrels began to put on full-length variety shows; before long, these spread throughout the United States and to England, where they joined other music hall acts. During the 1840s, the Virginia Minstrels were touring cities both in the United States and Europe.

Such blackface shows included comedy, dance and popular music, typically performed by white men wearing black face paint and singing and speaking like blacks. Indeed, the basis of such shows was the parodying of blacks, something that has made them anathema today. It also seems a bit strange today that such a widespread, popular form of entertainment could have at its heart such a narrow gimmick.

Minstrel shows typically consisted of three parts. In the first, the entire troupe sat on stage in a semicircle and sang popular songs (e.g., "Camptown Races," "Old Folks at Home," etc.), and engaged in riddles, puns and comedic one-liners. The second part, called the olio, was a variety show in which entertainers appeared and performed individually. The third part was farcical skit that combined comedy and music in what was often a parody of current fads or events. A master of ceremonies, or interlocutor, usually oversaw the events of the show.

Among the best known minstrel acts of the age were the Christy Minstrels. Formed by Edwin P. Christy, this troupe played in New York City from 1846 until 1854 and helped popularize the songs of Stephen Foster.

Minstrel shows dominated the American entertainment scene until long after the end of the Civil War. They reflected a preoccupation with slavery and the role of the freed black in society, and highlighted how racist much of white society was. As a form of entertainment, however, their days were numbered.

Variety Shows

Some impresarios saw a market for "clean" variety shows that left behind saloon environment and were suitable for women and children as well as men. One of these was Tony Pastor, the "father of American vaudeville," who abandoned his career as a circus clown for the variety show business. In 1865, he opened his first variety theater in New York City, which specialized in wholesome acts and songs that poked fun at the upper crust, aspects that made his shows popular with working-class family people.

Burlesque (shown above) and vaudeville replaced minstrel shows as a popular form of variety show during the nineteenth century.

Burlesque

There was still a market for the off-color show, however. Burlesque shows began as comic parodies of well-known people or subjects, but steadily evolved into "girlie" shows that included provocative displays of the female form. One of the most famous of these was Lydia Thompson and her British Blondes, who brought their burlesques of classical drama to America in 1868. In this all-girl show, the women wore tights and short tunics when playing male roles, outfits that were considered very risque at the time.

By the 1870s, American producers like M.B. Leavitt capitalized on the market for "**burleycue**" and "**leg shows**" by organizing female burlesque troupes who replaced parody with racy dance routines like the cancan. Before long, the buxom stars of these shows were being referred to as "burlesque queens." Increasingly, however, male comedians were also added to the acts and developed comedy routines designed to appeal to the sorts of crowds who came to burlesque shows.

Vaudeville

Vaudeville shows were a variety of unconnected musical, dancing, comedy and specialty acts that developed in the decades following the Civil War. To a large extent, they evolved from the olio, or variety portion of the minstrel show (minus, of course, the blackface). First built in the 1880s, vaudeville houses were ornate, opulent theaters with uniformed attendants where people of any class could feel like honored guests for an entry fee of 25¢.

Vaudeville, predecessor of the modern variety show, emerged in the 1870s as a popular form of urban entertainment and eventually came to replace the minstrel show. However, in its early years it was widely considered a lewd form of entertainment for men only, and it was not until the 1880s that it became a popular form of family entertainment.

Stars

Like celebrities today, the theatrical stars of the nineteenth century were well-known and loved. Most beloved of all was "Swedish Nightingale" Jenny Lind (1820–1887), a singer who appeared in every major European opera house between 1838 and 1849 and toured throughout the United States in the early 1850s, where she was lauded in the press. Other European stars, like William Charles Macready, were also well-known on both sides of the Atlantic, and frequently toured American cities during the mid-nineteenth century.

The New World also produced its own stars during this period. Stage divas were also popular during the Civil War and the years following it, and many were as well-known and popular as celebrities today.

Edwin Forrest (1806–1872) was perhaps the greatest, and certainly the most popular, American tragic actor of the nineteenth century. Known for his arrogance, short temper, booming voice and fierce looks, Forrest was famous for his many Shakespearean roles, especially Othello. He also offered prizes to encourage the writing of American plays, and as a result had many roles created for him.

Ira Frederick Aldridge (1804–1867), a free black from New York City, became the first famous black American actor, albeit in Europe. In 1825, he debuted with an acting troupe in London as the African prince Oroonoko in *The Revolt of Surinam.* Nicknamed the "African Roscius," he was also lauded for his roles as Othello, King Lear and Macbeth. Aldridge was popular throughout Europe, especially in Germany, and became a British citizen in 1863.

Other well-known American actors of the day included Charlotte Saunders Cushman; Edwin Booth, who also managed his own New York City theater; and his brother, John Wilkes Booth, most famous today as the assassin of Abraham Lincoln.

Directors and Playwrights

As stage productions became more complex, they increasingly required a director, a role which arose in its modern incarnation during this period. While he or she might still have a leading part in the play, the director was also responsible for overseeing every aspect of its production.

Playwrights also enjoyed improved status during the nineteenth century. They increasingly acted in or directed their own plays, benefitted from new copyright laws that protected their work in both the United States and Europe, and began to receive royalties.

Scenery and Lighting

New technology allowed for a revolution in lighting and scenery during the nineteenth century.

By the 1820s, candles and oil lamps had been replaced by gaslights in many theaters, and spotlighting effects through the use of limelight and the carbon arc were common by the 1850s. Many theaters were also fully trapped or even had hydraulic lifts, as did Edwin Booth's theater, allowing scenery to either be raised from below the stage or "flown in" from above.

Costumes, props and settings also reached a high level of realism and historical accuracy during this period, especially in renditions of plays with historical underpinnings, such as those of Shakespeare. Scenery had traditionally been painted on flats, a practice that gave way to elaborate settings, such as sinking ships, falling trees and erupting volcanoes. Such elaborate sets often required a long period between scenes to set up. Real animals, including dogs, horses and even elephants, joined actors on stage. Other innovations of the era included a completely enclosed, or "box" set, adopted for comedies, and moving panoramas to give the illusion of movement or travel.

Such elaborate production values meant that long-running plays also became increasingly common. As a result, the repertory system, in which theaters changed their performances almost nightly and under which a single theater might present dozens of plays in a single season, was largely replaced.

CIRCUSES AND CARNIVALS

Circuses of all sizes, both travelling and stationary, were increasingly elaborate and popular forms of entertainment during the mid-nineteenth century.

Travelling Circuses

Tent circuses started in America around 1830 and reached their peak in the early 1880s with the great traveling shows of Barnum and Bailey. Carnivals, smaller affairs that included games, rides and sideshows, also existed and increasingly began to set up camp in conjunction with state and county fairs.

American circuses typically featured three rings, with individual acts playing simultaneously in each of them. In between the rings and to the sides of them

Travelling circuses with three rings and a bigtop became increasingly popular during the nineteenth century, and largely replaced permanent, indoor circuses.

were platforms for additional displays. Surrounding all of these staging areas was a large hippodrome track used for pageants, parades and races.

Despite the familiar term "three-ring circus," American circuses could actually have anywhere from two to seven rings; many, few or no additional platforms; and lack the usual hippodrome track. In Europe, the multiring circus never really caught on, and most retained a single ring.

Indoor Circuses

During the nineteenth century, many circuses were housed within permanent, roofed buildings and did not travel from place to place. Among such indoor circuses were the amphitheaters of John Bill Ricketts in America, Astley's in England and the Cirque Olympique and the Cirque d'Hiver in Paris.

In addition to the ring, many of these circuses had a large scenic stage used for presenting spectacular theater dramas that included horses and other animals owned by the circus.

Circus Acts

Prior to and during the early part of the nineteenth century, circus programs consisted largely of trick horsemanship performed by costumed entertainers within a large circle, or ring.

Horses in such acts were trained to gallop within the circle at a constant speed, allowing a standing rider to maintain his or her balance by leaning inward slightly and making use of centrifugal force. To this basic act many variations were added, such as standing astride a pair of running horses, riding with one foot on the horse's head and the other in the saddle, and balancing head downward in the saddle while firing a pistol at a target.

More sophisticated acts included somersaults from one horse to another, human pyramids upon several galloping horses, pantomimes and *pas de deux* with partners. Female trick riders were also extremely popular during this period, leaping over broadcloth banners and through paper-covered hoops.

In between such strenuous acts, a "clown to the ring" performed acrobatic feats and comedy to give the riders and their mounts a needed rest.

In the years prior to and following the Civil War, trick horsemanship began to decline and was increasingly replaced with **dressage** and routines in which several matched, unmounted horses executed various evolutions at the behest of a trainer, rather than a rider.

During this period, many sorts of new, nonequestrian acts were also added to the circus, such as the flying trapeze. Wild animal acts also began to appear in circuses, performed by "lion kings" and "lion queens" and caged animals.

One of the most popular features of travelling circuses in the years following the Civil War was the exotic spectacle of the street parade, performed by a circus as it came into town. Such parades included brass bands; elephants; brilliantly painted, carved and gilded wagons; and costumed entertainers mounted on horses or in chariots, all to the sounds of a **calliope**.

America's most famous circus bears the name of and owes much of its success to Phineas Taylor Barnum (1810–1891), perhaps the most famous of all American showmen. In 1835 the self-proclaimed "Prince of Humbugs" launched his career as a showman with the purchase of Joice Heth, an aged black woman who he exhibited as the 161-year-old nurse of George Washington.

From 1841 to 1868, Barnum ran the American Museum, one of New York City's most popular attractions, a museum and menagerie that was home to thousands of curiosities, freaks and wild animals. And in 1871, Barnum took his show on the road, in the form of a huge travelling circus, museum, and menagerie.

Fairs and Expositions

Some of the most popular events of the nineteenth century were great national or international exhibitions showcasing culture or technological advancements. Among the greatest of the century were those held in the United States in 1876 (in celebration of the Centennial) and 1893, in England in 1851, and in France in 1855, 1878 and 1889. Scientists, captains of industry, arms manufacturers and futurists like H.G. Wells and Jules Verne were among the luminaries at such events.

In the United States, such fairs included all the elements of a carnival. For example, entertainers formed a kind of midway outside of the 1876 Philadelphia Centennial, America's first exposition. Likewise, state and county fairs, originally intended to promote trade and agricultural education, gradually began to include carnival amusements.

TOBACCO AND OTHER VICES

Partaking of tobacco and liquor were two of the ways soldiers and sailors on both sides passed the time and distracted themselves from the rigors and anxieties of military life.

Smoking and chewing tobacco were widespread among the soldiery and beloved pastimes for many. In the late 1840s, U.S. Army soldiers had returned from the Mexican War with a taste for the richer, darker tobacco of South and Central America, leading to an increased demand for cigars and other tobacco products, which in turn stimulated a U.S. tobacco industry.

During the Civil War, tobacco rations were given to both Union and Confederate soldiers; many Northerners were introduced to tobacco this way. During Sherman's 1864 march across Georgia, Union soldiers attracted to the mild, sweet "bright" tobacco of the South raided warehouses for chewing tobacco. Some of this bright tobacco made it back to the North, where it became extremely popular among tobacco users.

Contemporary diaries are replete with references to tobacco use, most of them positive. "Who can find words to tell the story of the soldier's affection for his faithful root-briar pipe! As the cloudy incense of the weed rises in circling wreaths about his head, as he hears the murmuring of the fire, and watches the glowing and fading of the hour pervading his mortal frame, what bliss!" wrote John D. Billings, a Union soldier who waxed poetic on the subject. "And yonder sits a man who scorns the pipe—and why? He is a chewer of the weed. To him, the sweetness of it seems not to be drawn out by the fiery test, but rather by the persuasion of moisture and pressure."

Shortages of tobacco constantly threatened to deprive soldiers of these pleasures, and a great many letters home include requests for tobacco. One of the few shortages to hit the North more profoundly than the South was of tobacco, which was produced primarily in Confederate, rather than Union, states. Union soldiers often compensated for this shortage by trading Confederate soldiers coffee or other items rare in the South for tobacco.

A Tobacco Industry

In 1849, in the aftermath of the Mexican War (1846–1848), John Edmund Liggett established the J.E. Liggett and Brother tobacco company in St. Louis, Missouri, and others soon followed. In 1852, matches were introduced, making smoking immeasurably more convenient. By 1860, nearly 350 tobacco factories existed in Virginia and North Carolina alone, virtually all of them producing chewing tobacco. Only a half dozen of them produced smoking tobacco, manufactured as a side product from scraps left over from plugs.

Cigarettes, originally a Turkish innovation, had for some years been imported from the Near East by English tobacconists. In 1854, however, London tobacconist Philip Morris began making his own cigarettes, and Old Bond Street soon became the center of the retail tobacco trade. Manufactured cigarettes appeared in America in 1860, a popular early brand being Bull Durham, and in 1864 the first domestically produced cigarettes were manufactured.

Tobacco was big business by the eve of the Civil War. In 1860, Lorillard wrapped $100 bills at random in packages of Century cigarette tobacco to celebrate the hundredth anniversary of their firm.

In 1862, the U.S. government capitalized on the lucrative nature of tobacco and imposed a tax on it to help fund the war efforts, realizing about $3 million in revenue by the end of the conflict. In 1863, to help facilitate taxation, the U.S. Congress passed a law calling for manufacturers to create cigar boxes on which IRS agents could paste Civil War excise tax stamps, a law that inspired the beginning of cigar box art. In 1864, Congress levied the first cigarette tax.

Tobacco use continued unabated after the Civil War. For example, from 1865 to 1870, there was a growing demand in New York City for exotic Turkish cigarettes, which prompted tobacconists to seek skilled tobacco rollers from Europe. And in 1873, Myers Brothers and Company marketed Love tobacco with a theme of North-South Civil War reconciliation.

In 1875, R. J. Reynolds founded R.J. Reynolds Tobacco Company and began producing chewing tobacco, including such brands as Brown's Mule, Golden Rain, Dixie's Delight, Yellow Rose and Purity. Also in 1875, Allen and Ginter began including picture cards in their cigarette brands, Richmond Straight Cut No. 1 and Pet, to stiffen the packs and serve as a premium, something that was a big hit with smokers. Themes included "Fifty Scenes of Perilous Occupations" and "Flags of All Nations," as well as boxers, actresses and famous battles. The cards were a huge hit. The same year, the company also offered a reward of $75,000 for a cigarette-rolling machine.

Indeed, at the 1876 Centennial Celebration in Philadelphia, Allen and Ginter's cigarette displays were so impressive that some contemporary writers thought the exposition marked the birth of the cigarette.

Opponents of Tobacco

Tobacco use was not enamored universally, however. In 1836, Samuel Green wrote in the *New England Almanack and Farmers Friend* that tobacco was a poison lethal to men and insects alike (it was often used as an insecticide component), in addition to being filthy. One of these, an 1859 tract by Rev. George Trask called "Thoughts and Stories for American Lads: Uncle Toby's Anti-Tobacco Advice to His Nephew Billy Bruce," said that "physicians tell us that twenty thousand or more in our own land are killed" every year by tobacco.

Indeed, contemporary doctors recognized it as a health threat as well, as evidenced by an 1845 letter of John Quincy Adams, who wrote that "in my early youth I was addicted to the use of tobacco in two of its mysteries, smoking and chewing. I was warned by a medical friend of the pernicious operation of this habit upon the stomach and the nerves." And in 1856 and 1857, there was a running debate among the readers of the British medical journal *Lancet* about the health effects of tobacco (which ran along moral as well as medical lines, with little substantiation on either side).

Some military diarists complained of how filthy camps became when a preponderance of men chewed tobacco and of the noxious quality of the smoke. There were also social movements, akin to the temperance movements, that decried the use of tobacco in pamphlets that were distributed to soldiers.

Alcohol

"No one agent so much obstructs this army," wrote Gen. George McClellan, "as the degrading vice of drunkenness." Complete abstinence among the troops, he continued, "would be worth fifty thousand men to the armies of the United States."

Indeed, a high number of insubordinations, camp brawls, sexual assaults and other crimes involved alcohol, as indicated by letters, diaries and official U.S. Army court marshal proceedings. Many other distasteful episodes from the war also involved drinking to excess. For example, on July 30, 1864, Union Gen. J.H. Ledlie hid behind the lines in a bombproof shelter while the troops of his division were massacred in the "Crater" outside of Petersburg, Virginia. Desperately seeking orders, some of Ledlie's subordinate officers eventually found him, drunk in his hideaway. And Ulysses S. Grant, Lincoln's champion general in the final phase of the war, had himself been forced out of the Army in 1854 on account of his heavy drinking.

Military personnel obtained alcohol at saloons when near towns and from **sutlers** when in the field, and were even issued it on occasion. "Someone at headquarters got the idea that a quantity of whisky issued to each man in the evening would be beneficial to the general health of the men," wrote John M. King, a soldier with the Ninety-second Illinois, in describing one such episode.

"There was not enough given each man to make him drunk . . . but there was just enough to make the men boisterous, excitable, talkative and foolish. After the drinks there was a sort of pandemonium in nearly every tent."

When soldiers could not buy alcohol or did not receive it with their rations, they would make it, and gave names like "Bust-Head," "Nockum Stiff," "Oh! Be Joyful," "Pop Skull" and "Tanglefoot" to such bootleg liquor. Ingredients in one Northern recipe for bootleg liquor included "bark juice, tar-water, turpentine, brown sugar, lamp-oil and alcohol." Southern recipes had similar ingredients and sometimes called for the addition of a piece of raw meat, which, after fermentation for a month, produced "an old and mellow taste," in the words of one veteran.

Prostitution

Despite the overt moral prudishness of the day, prostitution existed, then blossomed with the outbreak of war. Soldiers and sailors, far from home and family, frequently engaged the services of prostitutes. An unfortunate result of this is that at least one in ten Union soldiers suffered from some sort of venereal disease during the war, and a similar proportion was likely among personnel in other services and in the Southern forces. In an age before the introduction of antibiotics, the effects of such diseases could be terrible.

Brothels were available in urban areas of any size and common in places with high concentrations of troops, especially in the national capitals. In Washington, DC, in 1863, there were more than 450 brothels employing more than 7,000 prostitutes. And Richmond, Virginia, streetwalkers openly plied the streets, going so far as to solicit customers in the very shadow of the Capitol. Prostitution was often considered an activity plied by theater actresses, although this perception was probably more widespread than whatever reality it was based on. On the other hand, there are many documented cases of young women being forced into prostitution after finding they were unable to support themselves at low-paying jobs as clerks or factory workers.

With so many prostitutes operating in heavily populated areas during the Civil War, prices tended to be competitive, and $3 or $4 for a session was not uncommon.

TERMS

burleycue: A popular name for burlesque shows.

calliope: A set of steam-powered brass whistles operated by a keyboard or a pin-and-barrel mechanism that imitated the sounds of a train locomotive whistle. With sound that could carry up to twelve miles, the calliope was intended to attract attention rather than play music, and it was a familiar feature of circuses, fairs and riverboats. It was invented by J.C. Stoddard in 1855 in Worcester, Massachusetts.

dressage: The execution of precision movements by a highly trained horse in response to nearly imperceptible signals from its rider.

leg shows: One of the nicknames given to burlesque shows.

pas de deux: An intricate routine intended for two performers.

Prisoner's Base, Prison Base: A game played by children since at least the 1840s. Each of two teams has a home base that players are sent to after being tagged or otherwise caught and from which they can be freed only in some specified way.

sutler: A traveling merchant who sold goods to the soldiers and typically followed armies on the march. Sutlers were generally suspected of gouging soldiers and of selling substandard goods, and when they were robbed or otherwise caused mischief they tended to receive little sympathy from military men.

throwing the papers: A slang term that meant to play cards.

voltige: A form of trick riding that involved a rider leaping on and off a moving horse.

CHAPTER SIX

THE CIVIL WAR VIEWED FROM THE HOME FRONT

Tensions between the North and South had been building for nearly fifty years prior to the outbreak of war. Ironically, when armed conflict did erupt, it came as a surprise to many people. While the question had been raised several times in the past whether an individual state had the right to withdraw from the nation,or whether several could form a new confederacy, it had never so dramatically demanded an answer.

When civil war erupted in early 1861, it was thus not directly the right of people in some states to own slaves. Nonetheless, almost all the rifts of the preceding decades could be attributed to differences between abolitionists and radical Republicans in the North and proslavery Democrats in the South. And in the years immediately preceding the war, three historic events that set the stage for Southern secession were all concerned with the issue of slavery.

In early 1857, the U.S. Supreme Court declared that Congress had no power to prohibit slavery in the various U.S. territories, but Republicans and even many Northern Democrats refused to accept this opinion. Soon after, newly elected Democratic President James Buchanan (1857–1861) asked Congress to admit Kansas to the Union as a slave state, an act that enraged many Northern politicians and voters and contributed to the election of abolitionist Republican Abraham Lincoln in 1860. Tensions continued to smolder throughout Buchanan's

U.S. President Abraham Lincoln assumed broad powers in order to see the country through crisis of civil war, and was regarded by some as a dictator. His unwavering resolve, however, helped move the United States toward reunification and reconciliation.

unpopular presidency, and in 1859, fanatical abolitionist John Brown attacked the Federal arsenal at Harpers Ferry, Virginia (now West Virginia), hoping to ignite a general slave uprising.

After Lincoln was elected in November 1860, Southern states began to secede. Seven left the Union and formed the Confederate States of America by the time the new U.S. president was inaugurated in March 1861. Despite a conciliatory inaugural speech, the seceding states remained recalcitrant, seizing Federal forts and arsenals in the South, raising troops and granting commissions in their own forces to Southern officers who had or were willing to resign their commissions in the U.S. Army, Navy, Marine Corps and Revenue Cutter Service.

On April 12, 1861, Confederate forces commanded by Gen. P.G.T. Beauregard opened fire on the Union garrison at Fort Sumter, South Carolina, igniting war between the followers of the two opposing governments and flinging the country into turmoil. (An overview of the war can be found in Appendix I on page 215. Thousands of books contain descriptions of the various battles of the war, and several of the best resources can be found in Appendix II on page 234 and Appendix III on page 243.)

THE NORTHERN VIEW

Cries of "On to Richmond" resounded throughout the Northern states as war hysteria spread through them and the Union began to implement the **Anaconda Plan**. Thousands of ninety-day volunteers rushed to join state regiments, and the country moved to put down the rebellion and restore the Union. This goal marked the Northern struggle from beginning to end, as exemplified by Abraham Lincoln.

Unfortunately, many of the Union's other leaders were not so steadfast in their resolve. Gen. George McClellan, commander of the Army of the Potomac, the main Union army in the East, demonstrated great organizational talents in training troops and organizing military units. However, he consistently refused to engage the enemy in battle, and after he botched the 1862 Peninsula Campaign (a plodding attempt to capture Richmond) and refused to pursue and destroy the Confederate army after the September 1862 Battle of Antietam, Lincoln finally removed him from command in November 1862. Those who immediately followed McClellan, however, were not much more satisfactory.

As the death toll from the conflict mounted, Lincoln feared that preserving the Union alone might not be enough to maintain public support for the war, and he announced a preliminary Emancipation Proclamation in the wake of Antietam and followed it with a formal proclamation on January 1, 1863. From that point onward, the war was no longer simply a pragmatic one of national unity, but also a moral one of abolition.

Some Northerners, however, resented the idea that they might be forced to fight for the rights of blacks. When a draft was initiated in 1863, riots broke out in many Northern cities. The worst was in New York City, where they were led by Irish immigrants, who, being at the bottom of the social ladder, disliked the idea that blacks might advance socially and feared having to compete with them for jobs. Irish volunteer firemen attacked the officials drawing the names of those being drafted, battled with the police and assaulted blacks on the streets, hanging many from lampposts and even burning an orphanage for black children. In the course of the violence, stores and warehouses were looted and burned. Finally, heavy rains, the police and troops ordered in from Gettysburg were able to subdue the violence, which lasted for three days.

Various pro-Southern and antiwar organizations also worked against the Union cause or on behalf of the Confederacy during the war, mostly in the slave-holding border states and in the Midwest. Such groups included the **Copperheads** and the **Knights of the Golden Circle**.

For more than a year, Lincoln dealt with a series of senior generals, among them Hooker, Meade and Burnside, who he considered inadequate in terms of competence, aggressiveness or a desire to preserve the Union. By March 1864, however, he had found an able general whose attitudes about the war matched his own, and placed Ulysses S. Grant at the head of all the armies of the United States. Grant, along with William T. Sherman in the West, were concerned not with capturing Richmond, but with a strategy of total war, annihilating the Confederate military forces and destroying the South's infrastructure and ability to fight.

Early in the election of 1864, there was some notion that Union soldiers would rally around Democratic peace candidate George McClellan. However,

In the last years of the war, hard-edged generals like Ulysses S. Grant inexorably led the Union to victory against the Confederacy.

the Democratic platform was confused and at odds with itself, and many soldiers preferred to see the war to its conclusion, rather than acknowledge defeat and see all they had fought and suffered for thrown away. Lincoln won an undisputed victory in the North.

War ended within months of Lincoln's inauguration. When he was assassinated, just five days after Robert E. Lee surrendered the Army of Northern Virginia to Grant, he was elevated to the status of a martyr in the minds of many contemporary Americans.

THE SOUTHERN VIEW

In 1861, Southerners at all levels of society had a variety of reasons for linking their fates to the Confederacy. Loyalty to individual states, a burgeoning quasi-nationalism and a sense of states' rights all played a part in the decision of Southerners to secede from the Union and form their own government. Just as important, however, was that a relatively small, rich, very powerful landed aristocracy saw their wealth, lifestyle and other interests threatened. This land-holding upper class, along with most other whites in the South, feared that

Robert E. Lee, the Confederacy's greatest general, led the Army of Northern Virginia and drove it to perform almost superhuman feats.

antislavery forces in the North would eventually have slavery abolished, destroying the South's plantation-based economy.

Such feelings were by no means universal. Indeed, there were pro-Union elements in every Southern state, and in some, notably Virginia and Tennessee, large segments of the population were opposed to secession, mostly yeoman farmers who did not own slaves and ultimately had nothing to gain from rebellion.

Morale of soldiers and civilians was as important in the South as in the North. Shortages of staple food items and consumer goods contributed to sagging Southern morale, however, and bread riots erupted in Richmond and a few other Confederate cities in 1863. Soldiers increasingly received letters from home telling of the hardships their loved ones were suffering, something that led to higher rates of desertion amongst Confederate forces than in the North.

After the twin defeats of Gettysburg and Vicksburg in summer 1863, the Confederacy lost all hope of European support and much of its ability to take the war onto Northern soil. From that point onward, the war became a slow, bloody struggle for survival that the South saw it was less and less able to win.

116

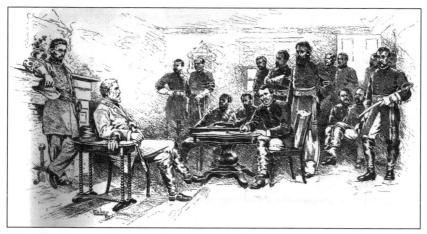

Confederate General Robert E. Lee surrendered his forces to Union General Ulysses S. Grant at Appomattox Courthouse, Virginia, on April 9, 1865. Influenced by Lincoln, Grant went out of his way to keep from humiliating the defeated Rebels.

Union forces intensified their operations in the South in 1864, destroying farms, cities, railroads and anything else the Confederacy needed to continue fighting. Desertions soared as soldiers abandoned the army and returned to their homes and families. On April 9, 1865, with his army starving and under-manned, General Lee surrendered to Grant at Appomattox Courthouse, Virginia. Other Confederate commands continued their increasingly hopeless struggle for several months, but before long war ended for the South and Reconstruction loomed ahead of it.

WHO FOUGHT?

It is easy to think of the Civil War as simply being a conflict between two great armies of white men, along with some blacks near the end of the war. Northerners and Southerners, however, could further be divided into men and women; officers and enlisted soldiers; whites and blacks; and many ethnic groups, including English, American Indians, Irish, Germans, Italians and Jews. And while a great many people came from families who had lived in America for several generations, there were also many people whose parents, or themselves, were immigrants. Consequently, many different sorts of people fought in or were otherwise affected by the Civil War.

Every state loyal to the Union provided regiments of soldiers to the U.S. military, every state that joined the Confederacy provided regiments of troops

117

for the defense of the South, and some states, notably the Northern slave states, provided regiments of troops to each side. And, within each state, there were individuals who chose to throw in their lot with one side or the other, based on a variety of personal reasons and circumstances.

Union soldiers and sailors were mainly white, but significant numbers of blacks and American Indians also served. Confederate soldiers were also mainly white and included some American Indians (policies preventing blacks from fighting in the Southern forces were not repealed until near the end of the war, too late for any to be put into uniform). In many cases, the Confederacy was so undermanned that it had to make do with anyone it could attract into the service. In the C.S. Navy, for example, many sailors were not Americans at all, but rather sailors and adventurers from a variety of nations, notably Great Britain.

Beyond simply being "white," many of the soldiers on both sides came from ethnic groups that if anything were more distinct during the Civil War than they are today. Soldiers often formed into regiments made up wholly or largely of troops from the same ethnic background.

Regional nicknames became common during the Civil War, as units from around the country came into contact with each other. For example, the name "Tarheel" was applied to anyone from North Carolina, "Dutchman" was anyone of German origin and "Mick" was a disparaging term for an Irishman. That such terms are listed in the following section should not be taken as a sanctioning of their usage.

Germans

About a million Germans lived in the United States when the Civil War broke out, about half of them having arrived since the German Revolution of 1848. These immigrants settled mostly in the large urban areas of Cincinnati, Milwaukee, Minneapolis and St. Louis. By 1860, the country had twenty-eight German-language daily newspapers in fifteen cities. Because of the areas they settled, Germans were widely represented in the Union armies, and much less so in the Confederate forces.

Several all-German regiments served in the Union forces, many in the Eleventh Corps, and there were also a number of German artillery units. Germans who fought for the Union included generals Franz Sigel, August von Kautz, Godfrey Weitzel and Carl Schurz, whose career as a professor at the University of Bonn was dashed by his role in the German Revolution. Among the most famous Germans to fight for the South were Capt. Justus Scheibert and Maj. Johann August Heinrich Heros von Borcke, both of whom served as Confederate staff officers (neither of them were Americans, however, and both ultimately returned to Germany).

Nicknames applied to Germans in the mid-nineteenth century included "cabbagehead," "sauerkraut" and "sausage." "Prussian," from the northern German region, had long been applied to Germans in general, but during the nineteenth century was also applied to arrogant or militaristic Germans. Similarly, "Junker," a word for a German nobleman, was used increasingly during the 1800s to mean an overbearing or militaristic German. "Dutch," from the German Deutsche, or "German," was also used in nicknames (e.g., a German bartender or neighbor might be referred to as "the Dutchman").

Hispanics

About ten thousand Americans of Spanish descent fought on both sides of the Civil War. In the Southwest, many Tejanos, Hispanic natives of Texas, fought in most of the ninety or so actions fought in Texas. It is uncertain if there were any non-Tejano all-Hispanic regiments, but there probably were not. There were individual Hispanic soldiers who became prominent during the war, however, among them Union generals Don Carlos Buell and Edward Ferrero.

In the 1800s, the most common derogatory term for a Hispanic was "Dago," from the common Spanish name Diego (it was not until the late 1880s that it was applied mainly to Italians). "Greaser" was a common epithet for Mexicans that originated in Texas during the 1830s prior to the Mexican War.

Irish

In 1846, the Irish Potato Famine caused a mass exodus of people from Ireland, and by 1860 more than 1.5 million Irish immigrants lived in America, as well as many people of Irish descent. Large numbers of Irish fought on both sides during the war, more than 150,000 of them for the North, which fielded a number of Irish regiments and an entire Irish brigade, and an uncertain number for the South. Fewer Irish immigrants lived in the South, and as a result colorful all-Irish brigades and regiments are a phenomenon associated with the Union armies.

After the war, many Irish soldiers were drawn to the Fenians, a quasi-military organization equipped with surplus Civil War weapons that made a number of abortive military attacks into British-controlled Canada.

Common terms used to refer to the Irish in mid-nineteenth century America included "Paddy," "Pat," "Irisher," "Irish American," and the disparaging "Mick."

Italians

Italians were one of the smaller European minorities in America at the time of the Civil War (although millions immigrated to the United States in the decades following the war). Nonetheless, Italians, many of them former followers of Italian revolutionary Giuseppe Garibaldi, fought on both sides during the war, especially for the North.

Many of these former republican revolutionaries identified with the Union cause, and some of them joined the Thirty-ninth New York Infantry Regiment. It was known as the Garibaldi Guard for its large number of Italian soldiers and was distinguished by red shirts similar to the ones they had worn when fighting tyranny in Italy.

Prominent Italians during the Civil War included Count Luigi Palma di Cesnola, whose military academy in New York City trained many young Italians for Union military service; Luigi Tinelli, a militia commander; and Francesco Spinola, who raised four regiments of Italian-Americans and led them as their general.

Women

Although women were not generally allowed to join the military at the time of the Civil War, a number found ways to serve the armed forces on both sides, some of them in uniform.

Most of these were vivandieres or cantinieres, women or girls attached mostly to Union armies who carried water and ammunition to soldiers in combat, helped the wounded and carried messages between commanders and their troops.

Notable women in uniform included Sally Tompkins, who ran a hospital in Richmond and was rewarded with the rank and pay of a captain, and Bridget Divers, who served as a trooper in her husband's unit, the First Michigan Cavalry. Quite a number of other women also served, almost always posing as men. When discovered, most were either honorably discharged or simply dismissed from service.

Blacks

In 1860, about 344,000 free blacks lived in the Northern states, while nearly nine times as many, about 3 million, were enslaved in the South (the South was also home to about 133,000 free blacks).

After the Emancipation Proclamation, blacks were allowed to enlist in the U.S. Army, and about 179,000 of them did, many of them former slaves from areas occupied by Federal forces. These black soldiers were not treated particularly well. Pay for their first year in service was about half that of white troops, something that caused many morale and pay problems; casualty rates in combat were about 35 percent higher than average white units, in part because Confederate troops were less likely to take black prisoners; twice as many succumbed to disease, largely because they were poorly clothed; and fewer than 100 were made officers, none of them greater than the rank of captain. About 37,300 of those who served were killed.

In the South, legislation was passed in March 1865 allowing the enlistment of blacks into the Confederate army, although it is not likely that many would have willingly joined. Before this effort could be organized, however, the war was over.

Free blacks were referred to as "negroes," "blacks" or "niggers," a term which, while never benign, did not acquire its most hateful connotations until the years following the Civil War.

SLAVERY

Slaves were a part of American society from its earliest days, and by the time the Civil War broke out, at least three million slaves lived in the Southern states.

Slavery as an institution had become unprofitable by the end of the eighteenth century and was waning. Introduction of revolutionary new agricultural equipment like the cotton gin, however, once again turned large-scale plantation slavery into a paying proposition. Prices of slaves rose throughout the nineteenth century, increasingly as slavery was curtailed in the North and the territories. A healthy, young black male slave, who cost $500 in the 1830s, cost $1,800 by the late 1850s. Even as antislavery sentiment strengthened in the North, a Southern aristocracy grew increasingly rich from slavery and determined to ensure its continued survival.

Because of the vested interest the South had in the plantation system, slavery remained viable in America well after it had been abolished by other nations. Britain outlawed the slave trade in 1807, authorizing the search and seizure of ships suspected of carrying slaves and payment for their liberation, and completely outlawed slavery in 1833. By 1840, Spain and Portugal had also officially outlawed the slave trade, but Portuguese ships remained a major source of smuggled slaves throughout the century.

Abolitionist sentiment had acquired momentum in America by 1831, with publication of the antislavery newspaper *The Liberator*. In 1833, the American Anti-Slavery Society was founded in Philadelphia, and by 1840 the Underground Railroad was actively helping slaves escape to the North.

While abolitionist sentiment continued to grow, however, spurred in large part by books like Harriet Beecher Stowe's *Uncle Tom's Cabin*, few people in the North actively opposed slavery until it became the major issue in the 1860 presidential campaign (e.g., in the 1857 Dred Scott decision, the U.S. Supreme Court ruled that neither slaves nor their dependents could be citzens of the nation or any state within it). In his speech accepting the Republican nomination, Lincoln summed up the political dilemma of slavery by stating that a country could not survive half-free and half-slave.

Thus, on the eve of the war, slavery existed largely in the South. Only about a quarter of Southern whites actually owned slaves, and of those who did, nearly nine out of ten owned fewer than twenty slaves. In the deep South, most slaves lived and labored on cotton plantations, most of which had fifty or fewer slaves, but some of which had several hundred. About half of all slaves in the South lived on plantations, working either as "field slaves" or in the homes of their masters as "house servants." Enslaved blacks were also referred to as "slaves," "negroes," "blacks," "niggers" or, by those squeamish about slavery, as "servants."

Slaves made up nearly a quarter of the population of many Southern cities, and in some, such as Charleston, South Carolina, actually outnumbered whites. Many of these slaves worked as house servants, but many others worked at trades, such as baking, blacksmithing, carpentry and cobbling. Skilled slaves were often hired out by their masters, and slaves were sometimes allowed to hire themselves out.

Sale was a constant threat to most slaves, and even those owned by a relatively benign master might be sold if he had to pay off debts. Fathers, mothers and children, not to mention grandparents, cousins, aunts and uncles, might be sold off individually and separated forever, without any recourse. Being sold to a more undesirable location was also used as a punishment.

Discipline on the plantation was maintained by the slave masters and their overseers through physical punishment or the threat of it. Even slave owners who were considered kind or lenient were likely to resort to whippings at times, and the harshest masters employed mutilation, torture and killing to enforce their rules. Offenses that could lead to a slave being beaten included talking back, working slowly, being late to the fields or trying to run away.

Nonetheless, thousands of slaves did run away. Many were subsequently caught and brought back to face punishment, while some grew fearful and returned on their own. Some escaped for good, to the North, Canada, or the territories, or lived in small communities in the wilderness.

Lincoln's Emancipation Proclamation laid the groundwork for ending slavery throughout the United States, and two years later, in 1865, passage of the Thirteenth Amendment made slavery illegal under the Constitution.

FILLING THE RANKS

Early in the war, volunteers flocked to join state regiments in great numbers, responding to the calls from presidents Lincoln and Davis and from their own local leaders.

Unfortunately, recruiters were not very selective, and many men with disqualifying factors, including physical disabilities, were nonetheless enlisted. Once units were formed, however, regimental surgeons tended to be fairly discriminating in removing unsuitable enlistees prior to combat.

As the war dragged on and stories of its horrors drifted home in letters and from soldiers maimed and discharged, enthusiasm waned among enlistees, and it became more and more difficult for states to form new regiments. Eventually, the opposing armed forces' personnel needs could not be met by volunteers alone and other methods were sought.

The Draft

Troop shortages were felt first in the Confederacy and then in the Union. This need for additional troops resulted in the passage of the Confederate Conscription Act of April 16, 1862, in the South and the Enrollment Act of July 1863 in the North.

The Confederate law required troops already in the army to serve an additional two years and subjected white males aged eighteen to thirty-five to three-year enlistments (later in 1863 the upper age was raised to forty-five and by 1864 the range was widened to ages seventeen to fifty). Initially, there were various exemptions, notably for slave owners. By 1863, however, slave owners had to pay a $500 "commutation fee" to be exempted, and substitutions were prohibited.

The Union conscription law made men aged twenty to forty-five subject to conscription. While no exemptions were allowed, Northern men could hire substitutes or pay a $300 commutation fee each time their names were drawn in the draft lotteries.

Whether or not the intent of substitutions, exemptions or commutation fees were to allow the more affluent to avoid military service, this was the practical effect, a fact that did not escape the attention of those who could not afford these options. Questions also arose on both sides as to the legality of draft laws. Southern governors, particularly Joseph Brown of Georgia, vehemently objected to conscription, and insisted that a central government did not have the power to enforce such laws over a confederacy of independent states. In the North, citizens reacted to the draft laws in many cases by rioting.

Ultimately, only about 2 percent of the troops in Union armies were draftees, while about 20 percent of Confederate soldiers had been drafted.

Bounties

In the North, soldiers were not drafted from districts that could fill their troop quotas with volunteers. Thus, local citizens, politicians and draft boards sought ways to entice enough people to join the military so that no one who did not

123

wish to go would be forced. Bounties were one of the most widespread methods.

Cities offered "volunteers" as much as $1,000 cash to enlist in their districts and often filled all of their troop requirements in this way. Unfortunately, the caliber of such men was almost uniformly bad. While many were family men trying to take advantage of a financial windfall, a disproportionate number were rogues or petty criminals who became **bounty jumpers**, taking a bounty, enlisting, deserting and then moving on to a new area and enlisting again in return for another bounty. Penalties for desertion could be as severe as execution, but bounty jumpers were actually caught so rarely that threat of death did not markedly curb the process.

When bounty jumpers did end up in units, they were almost always worthless as soldiers. They dragged down unit morale, caused excessive punishments to be instituted and often had to be assigned to noncombat duties by commanders (e.g., as hospital orderlies, where they routinely robbed the sick and wounded of their own armies).

Criminals

While most Civil War soldiers were decent men, a substantial number of criminals ended up in the ranks of both sides, particularly the Union army, which attracted an unsavory element with its bounty system. And, just as a criminal element found ways to profit from the war, so too was a brand of violent criminal created by the war. Men from both sides acquired a taste for killing and adventure during the Civil War, tastes that they sought to fulfill even after the end of hostilities.

Jesse James was one of the most famous of such outlaws. Born in Clay County, Missouri, in 1847, James was only fourteen when the war began. His family's farm was twice ravaged by pro-Union militia raids, and at fifteen he joined William Quantrill's band of Confederate guerrilla raiders. Quantrill's raiders were among the most savage irregular cavalry units of the war, and were, debatably, little more than heavily armed outlaws who took advantage of the chaos of war to ply their trade. After the war, many of these mounted raiders continued to use the skills they had honed during the war to further criminal careers, among them James, an outlaw until his death in 1880.

RECONSTRUCTION

As early as 1863, leaders in the North began to discuss how to "reconstruct" the South after the final shots of the war were fired. The Reconstruction period lasted for twelve years, from 1865 to 1877, during which Union troops occupied the secessionist Southern states and the Federal government strove to change the region's political and social institutions.

Many of the measures imposed under Reconstruction were intended to be retributive, and thousands of **carpetbaggers** flooded the devastated South seeking personal gain. These factors made Reconstruction a difficult, painful time for the South, and created many long-term resentments. Lincoln and his closest generals had favored a plan for Reconstruction that would have helped mend the rifts of the war; had Lincoln survived the country might have been more painlessly reunified. Andrew Johnson, however, a Southerner himself, did not have the popularity or political force to see Lincoln's plan through, and his attempts led to impeachment (although his opponents failed to remove him from office).

During this period, many white Southerners resented the ability of newly enfranchised black voters to put hated Republican politicians in power, and some of them reacted by forming white supremacy organizations like the **Ku Klux Klan**.

All of the seceding states were readmitted to the Union by early 1870, but violence, civil unrest and military occupation continued until 1877.

TERMS

Anaconda Plan: A plan for subduing the South formulated under Union General-in-Chief Winfield Scott in early 1861. It called for a naval blockade of Southern ports, military control of the Mississippi River Valley so as to split the South in two, and placement of Federal armies to contain the movement of Confederate forces. Scott estimated a year of such treatment would force the South to capitulate.

Lincoln initiated the first two components of the plan, but believed the third would be ineffective. Instead, he replaced Scott with young George McClellan and called for a massive military buildup.

bounty jumper: Volunteers who joined the Union Army in exchange for sizable cash bounties, offered in the latter half of the war, then deserted and reenlisted under a different name for an additional bounty. This process could be repeated almost limitlessly and with little fear of consequences; however, when bounty jumpers were caught, they were often shot.

carpetbaggers: A Southern term for unscrupulous adventurers from the North who swarmed into the South during Reconstruction in search of political offices and financial gain. This name derived from a popular form of cheap luggage, the carpetbag, which many of them carried.

Copperhead: A derogatory term used during the war to refer to Northerners with Southern sympathies who were considered capable of striking without warning (like the snake of the same name) against the Union war effort. People with such sympathies were strongest in the Midwest, which was home to many people of Southern descent. The most well-known Copperhead was Ohio politician Clement L. Vallandigham.

Copperheads tended to be antiblack, conservative "peace Democrats" who sensed that the war was forever changing the ideal of an egalitarian, rural America. They favored state's rights over a stronger central government and believed that Lincoln's policies were destroying constitutional government. While they did win some local elections and exerted some influence within the Democratic party, the Copperheads were not ultimately very influential. Nonetheless, for years after the war the Democratic party suffered from charges of "Copperheadism."

Fifteenth Amendment: An amendment to the U.S Constitution that prohibited the Federal or state governments from infringing on a citizen's right to vote on account of race, color or previous condition of servitude.

Freedman's Bureau: A government office established by Lincoln as part of the War Department in 1865 to help newly freed slaves obtain their own land and become self-sufficient. The bureau quickly became rife with corruption and extremely unpopular, especially in the South.

Knights of the Golden Circle: A secret pro-Southern organization that flourished in the Midwest during the 1850s. During the war, this organization was thought to have been active on behalf of the Confederacy and may have had connections with the Copperheads.

Ku Klux Klan (KKK): A secret society of white Southerners opposed to blacks, the Republican party and the Federal government that conducted terrorist activities during the period 1866–1872. Its members were sworn to secrecy and hid their identities behind white robes and hooded masks.

Many such organizations existed during Reconstruction, especially in North Carolina, South Carolina and Tennessee; the KKK came to include many of these smaller groups. Some former Rebel soldiers carried on the war in the guise of night riders, and for a time the KKK was led by former Confederate Gen. Nathan Bedford Forrest.

KKK groups, using the flaming cross as their symbol, were especially active during election campaigns when they used violence, rape, murder and intimidation to help sway votes and prevent Republican political victories in their states. Favorite targets were local Republican leaders (both white and black) and blacks who no longer conformed to antebellum standards of conduct.

In areas under Republican control, authorities were hard pressed to quell the violence and were loathe to send their mostly black state militias against the KKK for fear of provoking a full-blown race war. In areas under Democratic control, the authorities themselves were frequently KKK members or sympathizers. Even when local law enforcement authorities did take action, KKK members often sat on juries or the judge's bench and saw that little or no justice would be meted out.

By the 1870s, most Americans, Northern and Southern alike, agreed that the KKK was out of control; even Forrest renounced their activities. In 1871, the Republican-led Congress authorized President Ulysses S. Grant to use Federal troops to restore order in the worst areas, where they had the power to arrest suspects and hold them indefinitely without trial (under the provisions of *posse comitatus*, it is normally illegal for government troops to be used as police against U.S. citizens, a fact as true today as it was in the 1870s). By 1872, the KKK was dead as an organization, although there was a resurgence of violence as a political tool by smaller Southern groups from 1874 to 1877.

Missouri Compromise: An attempt by Congress to quell disputes between free and slave states by admitting to the Union Maine as a free state in 1820 and Missouri as a slave state in 1821. Another component of the compromise, the March 6, 1820 Missouri Enabling Act, prohibited creation of additional slave states north of Missouri's southern border, latitude 36°30' (this law was subsequently repealed by the 1854 Kansas-Nebraska Act.)

slave codes: Legal codes established in Southern states that defined slaves as property rather than people. The codes prevented them from testifying in court against whites, learning to read or write, making contracts, leaving a plantation without permission, striking a white, buying or selling goods, owning firearms, gathering without white supervision, possessing antislavery literature or visiting the homes of whites or free blacks.

Slave patrols, similar to local militias, enforced the codes and arrested slaves who had left plantations, broke up unauthorized gatherings, and searched slave quarters for contraband.

When slave insurrections were rumored or actually occurred, local slave codes were more strictly enforced and vigilance committees were often formed, beating, killing and terrorizing blacks.

CHAPTER SEVEN

BROTHERS AT WAR:
BILLY YANK, JOHNNY REB

N orth America has never seen battles, before or since, greater or more terrible than those fought by soldiers during the Civil War, nor has it seen larger armies mustered and sent against each other. During the four full years of warfare, more than ten thousand skirmishes or battles took place throughout the continent, an average of seven per day.

It is difficult to say how many men fought and died during the Civil War, and historians debate the specifics to this day. Because of a lack of records, this is particularly difficult to determine in the Confederacy. Most historians accept, however, that from a relatively small combined population of about 31 million people, from 2 million to 2.25 million men served through-out the course of the war in the Northern military forces and some 750,000 to 1 million served in the Southern military forces.

Not all of these men served at the same time, of course. When war broke out in 1861, the Union forces consisted of a mere sixteen thousand men, little more than a national defense force. The Union military reached a peak strength of about one million men under arms in 1863. Most of these men were very young, about two-thirds of them twenty-one or younger. The Confederate armed forces (which consisted almost entirely of its army—navy and marine forces were fairly negligible) reached a peak of about 500,000 men in 1863. As with the Union army, the majority of its soldiers were less than twenty-two years of age. On either side, about half the total men in uniform were present for duty at any given time (the rest being ill, wounded or on furlough).

Of the total number of combatants who served on both sides, an estimated 620,000 were killed (and hundreds of thousands more wounded and maimed). This is more than all the American military personnel killed in World War I, World War II, the Korean War, the Vietnam War and the Gulf War combined—about one in every five men who served, a horrifically high proportion.

THE ARMED SERVICES

Both the Northern and Southern military forces were composed of two major branches, an army and a navy. Smaller military or quasi-military organizations included a Marine Corps and a Revenue Cutter Service. The latter two services were much more significant in the Federal forces and played smaller roles for the South.

THE ARMY

Most of the military actions of the Civil War were fought between units of the U.S. Army and the C.S. Army. It was in these two opposing services that most combatants served.

Army Units

During the Civil War, the basic tactical and recruitment unit was the regiment, a unit that was supposed to number 1,046 men and be under the command of a lieutenant colonel or colonel.

In practice, regiments were perpetually understrength and usually consisted of three hundred to five hundred men. One reason for this among Union units is that after Northern states had raised regiments of troops, they made no effort to reinforce them once they were depleted and instead preferred simply to form new regiments when they had to provide additional troops. One exception is the state of Wisconsin, which recruited soldiers for service in existing regiments. For this reason, many generals liked to have at least a few full-strength Wisconsin regiments in their commands.

In descending order, regiments were further divided into **companies**, **platoons** and **sections**. In ascending order, regiments were grouped into **brigades**, **divisions**, **corps** and **armies**. The term **battalion** described a unit with only six companies, when it proved impossible to raise a full-strength, ten-company regiment of a specific type.

Company

Companies consisted of about one hundred men or two platoons plus company officers. A company's ranking **officer**, or company commander, was typically a captain, who was assisted by a 1st lieutenant and a 2nd lieutenant; its ranking **noncommissioned officer (NCO)** was generally a first sergeant. A full-strength regiment consisted of ten companies.

Platoon

Platoons consisted of up to fifty men, or half a company. In battle, the captain in charge of the company would take command of the first platoon and his 1st lieutenant would take command of the second platoon. If the captain was absent or a casualty, the 2nd lieutenant would also take charge of one of the platoons.

Section

Sections consisted of up to two dozen men, or half a platoon.

Brigade

Brigades were supposed to consist of three or four regiments and number about 3,138 to 4,184 men and officers at full strength. However, because regiments were perpetually understrength, brigades often included additional regiments to function effectively. Union veteran John D. Billings summed up the situation in his book *Hardtack and Coffee*:

> As a brigade became depleted by sickness, capture and the bullet, new regiments were added, until, as the work of addition and depletion went on, I have known a brigade to have within it the skeletons of ten regiments, and even then its strength [was] not half that of the original body. My camp was located at one time near a regiment which had only thirty-eight men present for duty.

A brigade was usually under the command of a brigadier general ("one star"); the ranking NCO in a brigade was usually a sergeant major.

Division

Divisions typically consisted of three or four brigades and included, at full strength, ten thousand to twenty thousand soldiers. In addition to infantrymen, a division had attached to it anywhere from a company to two regiments of cavalry and from one to four artillery batteries, as well as any necessary support troops.

A division was usually under the command of a major general ("two star").

Army Corps Badges.

1st ARMY CORPS.   2d ARMY CORPS.   3d ARMY CORPS.

5th ARMY CORPS.   6th ARMY CORPS.

11th ARMY CORPS.   12th ARMY CORPS.

Distinctively shaped badges were worn in most Union Army corps by the end of the war. Color of the badge was determined by division within the corps, and was usually red for the 1st Division, white for the 2nd Division, and blue for the 3rd Division (in the case of a 4th Division the color varied, but was often yellow).

Corps

Corps consisted of three or four divisions and at full strength were supposed to contain about fifty thousand men. Because none of its generals had the skills needed to command a corps, the Union army did not have units within its armies larger than divisions until March 1862. The Confederacy did not organize its divisions into corps until September 1862.

The term "corps" also referred to all the cavalry, artillery and signal troops in the army as a whole. Throughout the course of the war, the Union had twenty-five infantry corps in service at various times, in addition to the cavalry, engineer and signal corps.

Corps were subject to attrition just like brigades and divisions, and some of them consolidated after becoming too reduced. For example, in early 1864 the decimated First and Third Corps were deactivated and merged into the Second, Fifth and Sixth Corps.

A corps was generally under the command of a lieutenant general ("three star").

Army

Armies on either side consisted of up to five or more army corps, or some 100,000 to 200,000 men, and were responsible for military operations in a specific area or region. In general, Union armies were named for the major river in their area of operation or origin. Confederate armies tended to be named for geographical regions. Examples of several major Union and Confederate armies appear next.

An army was typically under the command of a lieutenant general ("three star") or a full general ("four star").

Union
Army of the Cumberland
Army of the James
Army of the Ohio
Army of the Potomac
Army of the Tennessee
Army of Virginia

Confederate
Army of Northern Virginia
Army of the Shenandoah
Army of Tennessee
Army of the Trans-Mississippi

Combat and Noncombat Troops

Each side's army was divided into three major combat arms: the infantry, cavalry and artillery. Ultimately, the Union army included at least thirty-four combat corps during the course of the war. There were also several noncombat arms, including the engineer, hospital and signal corps. Detachments of troops from these branches would be assigned to the various field armies and their subordinate units as needed.

The Infantry

Of all the branches of the army, the infantry was the oldest. Infantrymen, foot **soldiers**, represented the largest arm of the ground forces. They played a major role in nearly every battle and skirmish, and consequently inflicted and received the highest numbers of **casualties** throughout the war. Because of the role they served, infantrymen on both sides bore the brunt of the fighting, suffering and casualties, and often resented what appeared to be the easy lots of cavalry or artillerymen (particularly garrison troops, like the heavy artillerymen who guarded Washington, DC).

Most of the infantrymen on either side marched into battle as raw recruits and, if they survived, learned quickly and became veterans. New infantry regiments were often derided as green troops by their more experienced comrades, only to be hailed as veterans a day later following some particularly gruelling engagement.

While the competence of commanders who ordered masses of infantry into attacks that turned into slaughters can be questioned, the courage and esprit de corps of the men who took part in those attacks cannot. The widespread dedication and steadfastness of the Civil War infantry, ironically, contributed to the heavy toll of many battles. In some cases, advancing infantry from both sides fought each other at point-blank range, firing rifles and wielding mounted bayonets and clubbed muskets, stumbling forward across mounds of their own dead into ranks of enemy soldiers who were doing the same.

Naturally, the best infantrymen were those trained and experienced in the use of infantry weapons and tactics. In the absence of proper equipment or an appropriate mission, however, other types of troops were utilized as infantry. For example, cavalrymen sometimes fought on foot as skirmishers, and cavalrymen for whom remounts were unavailable were sometimes used as infantry if this was expedient.

One of the better-known Union infantry units was the Fifty-fourth Massachusetts, a black regiment that has gained recognition mainly from the movie *Glory*. Formed in 1863 a month after the Emancipation Proclamation, the Fifty-fourth consisted of 650 free blacks from Northern states. Later the same year during an assault on Battery Wagner, a Confederate fortification in South Carolina, nearly half of the Fifty-fourth were slain in combat, including its commander, Col. Robert Shaw. Nonetheless, its valiant performance laid the way for some 179,000 black troops to take the field as Union soldiers.

One of the most colorful Confederate infantry units was the First Special Battalion, Louisiana Infantry, a **Zouave** unit under the command of Maj. Roberdeau Wheat. Better known as "Wheat's Tigers" for its lack of discipline, this unit of mercenaries, New Orleans riffraff and second sons of plantation owners was, according to one officer, "so villainous that every commander desired to be rid of it." It fought well, however, suffered extremely heavy casualties, and had to be disbanded in August 1862, shortly after its commander was slain at the Battle of Gaines's Mill.

The Cavalry

Cavalrymen on both sides were used as scouts, raiders and, to a lesser extent early in the war, as battlefield soldiers. The mobility of cavalry allowed it to range far ahead of an army to serve as its eyes; to attack into the rear of an enemy army, destroying or plundering its supplies; and to serve as a highly versatile arm on the battlefield, either charging in to support a collapsing flank, fall upon an enemy's flank or pursue a retreating enemy.

While cavalrymen could fight from the saddle, most Civil War cavalrymen were used as mounted infantry, soldiers who would ride to battle and then, especially when a good defensive position was available, dismount, leave their horses behind the line of battle, and fight as skirmishers or as a loose screen of foot soldiers in front of massed formations of infantry. Cavalrymen used in this manner could be deployed more quickly than foot soldiers but still gain some of the advantages unavailable to mounted soldiers, such as being able to take cover behind **breastworks**.

At the start of the war, the Confederate cavalry was notably superior to that of the Union. This was due partly to an innate superiority of Southern horsemen, but was also a function of leadership and the ways that cavalry were utilized by the Northern leadership. As the war progressed, however, the gap between the Northern and Southern cavalry narrowed, and by the end of the war Union horse soldiers faced and beat the best the Confederacy could field.

Union cavalry were also ineffectively used from early in the war onward. At Bull Run, the first major engagement of the war, they were used merely as flank guards for infantry and artillery formations. Southern cavalry under the leadership of J.E.B. Stuart, on the other hand, was used adeptly at Bull Run, first defending the Confederate left flank, then sweeping in upon the retreating Union forces (Stuart was promoted to brigadier general as a result). This disparity, along with others, contributed to a prolonged war, rather than one that could have otherwise been ended quickly.

Less experienced as horsemen, many Union soldiers entered cavalry service because they believed it would be easier duty than serving in the infantry (it probably also seemed more dashing to many). To their chagrin, they learned otherwise. For one thing, cavalry tactics and fighting from the saddle are difficult enough to learn and employ, all the more so for soldiers learning to ride.

In the first years of the war, primary duties for Union cavalrymen included constant picket duty and service as mounted escorts and orderlies for general officers. Later, after Gen. Philip Sheridan took over the Federal cavalry corps, horse soldiers were largely relieved of such duties, and an effort was made to transform the corps into a powerful combat arm unto itself (as the Confederate cavalry corps had always been).

As a result of this limited role in combat, Union infantrymen often jeered at cavalrymen as they rode by, heading away from battlefields they had just scouted even as the foot soldiers were marching toward them. "Who ever saw a dead cavalryman?" was one quip employed by Union soldiers about their own horse soldiers, and became so widespread that Abraham Lincoln even once posed it to General Sheridan, whose response reportedly evinced no humor. However, by the time the Battle of Gettysburg had been fought (July 1-3, 1863), the Union cavalry had improved greatly and this reputation had been eclipsed.

As the war progressed and Northern cavalrymen gained combat experience, the disparity between the Union and Southern cavalry shrank. Eventually, too, the Union army produced able cavalry commanders like Gen. John Buford, hot-blooded Gen. Philip H. Sheridan, and George Armstrong Custer (who in June 1863 at age twenty-three became the Union's youngest general; he was killed in the Battle of Little Big Horn in 1876). Sheridan was ultimately the most important of these, after being appointed commander of the cavalry corps for the Army of the Potomac in April 1864. Pulling many of his cavalrymen from duty as sentries and orderlies, Sheridan formed them into a consolidated, heavy-hitting arm of the army that could provide a palpable presence on the battlefield or be used for raids in force, the likes of which only Confederate Gen. J.E.B. Stuart had ever led in the Eastern theater of war (although there were several large-scale cavalry raids in the West, as well).

An improved procurement process also led to improved Union cavalry. This process became more efficient as the Union cavalry acquired more conscientious officers with an eye for horseflesh. For example, Union Col. James H. Wilson, one of Sheridan's cavalry commanders, personally oversaw the acquisition of good horses at fair prices for Sheridan's troopers.

Overall, cavalry could play an important or even pivotal role in combat, and if used effectively, helped determine the results of major battles. Nonetheless, there were very few "cavalry battles" per se, but those that did occur were stirring in the extreme.

One such battle was fought on June 9, 1863, at Brandy Station, Virginia, an epic cavalry engagement that ranks among the greatest ever fought between mounted forces and the largest ever fought in North America. Union Gen. Alfred Pleasanton, at that time leader of the Army of the Potomac's cavalry corps, led his 11,000 mounted soldiers against the Army of Northern Virginia's 10,000 man cavalry corps under Gen. J.E.B. Stuart. For more than two hours, the twenty-one thousand men charged and countercharged each other, fighting stirrup to stirrup with pistols, sabers and rifles. Bugle calls and artillery fire added to the cacophony caused by neighing horses, barked orders and wounded men. Some 936 Northern and 523 Southern soldiers were killed or wounded in the battle. The field was held by the Confederates; therefore, tactically, Brandy Station was a minor Confederate victory. Strategically, however, it demonstrated that Union cavalrymen could effectively challenge their Confederate counterparts.

One of the most distinctive Union cavalry regiments was the Sixth Pennsylvania Cavalry, a unit of the Army of the Potomac, known for both its commander and weaponry as "Rush's Lancers." Initially, Col. Richard Rush's Sixth was equipped like any other cavalry unit, but eventually adopted a nine-foot lance as a primary weapon. Unfortunately, this somewhat archaic weapon did not see distinguished service.

Like many cavalry regiments in the North and South, the Confederacy's First Virginia Cavalry Regiment was originally a handful of independent cavalry companies that the commonwealth of Virginia formed into a regiment under J.E.B. Stuart. At the first Battle of Bull Run, they acquired the nickname "Black Horse Cavalry," and for the rest of the war gave exemplary service to the Army of Northern Virginia. Uniforms included broad-brimmed, plumed black hats and gray or butternut trousers and short jackets, the latter with black facings early in the war.

The Artillery

Of all the combat arms, artillery was the smallest in both armies. When war broke out, the U.S. Army had only four artillery regiments, which suffered the same levels of desertion to the Southern cause as the rest of the military. In early 1861, the government added the Fifth U.S. Artillery Regiment.

Light or "field" artillery soldiers provided support on the battlefield and were especially effective against tightly packed formations of infantrymen. Such troops typically used smoothbore artillery pieces that fired twelve-pound solid shot. Light artillerists could fire two rounds per minute or up to three if re-aiming the piece was unimportant.

Horse or "flying" artillery, trained to move and deploy quickly, was intended to accompany cavalry units and used the lightest sorts of artillery available. Such troops would fly into a firing position, unlimber and set up their guns, fire as many shots as would be effective, then limber up again and move forward to a better position or retreat in the face of an advancing enemy. Horse artillerists could maintain the same rate of fire as light artillerists.

Heavy artillerymen used massive, unwieldy artillery pieces to defend fortified areas or to conduct sieges against them. These soldiers typically used rifled
artillery pieces that could fire projectiles weighing one hundred pounds or
more. They were also armed with muskets and were expected to man ramparts
as infantrymen when necessary.

Lincoln and his cabinet were determined that Washington, DC, should be
safe from attack. They did this by ringing the Capitol with an interlocked chain
of fortifications manned by a garrison of up to forty thousand troops, particularly heavy artillerists. Because the capital was never attacked in force, these
troops enjoyed a much better lifestyle than did field troops, a fact that led to
them being much resented. However, after taking command of the Army of
the Potomac, Union Gen. Ulysses S. Grant pulled many of the heavy artillerymen from guard duty around Washington, DC, and used them as infantrymen
during the final year of the war.

The First U.S. Artillery, one of the heavy artillery units that guarded Washington, DC, was typical of such units. Like other heavy artillery units, it retained
its prewar uniform, the dark blue frock coat and light blue pants of the infantry,
along with a black Hardee hat and black leather accoutrements.

One of the most famous Southern artillery units was the Washington Artillery, a private or "fraternal" unit raised in 1838 and active in the Mexican War.
It consisted of five light artillery companies, four of which deployed to Virginia
early in the war and remained there for the duration, and one of which fought
in the Army of Tennessee. Early in the war, they wore fancy blue uniforms and
carried pistols and sabers, all of which were eventually abandoned.

Other Troops

Various sorts of troops were also attached to combat formations, or designated from within them, and tasked with performing specific functions. Pioneers and engineers are an example of such soldiers.

In addition to the soldiers of the combat arms (infantry, artillery, cavalry),
there were also many noncombat soldiers, including **chaplains**, commissary
sergeants, wagon drivers, engineers, signalmen and the Union's Invalid Corps.
Many of these noncombat support troops were organized into departments,
in contrast to field troops, which tended to be organized into corps. Army
departments at the time of the Civil War included the Quartermaster Department (responsible for supplying the army), a Medical Department, the Inspec-
tor General's Department, a Pay Department and the Adjutant General's
Department.

By the midpoint of the war, the Union army included great numbers of
such troops, more than some commanders thought necessary. Gen. Ulysses S.

Grant reacted to this imbalance by pulling many soldiers from their noncombat duties and assigning them to infantry units.

Pioneers: Pioneers were soldiers tasked with assisting a brigade or regiment by clearing obstructions in its path, building earthworks for light artillery pieces and similar tasks. A dozen men, chosen from the ranks, usually served as pioneers for a regiment; most served in this capacity temporarily, but the sergeant or corporal who led a detachment was usually permanently designated a pioneer and wore a small pair of cloth axes above his chevrons. Each pioneer carried an axe, a spade, a shovel or a pickaxe, along with a sling that allowed the tool to be carried over the shoulder. Like other infantrymen, pioneer's weapons included a rifle or musket, which was sometimes replaced, if possible, with a more manageable cavalry carbine fitted with a standard rifle sling.

Engineers: Engineers were a military corps trained in building or demolishing bridges, dams, fortifications and other structures. Engineer officers were attached to the staffs of unit commanders where they acted as advisors. During the Civil War, the engineer corps was very conservative and derided or refused to support engineering ideas that seemed radical or were not their own. Commanders with engineering backgrounds on both sides of the war were noted for their ability to dig in and fight defensively (e.g., Confederate Gen. Robert E. Lee, who was also exemplary on the offensive) and often for an inability to take the field and move decisively (e.g., Union Gen. George B. McClellan).

There was also a Corps of Topographical Engineers, charged with surveying and making maps.

Signalmen: Signalmen were troops that helped the various elements of an army communicate with each other in the field through the use of colored signal flags. Signalmen increasingly used telegraphy as a means of communication and could even tap into an enemy's telegraph wires to intercept his messages or send false information. This threat led to the creation of various ciphers and electronically transmitted information had to be decoded.

Congress acted to make the Signal Corps a separate branch of the U.S. Army on March 3, 1863.

Camp Followers: In addition to the soldiers, many civilians accompanied the army or followed in its wake, including photographers, vivandieres, sutlers, preachers and relatives of soldiers. Seedier folk often followed the army as well, among them gamblers, criminals and prostitutes, seeking opportunities for illicit profit amongst the soldiers. "Camp followers" was sometimes used pejoratively, particularly with regard to women.

Many officers, particularly those in the Union army, developed scandalous reputations for the company they kept in camp. For example, Union Gen. Judson Kilpatrick, a cavalry officer, reputedly kept a succession of mistresses with him while in the field, even going so far as to dress them in uniform so at a distance they could pass as young officers.

THE NAVY

Strategically, the most important role of the Union navy was to enforce the blockade of Southern ports, preventing goods from coming in or going out and attempting to slowly strangle the Confederate economy. Likewise, the most important role of the relatively small Confederate navy was to reduce the effects of this blockade.

Beyond such vital but rather mundane duties, however, the opposing navies fought each other everywhere their ships and gunboats were able to go—in coastal waters, inland waterways, rivers and on the ocean, where Union ships hunted Confederate commerce raiders. Often, navy operations were conducted in cooperation with the army (e.g., navy gunboats provided artillery support for troops camping, fighting or marching along the banks of major rivers).

At the beginning of the war, the Union navy consisted of some ninety warships, little more than a defensive force, but a framework that could be built upon. By mid-1864, the U.S. Navy had been built up to a peak strength of 670 ships and 50,000 **sailors**, a level that allowed it to operate without significant opposition by Confederate naval forces.

When compared to the Union's military forces, it is in its navy that the Confederacy can be seen to be most lacking. Throughout the course of the hostilities, the Southern navy never exceeded a strength of 130 warships and 4,000 men, a force far too small to break the Union blockade or face its ships in a head-to-head contest. Indeed, it was civilian or foreign blockade runners, typically coming up from the Caribbean with holds full of contraband, that were the biggest nuisance to the U.S. Navy.

Because of this relative weakness, the Southern navy developed different naval tactics than that of the North. A major component of the Confederate naval strategy was commerce raiding, attacking and looting United States merchant ships in international waters. This campaign was pursued globally and involved altercations literally on the other side of the world, as far away as Australia.

Nonetheless, the lack of telling Confederate strength limited the fruits of these efforts, and by the final year of the war the South had only three effective commerce raiders. These were *Alabama*, sunk in June 1864; *Florida*, which sur-

Armored vessels like the **CSS Virginia** *(formerly* **USS Merrimac***), used for some years by European powers, saw their first real action during the Civil War. This image of the ship in drydock shows how much of the ironclad vessel rode below the waterline.*

rendered at Bahia, Brazil, in October 1864; and *Shenandoah*, which survived the Civil War and surrendered to British authorities at Liverpool, England, in November 1865.

Most of the seafaring warships used by either side were steam-driven wooden craft, many of which could also function under sail. Most of the river-going vessels were gunboats, paddle- or screw-driven boats of relatively shallow draft that were well suited for riverine operations but less reliable at sea.

Armored vessels debuted during the Civil War, going into action against each other in the famous duel between the USS *Monitor* and the CSS *Virginia* (a.k.a. *Merrimac*) on March 9, 1862. Although these ships were the first and most famous of the American ironclad warships, they were by no means the only ones to be launched into action during the war. By the end of the war, the U.S. Navy had dozens of armored warships and used them as part of the blockade and to patrol rivers and coastlines. The South, hamstrung by its lack of heavy industry, was unable to construct nearly as many armored gunboats, but did manage to send a few into action, especially along the rivers flowing into the valley of the Mississippi.

Ships in Action

While the duel between the *Monitor* and the *Virginia* is the one most remembered from the Civil War, it was by no means the only high profile naval battle of the war. One naval battle widely covered by the press (coverage that was marked in many cases by sensationalism and inaccuracy) was the one fought between the USS *Kearsarge* and the CSS *Alabama*.

As a indicator of how effective Southern commerce raiders could be, in a period of not quite two years, *Alabama* had captured, burned or sunk more than sixty Union ships, mostly merchant vessels. Nonetheless, *Alabama* met its match off the coast of France on June 19, 1864, when the two ships sallied forth from the port of Cherbourg and fought a battle that caused very little damaged to *Kearsarge* but crippled and sunk the Confederate vessel.

Cannon made ship-to-ship combat brutal, lethal and often very quick. Maneuverability was paramount, as ships endeavored to align themselves to inflict the most telling damage against enemy vessels. Because warships' cannon face outward from the sides of the ship, the general goal was to maneuver into a position reminiscent of the letter "T," with the side of one's own ship, and half its major guns, facing the front or back of the enemy ship, and none of its major guns. Once so aligned, a warship could fire a "broadside," inflicting maximum damage with minimum risk. Solid iron shot and explosive shells, particularly those fired from the rifled cannon available in the latter half of the war, could blow the wooden ships to bits.

Once a ship was disabled from cannon fire, the victor would often send a boarding party to capture it, and hand-to-hand combat might ensue on the deck of the crippled ship (or, in rare cases, sailors and marines aboard the crippled ship might overcome the boarding party and fight their way onto the attacking ship). In shipboard combat, marines were armed with rifles or pistols, while sailors were typically armed with boarding axes, cutlasses, rifles and pistols.

Dramatic events, such as battles against other ships or bombardment of enemy positions ashore, were the exception to the rule. Sailors spent the majority of their time performing routine duties or combatting the effects of tedium. Running a ship required constant if monotonous activity; unlike soldiers, seamen tended not to have as much idle time on their hands. An exception to this was, of course, Union sailors on board blockading ships, who often complained of boredom in journals and letters. Like soldiers, sailors spent their free time playing cards or board games, mending clothing, singing and writing letters.

In addition to their shipboard duties, sailors sometimes took part in armed landing parties. Or, even more rarely than shipboard combat, sailors could actually be sent into battle on shore. For example, on January 15, 1865, Rear Adm. David Dixon Porter ordered 1,600 sailors and 400 marines into a frontal attack on Fort Fisher, North Carolina. In this rather cynical diversionary action, which was staged to allow an attack on the rear of the fort by Army infantrymen, the sailors were sent into combat before the marines arrived and suffered heavy casualties. Porter was widely criticized for his role in the operation, which nonetheless resulted in the taking of the strongly held Confederate fort.

THE MARINES

While **marines** played only a minor role during the Civil War, they were involved in military actions throughout the war—and on its eve, as well. In October 1859, eighty-six marines under U.S. Army Col. Robert E. Lee (future commander of the Confederate forces) stormed the engine house of the Federal arsenal in Harpers Ferry, Virginia, dislodging fanatic abolitionist John Brown and his followers.

When Southern states began to secede from the Union, the U.S. Marine Corps lost many of its **company grade officers**—about half of its captains, almost two-thirds of its first lieutenants, and half of its second lieutenants. Only one field grade officer, a major, resigned his commission from the corps.

After the U.S. Marine Corps appointed three dozen officers to replace those who had resigned, its strength was about 2,200 men total. In July 1861, Congress approved the addition of 28 officers and 750 enlisted men to the corps, raising its strength to about 3,000. Peak strength for the U.S. Marine Corps reached 3,900 men later in 1861 after Lincoln authorized two increases of 500 men each.

The Confederate Marine Corps played an even more marginal role and was never more then six hundred men strong.

For the most part, the primary role of marines was to serve in security detachments aboard navy ships. Beyond shipboard duty, small bodies of marines sometimes formed part of a ship's landing force, and in the Federal service others were assigned directly to the Union army.

Early in the war the Union marines' role was as inglorious as that of the rest of the Northern military's. At the Battle of Bull Run (July 21, 1861), the first major battle of the war, a small unit of marines broke and ran (along with the rest of the Union army) after sustaining repeated attacks from Confederate infantry and cavalry.

Such troops were better suited for coastal operations. For example, in August 1861, marines assigned to four Union ships (*Cumberland, Minnesota, Susquehanna* and *Wabash*) took part in amphibious operations along the North Carolina coast, assisting in the capture of forts Clark and Hatteras.

The Union marines' last major operation of the war was also an amphibious assault on an important Confederate fortification. On January 15, 1865, Rear Adm. David D. Porter ordered 400 marines to support a large body of sailors in a frontal assault on Fort Fisher, North Carolina. The marines arrived too late to help the sailors, suffered heavy casualties and were criticized, probably unjustly, for their performance in the action.

Throughout the course of the Civil War, 460 Union marines died from all causes (about 150 of them in combat). Casualty figures are harder to figure for the Confederate marines, but were probably proportionate. Overall, by the end of the war, both the reputation and the morale of the marines were at a low point.

THE REVENUE CUTTER SERVICE

In addition to the navy, the Federal government enforced its will on the seas through the Revenue Cutter Service, the forerunner of the Coast Guard (which today is an amalgamation of the Revenue Cutter Service, the Lighthouse Service, the Steamboat Inspection Service, the Bureau of Navigation and the Life-saving Service, all of which were originally independent).

In its role as a law enforcement agency, the service ensured that tariffs were not avoided, protected shipping from pirates and intercepted contraband. In 1794, the service was charged with keeping new slaves from being shipped in from Africa, and by 1861 had captured numerous slavers and freed almost five hundred slaves. Revenue cutters also performed rescue operations; from 1830 through 1870, immigrant packets proved to be the most vulnerable to disaster and received the most aid from the service.

During the Civil War, the service assumed quasi-military functions, and was charged with augmenting the Navy with men and cutters and with undertaking special missions in keeping with its peacetime experiences and unique skills.

As with the other military services, the sympathies of the cutter force were divided between North and South. Principal wartime duties of cutters serving the Union were patrolling for commerce raiders and providing fire support for troops ashore. Those serving the Confederacy operated primarily as commerce raiders.

In 1860, the U.S. Revenue Cutter Service consisted of twenty-four vessels, twenty-two schooner-rigged sailing ships, one brig and only a single steamship. In early 1861, six of its vessels defected to the Confederacy, reducing its strength by a quarter. Four years later, at the end of the war, service strength had increased to twenty-seven ships (with eight more under construction), two-thirds of which were steamers.

A typical schooner-rigged cutter was crewed by twelve or thirteen men plus three officers; a larger steamer or brig would have had a crew four or five times as large. Some 219 officers served in the U.S. Revenue Cutter Service during the war; total numbers of seamen and noncommissioned officers are unclear, but were probably about 800 to 900. Of these, one was killed and an unknown number were wounded. It is uncertain how many served in the equivalent Confederate service or how many vessels it included, but both would have been considerably less than in the North.

USS *Harriet Lane*, the service's only prewar steamer, under command of Capt. John Faunce, had the distinction of firing the first naval shot of the Civil War on April 11, 1861, when it challenged the steamer *Nashville* by firing a shot across its bow. Four months later, in August 1861, it participated in the first joint Federal amphibious operation, an assault on the strategic Confederate forts at Hatteras Inlet, North Carolina, a vital opening for Rebel privateers and blockade runners.

One of the service's most interesting Civil War cutters was *Naugatuck*, an ironclad semisubmersible that could be ballasted to sink almost three feet. Once semisubmerged and thus less vulnerable to enemy fire, it could still fire a single Parrott gun mounted above the water in its armored turret. In May 1862, *Naugatuck* led a naval assault up the James River in hopes of shelling into submission the Confederate capital, during which it fought a four-hour duel with a Confederate battery on Drewry's Bluff.

Revenue cutters took part in a variety of other operations. In December 1862, *Hercules* battled Confederate forces on the Rappahannock River; *Miami* carried President Abraham Lincoln and his party to Fort Monroe in May 1862, preparatory to the Peninsular Campaign; *Reliance* engaged Confederate forces on Great Wicomico River in Virginia in 1864; and on April 21, 1865, cutters were ordered to search all outbound ships for the assassins of President Lincoln.

TERMS

admiral: Although a familiar naval term, the U.S. did not have any officers of this rank prior to or during the Civil War. After his victory at Mobile Bay, David Farragut was promoted to the rank of vice admiral in 1864 and further promoted to full admiral in 1866 after the conclusion of the war.

army: A term that referred to the organizations known as the U.S. Army and the C.S. Army. Also, a major military organization of either side that operated at the strategic level and consisted of about five Army Corps, or a total of about 100,000 to 200,000 men. At least sixteen Union and twenty-three Confederate organizations were referred to, officially or unofficially, as armies.

A.W.O.L.: An abbreviation for "absent without leave." Apprehended deserters, particularly those from the Confederate forces, were frequently forced to wear placards emblazoned with the term. Pronouncing the initials as a word, rather than as individual letters, did not come into usage until eight decades later, during World War II.

battery: A basic unit of artillery, typically consisting of 6 guns and 155 men (55 drivers, 70 gunners and 30 officers, and NCOs, and other men). An artillery battery was the equivalent of an infantry company.

big thing: A term used by soldiers to describe any significant event, from a new shipment of shoes to a major battle.

blue jackets: Informal nickname for Union sailors, taken from their uniform coats.

boys in gray: Confederate soldiers.

breastworks: Field fortifications that, ideally, consisted of stacked timbers reinforced with earth. Time or availability of supplies sometimes resulted in less robust defenses of the same name. As their name implies, they were often chest high, so a rifleman could obtain maximum cover and still fire unimpeded. Soldiers might also rest their rifles on the breastworks when shooting for more stability or when they grew weary.

brevet rank: An honorary title conferred for meritorious action in wartime. During the Civil War, this system was done away with because of widespread abuse (e.g., in 1863 a single act breveted some 1,700 soldiers to the ranks of brigadier general or major general).

brig: A sailing ship with two masts, each equipped with a square-rigged sail. Most were also outfitted with two or more headsails and various other smaller sails.

bummer, Sherman's bummers: Used from about 1850 to refer to an army deserter, and from 1861 to refer to soldiers who would slip out of ranks prior to combat to loot or simply avoid fighting. Sherman's bummers were the rapacious bodies of foragers from the Union Army of the Tennessee that helped the army to live off the land as it marched eastward across Georgia.

Butternuts: A slang term for Confederate soldiers, who often wore brownish-gray uniforms dyed with butternut extract.

cantiniere: See *vivandiere.*

casualty: A soldier who can no longer be counted as a combatant, either because of injury, illness or death. Typically, about a quarter of battlefield casualties were actual deaths (although this typical three-to-one ratio could vary widely by battle).

chaplains: Uniformed clergy who served in the ranks on both sides during the Civil War. While there were many pious men on both sides—including generals like Lee, Jackson, Rosecrans and Polk, who was an Episcopal bishop—many commanders nonetheless viewed chaplains as extraneous, obstructive or even a bit suspect. In many cases, chaplains were indeed some-what seedy, and they seem to have run the gamut from those with a true sense of ministry to those looking for an easy job or some personal gain.

A black overcoat or untrimmed officer's frock coat was the main piece of regulation garb for chaplains.

chief: This term originated during the Civil War, but usually referred to the ship's cook with the most rank or authority rather than to a chief petty officer, a naval rank that was not introduced until the 1890s.

coffee coolers: Soldiers who hid behind the battle lines during combat, brewing and drinking coffee until the danger was passed.

company grade officers: Second lieutenants, first lieutenants and captains (i.e., those officers most likely to command a company or serve at the company level).

Confederate cruisers: The warships built by Britain and France for the Confederacy during the first two years of the war. By 1863, the Union looked like it was sure to win the war and pressured the European nations to stop providing them to the South.

contrabands, contraband of war: Term applied in areas under some Union generals (e.g., Gen. Benjamin F. Butler) to escaped slaves who made it into Union lines. Such slaves were considered to be "contraband of war" that could not be returned to their masters.

couter up: An informal command to put on one's equipment and get ready to fall into ranks, derived from the word "accoutrements."

cutter: A vessel sixty-five feet or more in length that could accommodate a crew for extended deployment.

department: A basic geographical organization that typically gave its name to the friendly army operating within its boundaries (e.g., the Army of the Potomac, the Army of Northern Virginia). This term was used to refer to a noncombat army function, such as the Pay Department.

doughboy: Although widely associated with World War I, this term for a soldier was used during the Civil War, albeit not widely.

dragoon, mounted rifleman: Soldiers who travelled on horseback and fought on foot. In 1861, the designations of dragoon and mounted rifleman were done away with, all such troops being redesignated cavalry. In general, cavalry was used as mounted infantry during the Civil War.

draftee: A citizen conscripted, or drafted, into military service.

ensign: The lowest commissioned rank in the U.S. Navy, established in 1862. In the British army, the term had been used to refer to various navy or army ranks for about three hundred years. Also, a flag, especially on a ship.

field grade officers: Officers bearing rank higher than captain (i.e., majors, lieutenant-colonels, colonels and general officers). The naval equivalents were lieutenant commander, commander, captain and admiral, respectively.

fougasse(s): A type of land mine, usually placed by engineers, made by packing explosives at the bottom of a sloping pit then covering them with boards followed by rocks or other debris. During an enemy attack, the explosives could be detonated, showering a large area with chunks of heavy shrapnel. Such devices generally used a ratio of 16 pounds of powder to one ton of rocks and affected a maximum area of about 150 yards in length and 100 yards in width.

general officer: The highest level of army rank, which included, in ascending order, brigadier general ("one star"), major general ("two star"), lieutenant general ("three star") and general, or full general ("four star").

the Gray: A term for the army of the Confederacy (or for the nation itself), taken from the official color of Confederate uniforms.

graybacks: A slang term for lice that was also applied disparagingly to Confederate soldiers (also, a slang term for Confederate paper money).

graycoats: Confederate soldiers.

gunboat: A type of shallow draft warship, used largely by the U.S. Navy, on inland waterways and rivers. Early in the war such vessels might be little more than armed steamers. After 1862, however, gunboats were more likely to be purpose-built warcraft after the models of the USS *Monitor* or CSS *Virginia*, riding low in the water; covered to just below the waterline with armored plate four or more inches thick; and equipped with a low, flat deck and a round pillbox that held a pair of guns or with sloping sides that housed a dozen or so guns in armored ports.

hayfoot: See *strawfoot*.

homeguard: A term used from 1861 onward to refer to militia and other local soldiers (on either side) who would only be used against invading forces or for local military duties.

ironclad: Warships armored with metal plate. While "ironclad" is now used to refer to the USS *Monitor* and the CSS *Virginia* (*Merrimac*) and the armored ships that descended from them, this term did not appear in print for the first time until 1867; during the Civil War, Northern warships of this sort were often referred to as "monitors." See *gunboat*.

Kentucky windage: A technique of compensating for range, wind or other conditions by aiming slightly high or just to one side of a target.

lobsterback: A derisive nickname for shipboard marines used by sailors.

Medal of Honor: A decoration awarded to military personnel for valor, established by Congress for Union heroes in 1862. Sometimes inaccurately referred to as the Congressional Medal of Honor.

marine: A naval soldier trained to fight on ship and take part in boarding and amphibious operations (although the role of marines went beyond shipboard activities; e.g., the troops that battled John Brown at Harpers Ferry were U.S. Marines).

militia: Civilians who formed military units and trained as local defense units that would fight in cases of enemy invasion or raids.

muster in, muster out: Terms that meant, respectively, to enter military service and to leave it. During the Civil War "mustered out" was also a euphemism that meant to be killed in action.

noncommissioned officer, NCO: An enlisted man elevated to a leadership position but given no commission from the government. Sergeants and corporals are noncommissioned officers.

officer: A soldier who is given a commission to serve on behalf of the issuing government. In ascending order, army officer ranks are second lieutenant, first lieutenant, captain, major, lieutenant colonel, colonel and general officer.

pickets: Soldiers tasked with guarding and patrolling an army's lines when it was encamped.

powder monkey: A young sailor, often a boy, who helped serve shipboard cannon.

provost, provost guard: Military police. A provost marshal would be the chief military policeman for a military command, and his office would be called the Provost Marshal's Office (PMO).

red badge of courage: Slang term for a wound.

redlegs: Nickname for Union artillerymen, inspired by the red stripes worn on such soldiers' trousers.

sailor: The military or civilian crewman of a ship, as well as the general term for any member of the U.S. or C.S. navies.

skirmishers: Troops who deployed in loose formation to the front and flanks of an army and were thus the first to come into contact with the enemy. Such troops were used to keep an army in the field from being surprised, and usually withdrew once the big formations moved into battle or they were driven away during the course of the battle.

sloop, sloop-of-war: A single-masted warship somewhat larger and more seaworthy than a gunboat that, because of its small size, carried all of its guns on a single deck.

soldier: A member of the Union or Confederate armies. This term cannot be accurately applied to all the combatants of the Civil War (i.e., navy personnel are sailors and Marine Corps personnel are marines).

spike, spiking: If gunners had to abandon their guns, the last thing they would do (if they were able to) was hammer a metal spike into the touchhole near the breech of the gun, thus making it temporarily unusable. Soldiers would also do this to captured enemy guns if they were unable to use them for themselves.

strawfoot: A term applied to a raw recruit or levy who had trouble learning to step off with his left foot. Training instructors dealt with this by having the soldier put a piece of straw in his left shoe or in his left hand, and possibly a bit of hay in his right shoe or hand, as reminders. They would then drill such troops by calling a cadence of "strawfoot, hayfoot," rather than the regulation "left, right." This term might also be used pejoratively to refer to any backwoods soldiers.

vedette: A mounted sentry (i.e., a cavalryman assigned to guard duty).

vivandiere, cantiniere: A woman or girl who accompanied an army for purposes of helping out with chores in camp, providing company for the troops or maintaining morale. Some accounts describe such women carrying water to the troops of their regiment, even while under fire from the enemy. Such camp followers often wore a feminized version of the regimental uniform.

Zouave: A member of one of the war's volunteer regiments that adopted the North African-style uniforms and precision drill reminiscent of the French Algerian Zouaves. Costume typically included baggy pants, vest and fez.

CHAPTER EIGHT

SLANG AND IDIOM

"A national language is a very large matter. It reflects everything that happens to a people, the cultural forces that create ideas and words, the content and form of regional and social expression."
—Mark Twain, "Concerning the American Language," 1880.

When reading material written during the Civil War, modern readers are often surprised that the writing is so similar to that of today, on the one hand, while containing so many idiomatic terms and expressions on the other.

A lexicon of terms is created during the course of any great conflict or period of change. This is especially true in the case of the Civil War, and many of the terms and expressions we take for granted today have their origins in the Civil War (while others that we continue to use today have their origins prior to the war, and would have been used during it, such as "bark up the wrong tree," which dates to 1832).

Contemporary idiom can also give modern readers some insight into what many people thought and felt during the Civil War. For example, Union soldiers referring to the U.S. flag as "God's flag" hints at the fervency felt by many of the combatants.

So, too, many words we use to describe the events of the Civil War have their origins in the years following the conflict, and writers should take care in using these words in stories set during the period, especially when putting them into the mouths of their characters. For example, Union Maj. Gen. William Tecumseh Sherman is widely known to have stated, "War is Hell." However, he did not say this until 1879, some fourteen years after the war had ended. Clearly, this is not a quote a careful writer would want to have him saying during the aftermath of a battle.

Likewise, some words were used widely during the war, but have now been lost to the ages. These are especially valuable for adding color to the dialog of contemporary characters. In addition, writers should keep in mind that the way even familiar words were used was sometimes quite different from the way they are used today. For example, today the word "supposed" is generally used to mean "should have," as in "He was supposed to have been promoted." During the Civil War, it was generally used to mean "thought," as in "His family supposed he had been promoted."

Writers are probably better off avoiding too many period terms, slang or idiomatic expressions in their narratives. After all, as twenty-first-century people writing for other people from the same period, our use of such words is necessarily going to be imperfect, maybe even confusing or annoying. However, when worked into the dialog, letters or thoughts of the characters in a story, such terms and expressions can add color and authenticity.

Those who choose to set a story during the Civil War have an unlimited variety of themes to chose from. Yes, an uncanny number of such stories now in print do include the major battles of the war and do seem to focus on the actions of generals, other high-ranking officers and military units. But a story set during the Civil War can just as easily revolve around individual enlisted troops or company-grade officers, skirmishes and special military operations, or even nonmilitary subjects, like a murder mystery, espionage, business and trading, romance or anything else that makes a good story, with the war itself serving as a colorful background. Use of appropriate slang and idiom can convey a lot about such people and situations. For example, troops in a regiment recruited from a tough part of town might use slang terms related to criminality and law enforcement.

A NATION OF MANY TONGUES

Since Colonial times, the American language diverged from the language spoken in England and began to acquire a variety of what are known as Americanisms. Such Americanisms were often the products of local conditions and the influences of other languages, and by the 1800s America was a country of many distinct dialects. Not only did people in the North and South speak languages with different words, grammar and forms, groups of people in pockets or entire regions also had their own ways of speaking the English language. Wilderness, lack of roads or means of communication, and no centralized education helped propagate this fragmentation of the national language. Such dialectical differences generally manifested themselves in speech rather than in the written word.

Beyond this, of course, were ethnic enclaves that did not speak English at all. For examples, the German-speaking Pennsylvania Dutch, immigrant populations in many large cities, communities of Spanish speakers in the far West and American Indians throughout the country. These non-English-speaking populations also influenced the evolution of the American language.

In the decades following the Civil War, many factors combined to erode the clearly differentiated American dialects and homogenize the language. Regional differences were smoothed over by factors that allowed people from different regions to more effectively communicate with each other, such as improved roads, rail transportation, telegraphy, rise of public education and increased literacy because of more widespread newspapers and publications like Noah Webster's *The American Spelling Book* and William McGuffey's *Eclectic Readers*.

LANGUAGE IN THE NORTH

People in the North, including all the non-Confederate states of the West, spoke a wide variety of distinct dialects during the Civil War. These included dialects spoken by people in Appalachia (influenced by Scottish), the Hudson River Valley (influenced by Dutch) and Minnesota (influenced by various Scandinavian languages).

The two largest and most distinct dialects spoken in the North, however, were the New England dialect and what is often referred to today as Standard American English.

New England Dialect
This New England dialect was (and to a great extent still is) spoken in Connecticut, Rhode Island, Massachusetts, Vermont, New Hampshire and Maine. At the time of the Civil War, it was closer to the English spoken in England than any other major American dialect.

Idioms peculiar to the New England dialect included using *angleworm* for *earthworm*; *brook* for *creek* or *stream*; *buttonwood tree* to mean *sycamore tree*; *clothes press* instead of *closet*; *pail* instead of *bucket*; *to home* instead of *at home*; and *trading* instead of *shopping*. Other idiomatic words included *pesky*, *scrimp* and *snicker*.

Several other characteristics distinguished the New England dialect. One of the most noticeable is pronouncing the "a" in words like *ask, class* and *fast* or the "o" in words like *box, hot* and *pot*, like the "a" in *father*.

Also notable in this dialect was the lengthening of the "a" in words like *barn, park* and *star* to something in between the sounds "a" found in *fat* and *father*.

Another characteristic of the New England dialect was the shortening or omission of some "r" sounds. For example, *bar* would sound like *bah, dear* would sound like *deah* and *poor* would sound like *poah*.

Standard American English

Most English-speaking people in the areas controlled by the Federal government spoke the standard American dialect of English. However, this dialect could still be divided into several other regional subdialects that featured their own idioms and accents.

Distinguishing characteristics of Standard American English include using a flat, short "a" in words like *ask, class* and *shaft*; pronouncing the "o" in words like *box, knot* and *shot* similarly to the broad "a" sound in *father*; and retaining a strong "r" sound in most words.

LANGUAGE IN THE SOUTH

A distinct Southern dialect was spoken by people in all of the Confederate states (except for western Arkansas and Texas), as well as Maryland, Kentucky and southern Missouri.

This Southern dialect could be further divided into the modes of speech in the upper and Deep South, and even further into regional dialects, such as those spoken in the South Carolina Low Country, in the Virginia Tidewater region, and in the vicinity of major population centers like Atlanta, Charleston or New Orleans. And altogether beyond the Southern dialect were other regional dialects, including those spoken in the Florida Keys and by Cajuns in the bayous of Louisiana.

Words and terms peculiar to the South include *you all* and its contracted form *ya'll; bucket* to mean a *pail; heap* or *right* for *very; pine tags* instead of *pine needles; raise children* instead of *rear children; reckon* to mean *judge* or *think; right* to mean *very; snap bean* to mean *string bean; tote* to mean *carry;* and *toboggan* to mean a knitted hat rather than a sled.

Beyond its unique vocabulary, the Southern dialect also has several distinct characteristics. Foremost among these is a "twang" or drawl, that manifests itself in slower enunciation and an elongation of stressed vowels. Examples include *clae-is* for *class; dyu* for *due; fi-ahn* for *fine; I-ah* for *I; a-out* for *out; nyu* for *new; ri-ahd* for *ride; ti-ahm* for *time; ty-une* for *tune;* and *yea-is* for *yes*.

Another characteristic of Southern speech, caused by the elongation of words by the drawl, is a weakening of the final consonant in words, especially the letters "d," "l," "r," and "t." This leads to such pronunciations as *bes'* for *best*, *fin'* for *find*, *fo'* for *for*, *flo'* for *floor*, *he'p* for *help*, *kep'* for *kept*, *las'* for *last*, *mo'* for *more*, *nex'* for *next*, *po'* for *poor*, *se'f* for *self* and *yo'* for *your*.

ETHNIC INFLUENCES

African Influences

African slaves came from hundreds of different tribes and subtribes and spoke scores of different languages. Many of the words from these languages remained or worked their way into the everyday speech of slaves, and ultimately into the language as a whole. During the Civil War, these influences were greatest in the South, where the vast majority of blacks in America lived.

Many slaves were not formally taught English and as a result developed their own synthesis of English and African words, pronunciations, speech patterns, syntax and tones. This spoken language was generically referred to as Nigger by 1825 and both influenced and was influenced by the dialect spoken by white Southerners. It also included pidgin English words like *sickey-sickey* for *sick* or *workee* for *work*; altered pronunciations and forms, such as *de* for *the*, *dis* for *this*, *dat* for *that*, *berry* for *very*, *gen'l* for *general* and *gen'man* for *gentleman*; dropped auxiliary verbs, such as *can*, *have*, *may*, *must*, and *will*; and simplified conjugations of many other verb forms or using them unconjugated (e.g., the verb "to be").

In some areas, this sort of black English was mixed with other languages, such as French in Louisiana and Spanish in Florida. One of these sublanguages, Gullah, was spoken by a black people of the same name who lived on the Sea Islands of South Carolina, Georgia and Florida.

Direct introduction of African words into American English by enslaved blacks dropped off in the early decades of the nineteenth century, after the importation of new slaves was banned in 1808. Other African words entered English indirectly, however, from Dutch, Portuguese and Spanish traders, from England, and from black slaves in the Caribbean. English words with African roots include *banana*, *banjo*, *gris-gris*, *okra*, *tote*, *voodoo*, *yam* and *zombie*. Several others are included in the term list at the end of this chapter.

German Influences

As early immigrants to the Americas, Germans have influenced the language of the United States since its earliest years. It was in the decades immediately before and during the Civil War that they made their greatest contributions, however, driven from Germany by the failed German Revolution of 1848 and by the same European potato blight that caused so many Irish to abandon their homes.

The German influence was most palpably felt in the North and East and what was then known as the West (and today as the Midwest).

A great many terms Americans take for granted today entered the language during the nineteenth century or earlier, either in their original form, as translations or as modified German words or phrases. For example, *concert master* (as opposed to the British concert leader) was a translation of the German *Konzertmeister*, *cylinder*, a slang term for a plug hat, was a modification of the German *Zylinder*, and *pumpernickel*, the same word in either language for a type of coarse bread.

Other terms taken from German in the mid-1800s or before included *beer cellar, beer garden, bock beer, coat, dachshund, ecology, gesundheit, hoodlum, kindergarten, klutz, lager, liverwurst, nix, pinochle, pretzel, sauerkraut, schnapps, shyster, wanderlust, wisenheimer* and *zweiback*.

Other words that seem to have two meanings often derive one meaning from their German genesis and another from their British. For example, *dumb*, meaning stupid rather than mute, comes from German, as does *check*, meaning a restaurant tab rather than a bank check; or *fresh*, meaning impertinent rather than the opposite of stale.

Some words have also been influenced by German forms, prefixes or suffixes. For example, words starting with ker-, like *kersplash* or *kerplunk* that entered the language in the 1800s, are thought to have come from the German prefix ge-.

The word "German" was also used during the nineteenth century to identify the origin of specific groups, as in *German Jew* or *German Lutheran*, or other things, such as *German measles*, a condition prevalent in Germany and sometimes brought to the United States by immigrants.

Irish Influences

Although the Irish have been present in America since early Colonial times, it was waves of immigrants fleeing the 1846 Irish Potato Famine that led to their greatest influence on the American language. At the time of the Civil War, this influence was felt most in the North and East, especially the great urban areas like Boston and New York City.

As with other ethnic groups, the Irish contributed a variety of words to the nineteenth-century American vocabulary, including *shanty, shebang, shenanigan* and *smithereens*. As recent immigrants at the time of the Civil War, the Irish also inspired a variety of unfortunate terms and disparaging nicknames. For example, a slang term for a bullfrog was *Irish nightingale*, a play upon "Swedish Nightingale," nickname of the popular diva Jenny Lind.

However, beyond their influences upon the American vocabulary, the Irish's greatest influence was not so much upon what people said but rather how they said it—through grammar, pronunciation and syntax.

One of the most noticeable contributions is in the addition of the definite article and pronoun, something not used in England. For example, while an Englishman might say "Invalid soldiers were sent to hospital to recover," Irish influence led Americans to specify "the hospital."

Use of idiomatic forms like *shall* instead of *will* and *I seen* instead of *I saw* are also products of the Irish influence.

Spanish and Mexican Influences

The influence of Spanish on the language of Americans is not surprising considering the Spanish had settlements in Florida and the Gulf states decades before English settlers ever landed in Massachusetts or Virginia. Also, Spain or Mexico controlled all of what became the states of Texas, California, Arizona, New Mexico and Nevada. Because of this geographical influence, Spanish words and phrases were most common in the Southwest and on the West Coast.

Spanish words that entered the English language prior to or during the nineteenth century include *adobe, alfalfa, alligator, bonanza, breeze, buffalo, burro, canyon, cockroach, incommunicado, loco, machete, mesa, mosquito, patio, pickaninny, plaza, pronto, sassafras, savvy, sierra, serrated, tornado, vamoose* and *vigilante*.

During the 1800s, the words "Mexican" and "Spanish" also appeared in conjunction with other words and phrases, including *Mexican dollar, Spanish America, Spanish American, Spanish Creole, Spanish dance, Spanish fly, Spanish Mexican* and *Spanish moss*.

Spanish terms and phrases might turn up in the words of veterans of the 1846–1848 Mexican War, of soldiers formerly stationed in California, or of those who took part in the Gold Rush of the late 1840s.

A WAR OF MANY NAMES

Few wars have been referred to in quite so many ways as this one, and its various names reflect a wide range of attitudes toward the conflict. The official name given to it by the victorious Federal government is, of course, the Civil War, a term that came into use in 1861. In the Southern states, however, the terms used in 1861 included the Revolution, the Second War for Independence, and the War of Secession.

A variety of other names came into use during the war and in the decades following it, most of which reveal partiality to one side or the other, a tone of reconciliation, humor or an emphasis on some aspect of the conflict. These include the Great Fratricide, the War of Northern Aggression, the War for Constitutional Liberty, the War Between the States, the War Between the North and the South, the War for Southern Independence, the Second American Revolution, the War for States' Rights, Mr. Lincoln's War, the Southern Rebellion, the War for Southern Rights, the War of the Southern Planters, the War of the Rebellion, the War to Suppress Yankee Arrogance, the Brothers' War, the Great Rebellion, the War for Nationality, the War for Southern Nationality, the War Against Slavery, the Civil War Between the States, the War of the Sixties, the War Against Northern Aggression, the Yankee Invasion, the War for Separation, the War for Abolition, the War for Union, the Confederate War, the War of the Southrons, the War for Southern Freedom, the War of the North and the South, the Lost Cause, the Late Unpleasantness, the late Friction, the Late Ruction, the Schism, the Uncivil War and, especially in the South in the years since it ended, simply as the War.

Overseas, the conflict was given still other names. For example, contemporary German writers refer to it as the North American War.

THE WRITTEN WORD

During the era of the Civil War, people often wrote in a manner that would seem melodramatic or even unnatural today. Examples of this are easy to find. One of the more striking is an article in the *Baltimore American and Commercial Advertiser* about Confederate Maj. Gen. Joseph Johnston's burning of Baltimore and Ohio property in June 1861, in which he is said to have performed an "act of diabolism" and performed a crime "effected by means worthy of the spirits tenanting the nether world."

Other idioms that turn up in contemporary writing include capitalization of many or most nouns, even nonproper nouns (e.g., Rail Road, instead of railroad). Also, many words that today would be contracted to one word were written as two, as in the previous example.

TERMS

Following are some of the words and phrases that were in use, or originated, during the Civil War. Also, see the term lists at the end of many chapters, which contain specialized terms specific to the material in those sections. For example, in the chapter on the opposing armies there are many terms which refer specifically to soldiers.

Some of the words derived from African, Irish, German and Spanish dialects are marked for ease of reference, with an A, I, G or S, respectively. Many of these words were used predominantly by the ethnic group in question or in certain geographical areas. For example, most of the Spanish words would have been used only in areas once controlled by Spanish speakers.

abatis: An obstacle made from sharpened stakes or timbers, especially for blocking roads and impeding cavalry.

"All quiet along the Potomac": A phrase used by Northern newspapers in the weeks after the Union defeat at Bull Run, making fun of General McClellan's interminable delay in attacking the Rebel forces. This phrase also became the name of a popular Union song.

ante-bellum: A Latin term that means "before the war," specifically before the Civil War. It first appeared in print in 1867 and eventually came to be written without a hyphen.

(S) arroyo: A brook or gully.

(I) belave: A variant of believe.

big thing: A term used to describe any significant event, from a new shipment of shoes to a major battle.

(I) bile: A variant pronunciation of *boil*.

Black Maria: From the 1840s, a wagon used to transport people arrested by the police.

(S) bodega: A wine shop or liquor store.

book: From 1846, to enter charges against a suspect into a police registry.

(A) buckra, buccara, boccra: A word used by slaves to address their masters that remained in use through the 1860s. In Colonial times, buckra was used to refer to any whites, and eventually to a gentleman.

cablegram: A telegram sent via undersea cable, a service that began to appear reliably in the late 1860s.

(S) cafeteria: Since about 1830, a coffee house. Its usage for a self-service restaurant did not arise until the 1890s.

(S) calaboose: From the Spanish *calabozo*, or dungeon, this colloquial word for a jail was popularized by American cowboys in the 1860s.

(S) cay, key: A low island.

chain gang: This practice of using manacled prisoners to perform labor, and the term for it, came into use around 1835.

(I) chaw: A variant of *chew*.

chief of police: A term from the 1840s that refers to the head of a police department.

(A) chigger, chego, chiego: A chigger or a flea.

(S) chinch, chinch bug: Used variously to describe an insect that destroyed wheat and corn or a bedbug.

the Confederacy: Prior to 1829, this term referred to the confederation of all the United States. From 1829 to 1861, as secession of Southern states from the Union became more and more widely discussed, this term came to refer to the states of the South, and, ultimately, to the Confederate States of America.

Confederate: The use of this word as a modifier or qualifier began in 1861, as in the Confederate Capital, Confederate money and Confederate stamps.

constable: A policeman. "Police" and "policeman" were also in wide usage.

(A) cooter: This word for a box turtle entered the Southern dialect of English from Gullah.

cop: To arrest.

cotton black, cotton slave: Terms that arose in the early 1860s for blacks who worked the cotton plantations.

(A) Cuffy, Cuff: A common black male name, which, at the time of the war, was used to refer to any black man. From *Kofi*, a name often given on the Gold Coast of Africa to boys born on Friday.

(A) cush, cushie: A sweet fried cornmeal cake. From the Gullah word *kush* or *kushkush* and ultimately derived from the Arabic *kusha*, or *couscous*.

cut off: A euphemism for being killed.

(S) dobie, doby: Informal term for a house made of adobe.

do time: A slang term for spending time in jail that came into use around 1860.

dower negro: A slave owned by a woman at the time of her marriage or given as part of her dowry.

draftee: A citizen conscripted, or drafted, into military service.

(S) embarcadero: A landing place or wharf.

free papers: Papers, first used in 1838, issued to freed blacks as documentation of their status.

fugitive slave: A term originating in 1793 with the Fugitive Slave Act that became familiar in the 1840s, when conditions on large plantations became increasingly oppressive.

German corn: Rye.

German cotillion, German: A complex round dance popular in the 1830s and 1840s.

get one's Irish up: To get angry.

God's country: Term used by Union troops to refer to the North, especially when suffering from heat, humidity, mosquitoes and other unfamiliar conditions while campaigning in the South.

God's flag: Term used by Union troops to refer to the U.S. flag.

(A) goober: A peanut.

the Gray: A term for the Confederacy or its army, taken from the official color of Confederate uniforms.

graft: From about 1859, this meant to earn a living dishonestly as a con artist, robber or thief.

(A) gumbo: A soup made from okra, shrimp and powdered sassafras leaves.

(G) Hessian: Taken from the mercenary German soldiers from Hesse who fought for the British during the American Revolution, this term was applied to Germans, to any person of low character and, during the Civil War, by people in the South to Union soldiers.

(G) hold on!: An expression meaning "wait" or "stop" that comes from the German *halt am*.

hoodlum: Used from about 1871 to refer to a tough or rowdy person.

(S) hoosegow: A cowboy slang term for a jail, taken from the Spanish *juzgado*, meaning sentenced or jailed.

house negro: A term applied to slaves who worked in their masters' houses.

Irish hoist: A kick in the pants.

ironclad: Warships armored with metal plate. While this term now refers to the *Monitor* and the *Virginia* (*Merrimac*) and the armored ships that descended from them, it did not come into use until 1867.

jailbird: A term for a habitual criminal (although spelled "gaolbird" until about 1814).

jail fever: An informal term for typhus, contracted by many prisoners through lice infestation.

jailhouse: A common term for a jail since the early nineteenth century.

(I) jine: A variant of *join*.

Josh: Nickname for a person from Arkansas.

(A) juba: A group dance of African origin popular with plantation slaves that included complex routines of clapping and knee- and thigh-slapping.

(S) jug: A slang term for a jail used since the 1810s, probably taken from the Spanish *juzgado*.

(S) junta: A Spanish or Italian legislative council. Its meaning of a military government did not arise until the end of the century.

(G) katzenjammers: A term that referred to the effects of a hangover.

(G) liederkranz: German American men's social groups that met to sing and drink beer.

(G) loafer: A lazy person.

lockup: A term for a jail in use since the late 1830s.

(S) mosey: A word used to mean both "to move quickly" and "to move slowly."

old soldier: Although this term could simply mean a veteran, it could also be used sarcastically to refer to soldiers who had learned all the tricks of malingering and avoiding work and combat.

operator: Since the 1840s, a telegraph operator.

paper collar: Derisive term used by western Federal soldiers to refer to eastern Federal soldiers, who they often thought looked like fancy dandies.

patrolman: This term for a policeman originated in the 1860s.

pen: An informal abbreviation for "penitentiary" that came into use around 1870.

pinch: A slang term meaning "to arrest."

(A) pindal, pinder: A peanut. From the Kongo word *npinda*.

(S) placer, placer mine: A deposit of gravel or sand or the means of mining it.

police commissioner: From the 1850s onward this term referred to the official at the head of a city's police force.

(A) poor jo, poor Job: Name used, mainly in Georgia, to refer to the great blue heron.

(S) presidio: A fortress or garrison, the central feature of many early Spanish settlements.

prison pens: The outdoor stockades used to house prisoners of war. Conditions within these were often horrible, and thousands of soldiers on both sides suffered and died from exposure, malnutrition and disease. For example, more than thirteen thousand died at the Andersonville prison in Georgia, considered the worst such facility of the war.

rap: Since 1777, a term that meant blame or rebuke (i.e., "a rap on the knuckles").

(G) rathskeller: This term for a beer hall or restaurant entered the American vocabulary during the Civil War but was not commonly used until several decades afterwards.

reformatory: This term for a jail came into regular usage after 1807, when the reformatory in Elmira, New York, opened.

(A) Sambo: A common black male name that by the early nineteenth century was loosely used to refer to any black man or boy. From a name given to a second son in northern Nigeria.

sandwich man: A person wearing two signboards, strapped together and hung over their shoulders, one in front and one behind, as a form of advertisement.

Sanitary Commission, U.S.: A civilian commission, strongly supported by the Federal government, that looked after the well-being of troops by providing them with food, medicine and clothing; helped to oversee their living conditions; and established field hospitals for them. The commission had more than four thousand local branches and held fund-raisers, such as art exhibitions or teas, which they called Sanitary Fairs. For many women volunteers, working with such activities in the U.S. Sanitary Commission or similar organizations was their first experience with work outside the home.

(l) sass: A variant of *sauce*.

screw: A harsh disciplinarian, martinet (i.e., someone who applied thumbscrews).

secesh, seceshers: Term used by Northerners to refer to those who had seceded from the Union.

Sherman's neckties, Sherman's hairpins: Railroad rails that had been heated in fires then wrapped around trees to make them useless. From the practice employed by Sherman's troops during their rapacious march across Georgia.

Sherman's sentinels: The still-standing chimneys of buildings burned down by Sherman's troops. Called "Sherman's monuments" after the war.

(l) shillelagh: A cudgel, especially one made from oak or blackthorn.

shoddy: A word for a type of cheap cloth that in the 1860s came to describe anything of low quality.

skedaddle: Although it had entered the U.S. lexicon in the 1820s, this word did not come into wide usage until 1861, when it became popular after Union troops used it to describe fleeing Confederate soldiers. (Its origin is a bit obscure, and could be derived from some Scottish or Northern English idiom or even from the Greek *skedannunai*, "to split up").

(G) slim: In its meaning bad, as in "slim chance," this term is derived from the German *schlimm*.

(G) smearcase: A type of spreadable cheese, from the German *Schmierkaese*.

solitary confinement: This punishment and the term for it, originally thought to be a humane alternative to flogging, came into use in the 1780s.

Spanish fever, Texas fever: A cattle disease transmitted by ticks.

Spanish trail: Name applied to various routes in the far West, including that between Santa Fe, New Mexico, and Los Angeles, California, and that between New Orleans, Louisiana, via El Paso, Texas, to Los Angeles.

stationhouse: A police station.

stars and stripes: The primary nickname for the United States flag.

switchboard: An term used in the 1860s to describe telegraphy routing equipment.

Tarheel: Nickname for a person from North Carolina.

(l) tay: A variant of tea.

telegram: A term that came into use about 1850 to describe a message sent by telegraph. Prior to this, such messages had been variously called telegraphic dispatches, telegraphic communications and telegraph messages.

telephone: Until being applied to Alexander Graham Bell's invention in the 1870s, this referred to a kind of nonelectronic megaphone used for carrying music or voices over a distance.

"10 acres and a mule," "40 acres and a mule": From about 1862 onward, Union propagandists spread the word among slaves that after the war was won, their masters' plantations would be parceled out to the former slaves. Union Major General Sherman exacerbated this idea on Jan. 16, 1865, when he stated in a field order that "every family shall have a plot of not more than forty acres of tillable ground." When the war ended the Federal government made no attempt to fulfill such promises, which it had not itself explicitly made.

traffic police: A term that dates to 1860, the year New York City's Broadway Squad was established to manage horse-drawn traffic and help people cross the streets.

tumbled over: A euphemism that meant to be killed.

unconditional surrender: Although widely associated with the Allied ultimatum to Nazi Germany during World War II, this term traces its roots to the Civil War. When on February 16, 1862, Confederate Gen. Simon Bolivar Buckner, commander of Fort Donelson, Tennessee, requested terms for his surrender from Union Gen. Ulysses S. Grant, the Northern general responded with, "No terms except unconditional surrender." Because "unconditional surrender" also matched Grant's initials, it became his wartime nickname.

Union League: A society founded by Northern patriots in November 1862 to encourage loyalty to the Union and boost flagging morale. During Reconstruction, this name was adopted by a secret political organization of blacks in the South.

war correspondent: The widespread accompaniment of armies by journalists took place during the Civil War. The most famous of these was Winslow Homer, a writer and artist for *Harper's Weekly* who accompanied the Federal forces during the war. The term "army correspondent" came into use in 1863.

war widow: A woman whose husband was away for military service (but not necessarily dead, as the term might imply).

"The war will be over by Christmas": A popular expression in 1861 that became progressively less popular (or believable) each year the war progressed.

yard: A prison yard.

CHAPTER NINE

TECHNOLOGY

One of the great ironies of history is that the greatest advances in technology, thought and the arts often occur during times of warfare and strife. America's Civil War is certainly no exception to this rule. It saw the introduction or improvement of weapons, inventions and industrial processes. Technological advances like mass production, railways and telegraphy made it possible to raise, transport and supply the huge armies that fought the Civil War.

America at the time of the Civil War was in the midst of its Industrial Revolution, being transformed by advancing technology into an industrialized rather than an agrarian society. When war broke out, each side was driven to bring to bear whatever advantages it could. Ultimately, the North, a more industrialized region and the beneficiary of more and greater modern technology, prevailed and won the war. And, as horrible as the Civil War was, the technology advanced and produced during the conflict subsequently helped the United States become the world power it is today.

Like so many other conflicts, the Civil War proved that technological superiority alone is usually not enough to win a war; if it had been, the war would have ended in 1861 and not dragged on for four long, bloody years. However, Northern superiority meant that the war was an uphill battle for the South from the beginning, one that it eventually was unable to continue.

Many inventions associated with later ages saw their earliest incarnations during the Civil War, and writers who are so inclined have ample opportunities to include "cutting edge" technology in their stories (like Tom Clancy does in his twentieth-century novels). An element of science fiction can even be added if desired; indeed, many of the works of nineteenth-century science fiction writer Jules Verne are set during or shortly after the Civil War.

Military advances included the introduction of many new types of weapons and equipment, among them land mines, repeating rifles, automatic weapons, revolving gun turrets, armored warships, long-range sniper rifles, railroad artillery, double-barreled cannon and the first naval mines (many of these weapons are discussed in chapter ten). Great advances were also made in the usage of existing types of weapons and equipment, including observation balloons, hand grenades, submarine and semisubmersible vessels, mobile siege artillery and rockets.

Medical advances included vast improvements in medical care, improved prosthetic limbs, the first orthopedic hospital, improvements in pharmacology, techniques for handling infection and the spread of disease, and anesthetics for the wounded.

Other technological advances included the first fire extinguishers, periscopes, the first railroad signal system, the first oil pipeline, great advances in photography, improved telegraphy, mobile field communications, canned food, improvements to the factory system, instant coffee and rudimentary refrigeration.

TECHNOLOGY IN THE NORTH

In the North on the eve of the Civil War, more than 1 million Northerners worked in some 100,000 factories of varying sorts and sizes, which included virtually all of the nation's weapons manufacturers and shipyards. Several parts of the North, notably New England and New Jersey, were also noted as being sites of particular innovation and inventiveness.

Northern ability to produce whatever it needed, rather than import it from other countries, simply eclipsed that of the South. A striking example of this is that in 1860, the textile factories of a single Northern city, Lowell, Massachusetts, had more spindles turning thread than did the entire South.

TECHNOLOGY IN THE SOUTH

At the outbreak of the Civil War, the South had about 100,000 workers employed in a mere 20,000 factories and workshops. Some of these were very technologically advanced, such as Augusta Powder Works, which produced some of the best gunpowder used on either side. Overall, however, the South probably had about a tenth the industrial capability of the North. This capacity diminished as the war progressed, too, as the South was unable to furnish the raw materials it needed to produce goods in its factories, and Southerners had to become adept at improvisation and devising substitutes as needed.

For example, at the beginning of the war, the Confederacy had only two major metal foundries, Leeds Company in New Orleans and Tredegar Ironworks in Richmond, Virginia. It lost Leeds when Union forces captured New Orleans in April 1862, and less than a year later Union forces occupied Tennessee, depriving the Confederacy of its primary source of iron. This left Tredegar, as well as many smaller factories, at a standstill for months at a time for want of raw materials to work with. Nonetheless, throughout the course of the war Tredegar produced thousands of artillery pieces, as well as armor plating for ironclad warships. Southern ironworks produced only a quarter as many cannon as did factories in the North, but this still represents a high level of ingenuity and dedication. A side effect of this was that even the limited numbers of consumer goods that had been produced prior to the war were no longer manufactured in the Confederacy.

Prior to the war, of course, the South was able to import whatever products of technology and industrialization it needed. Indeed, it was technology that had made the institution of slavery profitable by the time of the Civil War. By the early 1800s, slaves could not pick or process enough cotton to make them highly profitable. The invention of the **cotton gin**, however, allowed far more cotton to be grown and processed by fewer slaves, ensuring the economic viability of the slave-based plantation system, which otherwise would have likely died a natural death within a few generations. Cotton became the world's cheapest and most widespread textile fabric.

MILITARY TECHNOLOGY

Military technology is very reactive and tends to improve only in response to specific threats, conditions or needs; technological advances in some areas require corresponding advances in others. For example, the heavy rifled artillery pieces of the Civil War, which were able to blow apart existing masonry fortresses, necessitated improvements in fortification. And the war's deadly weapons in general prompted improvements in many areas, from battlefield medical care to prosthetic limbs for soldiers who had been horribly maimed.

Military tactics, too, had to change in the face of improved technology. Battlefield tactics at the beginning of the war were based on principles that had been modified little since the Napoleonic Wars (1793–1815). Commanders studied the strategies, tactics and maxims of those wars, and soldiers on both sides were taught corresponding drill and maneuver from a variety of training manuals. One of the foremost was *Rifle and Light Infantry Tactics* (subtitled *For the Exercise and Manoeuvres of Troops When Acting as Light Infantry or Riflemen*), written in 1855 by William J. Hardee, a veteran of the Mexican War who served as a Confederate general during the Civil War. It was better known among soldiers as "Hardee's Tactics" or the "Hardee Manual." Other contemporary texts included *Scott's Tactics*, "Casey's Manual," (*Infantry Tactics for the Instruction, Exercise, and Maneuvres of the Soldier, a Company, Line of Skirmishers, Battalion, Brigade or Corps D'Armee*), "Gilliam's Manual" and a manual on bayonet fighting that had been translated from the French by Union Gen. George B. McClellan.

Unfortunately, these strategies and tactics assumed an antiquated level of technology in which soldiers bearing smoothbore muskets with limited accuracy and range had to line up on open ground in tight formations within a few hundred yards of the enemy and blaze away at each other in volleys, eventually following up with a spirited bayonet charge. Rifled muskets, however, allowed defenders to shoot apart tightly packed enemy formations while still hundreds of yards away. Many commanders, nonetheless, persisted in employing the tactics of a previous age right through until the end of the war, something that contributed to it being the United States' costliest war ever.

Tactics did evolve, of course, in response to the new technology. Referred to as "skirmisher tactics" or "Zouave tactics," they emphasized fighting in small groups and loose formations, making good use of cover and charging for short distances before dropping behind cover.

Improvements in Artillery

Industrialization allowed for the manufacture of more powerful, accurate artillery pieces than had ever before existed, and for vast improvements upon explosive shells and other types of artillery ammunition. Such improvements included breech-loading mechanisms, rifled barrels, smokeless gunpowder, systems for absorbing recoil and vastly improved metallurgy.

Cannon makers also developed new ways to construct guns so that they could withstand heavier powder charges, firing heavier projectiles further and with greater velocity. Thomas J. Rodman developed a process for producing incredibly strong gun barrels by casting successive layers of the tube around a removable metal core that was cooled by water. As each layer cooled, it shrank and further compressed the layer beneath it. Robert Parker Parrott created artillery barrels by wrapping wrought iron or steel hoops around a central tube made of cast iron or steel.

Redoubts, trenchworks, and other forms of modern fortification were used extensively during the Civil War for the first time.

Fortifications and Siege

In addition to modern tactics, soldiers who survived their first experiences in battle learned to take cover behind trees, fences, walls and anything else available, and to make use of **firing pits**, **trenches** and other means of defense. Although it had existed in a much simpler form since the seventeenth century, trench warfare was adopted and refined throughout the course of the Civil War, foreshadowing the way conflicts of the future would be fought. And, just as the trenchworks were a reaction to highly lethal small arms, weapons were developed during the Civil War to harry or kill soldiers within such defense works, including hand grenades and relatively light mortars.

Just as infantrymen had to react to the power of modern small arms, so too did engineers have to react to the power of the newest artillery pieces. Most of the forts in existence when the Civil War began were "Third System" fortifications, planned in the decades following the War of 1812 and constructed according to the canons of the early nineteenth century. These polygonal brick forts were designed to withstand the weapons of an earlier age and not heavy, rifled artillery pieces firing explosive shells; such guns, especially when used in mass, wreaked havoc on the outdated fortifications. Fortifications built after the war utilized low, earthen walls that would absorb the force of artillery projectiles, rather than try to resist or deflect them with high stone walls.

After making history as the flash point for the Civil War in 1861, Fort Sumter

Many sorts of obstacles were used on Civil War battlefields, including **chevaux**, *sharpened stakes affixed to logs that were especially effective at impeding cavalry.*

came under fire again in 1863, this time from Union siege artillery. For twenty-two months the fort withstood bombardment and was almost completely reduced to rubble. Pounded into small pieces, however, Sumter became even more defensible, and Southern defenders burrowed into the rubble, living in subterranean bombproofs and firing their guns from behind berms of smashed masonry.

MEDICAL TECHNOLOGY

When the Civil War broke out, contemporary medical technology proved unable to adequately cope with the widespread diseases and horrific wounds it was faced with over the ensuing four years. Blood transfusions, penicillin and other antibiotics, antiseptics, hypodermic needles, X-ray machines and innumerable other innovations that could have helped save innumerable lives, did not yet exist.

In 1861, the U.S. Army Medical Corps consisted of a mere ninety-eight surgeons and assistant surgeons (in the mid-nineteenth century, doctors were usually referred to as surgeons). Equipment consisted of a few dozen thermometers, no microscopes (not until 1863), and no working knowledge of devices like the laryngoscope, stethoscope or ophthalmoscope.

Hypodermic syringes did not exist either. When painkilling drugs had to be administered, they were generally rubbed or dusted into open wounds, or administered in pill or solution form. Morphine and other opiates were the most common sort of painkillers, and many soldiers became addicts as a side effect of their widespread usage. After the war ended, however, they could easily obtain such drugs at local drugstores.

By the end of the war, surgeons had learned much about wounds, diseases and drug addiction, much more than they ever could have learned spared the horrors of the war, and medical technology advanced as a result.

Hospital design was one area of improvement. Hospitals were designed as a series of pavilions connected by covered or enclosed walkways. Soldiers were separated based on their particular wounds or afflictions, reducing the spread of disease. Modern hospitals are based on this model today.

Advances were also made in areas peripheral to the treatment of wounds and illness. For example, improvements in photography allowed for wounds and their treatment to be studied by doctors after the war. Also, because many families wanted their dead loved ones shipped home, great strides were made in the science of embalming during the Civil War. A whole new profession concerned with embalming developed during this period, and families who could afford it could hire an "embalming surgeon" to embalm the body of a dead soldier and bring it back home for burial. The role of medical personnel on the battlefield changed, too, and one important concept advanced during the war was the idea that doctors, nurses and orderlies were neutrals who should not be shot at or taken prisoner.

Medical Training

Medical schools were common during the Civil War, but, unfortunately, many of them provided little practical training. In the nineteenth century, training for surgeons typically consisted of three, thirteen-week semesters of medical school. Some fairly good medical schools did exist, mainly at established colleges and universities, like Princeton and Yale. Programs at such schools lasted one or two years and consisted almost entirely of classroom instruction, with just a few weeks of medical residency. Training during each year was identical, and some students did not bother to study a second year, although this was generally recommended.

No sort of medical licensing board existed, however, so little could be done to regulate doctors. In fact, no training or certification of any sort was required for someone to call themselves a surgeon or doctor, and quacks and incompetents were not uncommon.

Causes of Death and Injury

Although battlefield injuries were among the most dramatic and horrible ways soldiers were killed, more actually perished from disease than from any other causes during the Civil War. In general, for every man who died from wounds, there were two who succumbed to disease. In camps and prisons alike, soldiers suffered the effects of overcrowding, inadequate waste disposal, malnutrition or starvation and parasitic infestation, all factors that caused diseases like influenza and cholera to spread almost unchecked.

Wounds, of course, were not to be underestimated. Because no sorts of antibiotics or antiseptics were available, even a minor wound could easily become septic or gangrenous, killing a soldier within days or requiring the amputation of an infected limb.

Nearly nineteen out of every twenty wounds were inflicted by small-arms fire, and the worst of these were caused by cone-shaped, soft lead rifle slugs called minié balls. Minié balls could be fired at much higher velocity than the round musket balls of a generation before, and were thus far more destructive to internal organs. Such projectiles would flatten out upon impact with the long bones of the legs and arms, blowing them into splinters and requiring them to be amputated. Even wounds that did not require amputation or were not immediately fatal often became infected and ultimately proved mortal.

Amputation

During the Civil War, three out of four operations performed on soldiers by surgeons were amputations. It might seem to a casual observer that surgeons were taking the easy way out with amputation, that they were indifferent or incompetent, or that limited resources forced them to fall back on amputation rather than perform more delicate surgery. Unfortunately, while some contemporary doctors were truly incompetent, even the best doctors simply had no choice but to remove limbs irreparably mangled by minié balls, explosive shells and other weapons of the age.

Surgery in the field was usually performed in makeshift field hospitals, sometimes on operating tables consisting of a few boards laid across a pair of barrels. Chloroform was often available (more so in Union hospitals than those of the Confederacy), and a rag or sponge soaked with it would be held over the face of the soldier being operated on. This was in itself a dangerous procedure, and could result in chloroform poisoning if not removed often enough. In the absence of chloroform, a few shots of whisky might do; in any case, some sort of anesthesia was usually administered, and it was uncommon that nothing was available but a bullet or stick to bite down on. In such cases, the risk of a soldier dying from shock was much greater.

Amputation usually consisted of the following steps. First, the surgeon would cut off blood flow to the afflicted limb with a tourniquet. Then, after selecting the place where he would have to cut through the limb, he would slice through the surrounding flesh and connective tissue with a scalpel. He would then use

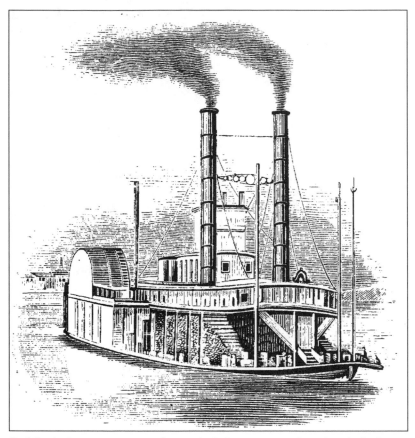

Paddlewheel steamers were used extensively for commerce along America's rivers and inland waterways. During the war, such vessels were used for ferrying troops, as hospital boats, and were sometimes armed and used as warships (although they were not generally considered sturdy enough for this role).

a "capital saw," a saw with replaceable blades that looked much like a hacksaw, to saw through the bone. Once the limb was completely removed, the surgeon would toss it onto a pile of other arms and legs, and sew up the major veins and arteries with sutures (silk thread in the North, cotton thread in the South). The soldier would immediately be removed so another could take his place. The entire process took about fifteen minutes, although some doctors were noted for performing amputations even more quickly.

Amputation was most effective if performed immediately after a wound occurred. Mortality rate for soldiers who received an amputation within twenty-four hours of being wounded was 25 percent, a rate that doubled to 50 percent for soldiers who received an amputation more than a day after being wounded. Nonetheless, and as horrible a solution as it was, amputation saved the lives of many soldiers for whom there otherwise would have been no hope at all.

Medical Transportation

Medical personnel had to deal with greater numbers of wounded soldiers than they ever had before, and numerous means of transporting the injured were developed.

Ambulances were among the most common. Two-wheeled varieties provided a very bumpy ride, and many severely wounded soldiers died after being transported in them. Four-wheeled ambulances were also used, and these provided a more comfortable ride. Horses were preferred to mules for ambulances, as they were provided steadier service.

Steamboats, train cars and barges were also modified as conveyances for the wounded. Converted passenger cars could carry up to three dozen wounded soldiers, the least seriously wounded in stretchers hung from the ceilings and the most severely wounded on wooden slats inserted across the seats.

FARM TECHNOLOGY

Agriculture in the United States had been transformed in the late eighteenth and nineteenth centuries. Improved understanding of chemistry helped fertilization and livestock feeding practices; productivity was increased through improvements in plant and animal breeding; inventions like steam-powered grain-threshing machines, sugar mills and the cotton gin radically improved the yield of crops that had once been highly labor-intensive; and canals, railroads and steamboats allowed surplus produce to be shipped into the growing urban areas and encouraged farmers to increase their production for profit.

Horse-powered farm machinery dominated American agriculture throughout the nineteenth century and reached the height of its effectiveness during this period. Elaborate horse-powered agricultural equipment increased labor productivity immensely and allowed new land to be brought under cultivation. Horses pulled cultivators, harrows, mowers, plows, hay rakes and reapers; activated combines and threshing machines; and performed many other useful tasks.

RAIL TRANSPORT

In 1861, most of the country's railroad track and rolling stock, along with the workshops needed to manufacture and repair them, existed in the North. As

Improved agricultural machines, such as this thirty-three-horse harvester, revolutionized American farming in the decades leading up to and following the Civil War.

a result, the Union was able to use the railways as a significant tactical, strategic, and logistical tool.

The South had fewer miles of rail line, much less rolling stock, an inability to replace either and handicaps in maintaining them; nonetheless, the Confederacy used the railways to accomplish a handful of impressive results, including their victory at the first Battle of Bull Run and the transfer of Lt. Gen. James Longstreet's corps in time for the Battle of Chickamauga, widely considered a master stroke. However, as Jeffrey N. Lash explains in *Destroyer of the Iron Horse*, a difference between the philosophies of Northern and Southern generals led the latter to not fully take the railways into consideration to the extent that their adversaries did, nullifying even the limited resources at their disposal.

Many otherwise exemplary Southern generals (notably Joseph Johnston, who had a strong background in railway construction, technology and design) had a blind spot when it came to the possibilities offered by the railways. Some Confederate generals did try to make the most of railway resources, and Leonidas Polk was their most proficient rail general. Overall, however, this inability to exploit such an important resource tarnishes to a great extent the popular notion that Confederate generals were vastly superior to their Union counterparts.

This deficiency was not limited to the Confederacy, however. Several high-ranking Union generals also failed to use rail to its fullest advantage, among them Henry Halleck, George McClellan and William Rosecrans.

When used properly, railways could quickly transport fresh troops to a new theater, evacuate worn units or supply garrisoned areas. As a result, rail lines were often military targets. Quick ways to disrupt rail transit, employed especially by raiding troops, included tearing up railway tracks and ties, tipping over locomotives and cars, and blowing up railway bridges. Possible disadvantages to these methods were that they could make a section of line unusable to the side doing the destruction (which was not an issue if they would not have opportunity to use it anyway), and that their effects could be undone with relative ease once the vandals had retreated back to their own lines. Indeed, some Union army engineers made prefabricated bridge components and reached the point where they could replace demolished bridges within twenty-four hours.

More lasting methods of disrupting rail traffic included pushing rolling stock off bridges or into ravines; packing wood or coal in or around rolling stock and igniting it; and pulling up railroad ties, heating them in a fire, then wrapping them around trees to make them permanently unusable (a method employed by Sherman's troops when marching through Georgia in 1864).

Railroad equipment was expensive, and its destruction could prove costly. In 1861, a heavy locomotive cost $9,000 and a passenger or freight car cost $2,200. As the war progressed, prewar costs became moot, and a new locomotive could not be had in the South at any price in the latter half of the war.

COMMUNICATIONS

Many new forms of communications were developed prior to and during the Civil War, most notably the telegraph, while other innovations of the period were not widely used. For example, in 1843, Scottish physicist Alexander Bain invented a facsimile machine that could send an image and printed material over telegraph lines. A working version of the system was built in 1861 in Paris, but practical models were not built until the invention of photoelectric cells, which could convert light and dark areas on paper into electrical impulses.

Telephones came into limited use in 1877, during the last year of Reconstruction.

Mail

The amount of mail being sent increased dramatically during the war, as thousands of soldiers and their families tried to stay in touch with each other. One measure the Federal postal service employed to cope with this increased demand was to divide posted materials into first-class, second-class and third-class mail. During this period the postal service also began to provide free delivery in cities.

The famed but short-lived Pony Express reached its peak during the Civil War. Established on April 3, 1860, in hopes of winning a mail contract from the Overland Stage company, the mail service strove to deliver mail from St.

Joseph, Missouri, to Sacramento, California, about two thousand miles, in a mere ten days. Pony Express employed some eighty riders during its brief tenure, including the famous "Buffalo Bill" Cody. Each rider rode seventy to eighty miles at a time, stopping to change horses at stations along the route, which were built at intervals of about ten miles. Despite its success, the Pony Express lasted little more than a year and a half (October 24, 1861) and was rendered obsolete by the linking of the East and West Coasts by telegraph, a considerably faster and cheaper means of communication.

Telegraphy

Message transmission during the nineteenth century was fairly simple. An operator used a key or switch to send short pulses of electricity to the telegraph line from a battery. Messages were sent by dispatching these pulses in patterns that formed codes representing letters and numbers.

Inventors Samuel Morse and Alfred Vail made great improvements to this early sort of receiver and modified it to print dot and dash symbols corresponding to electric pulses of short and long duration, creating what became known as Morse code. In 1844, Samuel F.B. Morse sent his first famous message, "What hath God wrought," from Baltimore to Washington, DC. His receiver was widely adopted, and telegraphy soon achieved a central role in communications. Western Union was founded shortly thereafter to provide telegraphy services, and it extended its lines to California by 1861.

This was facilitated by relays, electromagnet receivers that operated switches and allowed power from a local battery to key a further length of telegraph line. At the time of the Civil War, relays were the only form of amplifier available to telegraph engineers.

Because telegraphers could easily distinguish and transcribe Morse's dot-and-dash signals onto paper by hand, devices for recording signals directly onto paper, used earlier in the century, were largely abandoned. However, new methods were devised by other inventors.

Publications and Print Media

People learned about the major events of the war through a wide variety of publications. In many cases, newspaper stories were sensationalized, inaccurate or even outright fabrications, and soldiers often commented that what was going on around them bore little resemblance to what the newspapers and newsweeklies were reporting. Nonetheless, people on the home front were better informed about what was happening on the battlefields than in previous conflicts.

Contemporary news publications tended to be much smaller than their modern counterparts in both length and dimensions. "Tabloid"-size publica-

A wide array of daily and weekly newspapers were available during the Civil War, providing detailed coverage of the war that had previously not existed.

tions were more common for mainstream daily publications than today, and many dailies were eight pages long (i.e., two folded broadsheets, each comprising four pages) or shorter. Southern papers, in particular, shrunk in size along with available resources in general, and were often printed on less-than-ideal materials. For example, because of a shortage of newsprint, an 1863 edition of the *Opelousas Courier* was printed on wallpaper.

Civil War-era news publications were also text heavy, and frequently the front pages included no illustrations. There were exceptions to this, most notably *Leslie's Illustrated Newspaper*. When publications such as Frank Leslie's did include artwork, the most common sorts were engravings and lithographs of scenes from the war, maps and political cartoons.

During the war, reporters near the front would file their stories with their newspapers via telegraph. Because telegraphy was subject to so many vicissitudes, such as lines being cut by enemy raiders, reporters developed an "inverted pyramid" style of story writing, in which the lead paragraph of a story included its most critical information, and each subsequent paragraph contained information of decreasing importance. Thus, even if only the first paragraph went through, a newspaper might still have the basis for a story.

Following are some of the publications available to people during the war (many are still read today). Many of these are available on microfiche at libraries, particularly in the areas where they were originally published, and can be a valuable resource for writers. Frequency and a publication's affiliation with a particular city are noted, unless such information is obvious from the name.

Northern News Publications
Cincinnati Daily Gazette
Harper's Weekly
Hartford Evening Press
Hickman Daily Courier
National Police Gazette
Newark Daily Advertiser
New York Daily Tribune
New York Herald
New York Tribune
New York Semi-Weekly Tribune
New York Times (daily)
Philadelphia Enquirer
The Oregonian Statesman (daily)
Rochester Daily Union and Advertiser
Rochester Evening Express

Southern News Publications
Army & Navy Messenger
Charleston Daily Courier
The Charleston Mercury
Chattanooga Gazette (daily)
Columbia Guardian (daily)
The Daily Press (Nashville)
Daily Union (Nashville)
Galveston Tri-Weekly News
Houston Daily Telegraph
Houston Tri-Weekly Telegraph
Louisville Daily Journal
New Orleans Daily Delta
Opelousas Courier (daily)
Republican Banner (Nashville; daily)

Richmond Enquirer (daily)
Southern Enterprise (Greenville, South Carolina; daily)
True Union (daily)
Weekly Union (Nashville)

Photography

Photography emerged as a significant new medium during the Civil War. Photographers followed in the wake of the armies and provided a visual record of units in the field, troops in camp and the aftermath of battles. Photographers provided a previously impossible coverage of the war, its participants and its effects.

Indeed, after the Battle of Antietam in September 1862, the Army of the Potomac held the field, allowing Northern cameramen to thoroughly photograph the aftermath of the battle. And, in the days following the battle, photographers recorded Lincoln's visit to McClellan's headquarters and then followed the Union army across the Potomac and into recaptured Harpers Ferry, Virginia.

Notable Civil War-era photographers include William R. Pywell, Alexander Gardner (who photographed Richmond after it was destroyed by Federal troops), Timothy H. O'Sullivan (who accompanied the Union army in the western theater and recorded the course of its operations) and perhaps most famous of all, Mathew Brady (who had employed both Gardner and O'Sullivan until 1863).

Beginning in 1845, Brady had made daguerreotypes of several famous Americans and published it in 1850 as *The Gallery of Illustrious Americans.* By 1860, he was making a good living through his three **daguerreotype** studios, two in New York City and one in Washington, DC. War offered Brady new opportunities. At the expense of nearly his entire fortune, he outfitted a score of photographers with camera equipment and mobile darkrooms and sent them off to cover all fronts of the war. Contemporary equipment was too primitive to take action shots, but the thousands of photographs they took depicted the war in a shocking, brutal way. Brady's name appeared on all of the photographs, in keeping with the convention of the day, something that has helped identify the work of his studios (e.g., more than a third of the one hundred known photographs of Abraham Lincoln bear Brady's name).

Official military photographers, too, added to the pictorial archive of the war. For example, George N. Barnard, official photographer of the Chief Engineer's Office, created the best photographic record of the war in the West and made many pictures of Atlanta, Georgia, just prior to its destruction by fire upon Sherman's departure from the city.

TERMS

ambrotype: An underexposed, negative photograph on a glass plate that appeared positive when set against a black background. Used primarily for portraits, glass photo plates had been invented in 1851 by Englishman Frederick Scott Archer.

banquette, firestep: A small mound of earth below the crest of a parapet that allowed shorter soldiers to fire over it more easily.

Barton, Clara: This "Angel of the Battlefield" played a significant role in providing medical care throughout the course of the Civil War. Her wartime activities included collecting and distributing supplies to soldiers, caring for the wounded and gathering identification records for soldiers who were missing or dead. In 1881, she founded the American Red Cross, basing it to some extent on the Swiss-based International Red Cross.

cotton gin: A device for removing seeds from cotton fiber. Devices for removing the seeds from long-staple cotton had long existed but were ineffective at removing seeds from the short-staple cotton of the Americas. This task had traditionally been performed by slaves.

In 1793, Eli Whitney invented a machine for removing the seeds from short-staple cotton. This device consisted of a boxed, revolving cylinder set with spiked teeth that could be turned by a crank, pulling the raw cotton through small slots, thereby separating the seeds from it. At the same time, a rotating brush operated pulleys and a belt removed the cotton lint from the spikes.

Many variations on Whitney's design appeared in the following years, including horse-drawn and water-powered gins, which radically speeded up the ginning process and lowered production costs.

daguerreotype: Invented by Frenchman Louis Daguerre in 1837, this first practical means of photographic reproduction created detailed images on silver-plated copper sheets. Although popular, this process was also expensive and time consuming, and was soon replaced.

diplex: An innovation that allowed two telegraph signals to be transmitted simultaneously in the same direction.

duplex: An improvement in telegraphy that allowed signals to be simultaneously transmitted from opposite directions over the same line.

fascines: Bundles of branches or saplings used to line earthworks or trenches.

Elaborate trenchworks, reinforced by obstacles and traps and often stretching for miles or encircling entire cities, were utilized extensively during the Civil War.

firing pit: A shallow pit dug out by hand and used to protect one or more infantrymen in combat. Veteran soldiers learned to begin digging such defense works whenever they stopped for an extended period of time, and continued to improve upon them as time and resources allowed.

"laudable pus": A term used by nineteenth-century doctors to describe the pus that formed in a wound after surgery or amputation, thought to be a beneficial sign of healing. In actuality, of course, it was a sign of massive bacterial infection, which often proved fatal.

plank road: A road wide enough for two wagons, one side of which was dirt and the other side of which was covered with thick wooden planks. Conventions of the day dictated that heavily laden wagons had right-of-way on the plank-covered side and that less full wagons should move on to the dirt side. As with other dirt roads, the parts not covered with timbers often became mud tracks in wet weather.

quadruplex: A combination of **diplex** and **duplex** technology that allowed a total of four messages, two coming from each direction, to be sent simultaneously along a single telegraph line. Invented by Thomas Alva Edison in 1874.

tintype, ferrotype: A photograph made by exposing a thin, black-enameled metal plate coated with a chemical compound called collodion. Small tintypes were the most common and inexpensive form of portraiture prior to the Civil War.

trenches: Narrow, deep holes excavated to protect infantrymen. Ideally, a trench would be deep enough so a man could stand erect within it and still not be exposed to enemy fire. To fire from within a trench, a soldier would step up onto a one- to two-foot high parapet called a firestep. Civil War trenchworks, especially around besieged cities, often stretched for several miles, anticipating the style of warfare now most often associated with World War I.

CHAPTER TEN

ARMS, EQUIPMENT AND UNIFORMS

mind-boggling variety of weapons, equipment and uniforms were used during the four years of the Civil War. While the military forces of either side would have preferred equipment and weapons to be standardized for logistical reasons, this was not always possible, especially when war materiel was being produced by scores of domestic manufacturers and being imported from abroad.

Equipment and uniforms, and weapons to a lesser extent, were often cheaply made by profit-hungry government contractors and of substandard quality, something that contributed even more to the suffering of soldiers in the field.

Arms, equipment and uniforms, those prescribed by regulation and those actually worn and used by troops, are covered thoroughly but not exhaustively in the following section. For most readers, this information will be more than enough, but those who require extensive detail should check with more specialized sources. Several of these are listed in Appendix II on page 234.

NOMENCLATURES

Military equipment differed from civilian equipment in that it had both a name and a nomenclature, an identifying combination of letters and numbers.

Often, the nomenclature identified the year a particular weapon or piece of equipment was produced, or its place in a sequence. For example, the sword carried by Union light artillerymen was labeled as the "M1840 light artillery saber''; because the original pattern was first produced in 1840, all swords of that pattern are identified as an M1840, regardless of the year they were actually manufactured. A piece of military equipment might also be described in terms of its pattern, or model, as in an "1858-pattern hat."

Nomenclatures were not generally used in everyday speech and not all items were assigned one.

SMALL ARMS

Small arms are those firearms used by individuals, as opposed to artillery pieces or other crew-served weapons, and include rifles, muskets, **carbines**, **pistols** and shotguns. Such weapons, notably rifles firing minié balls, inflicted 94 percent of all fatal battlefield injuries during the Civil War.

For many logistical and practical reasons, military systems prefer to have their small arms be as standardized as possible (e.g., the rifles used by almost all modern U.S. military personnel are part of the M16 series of weapons, including the M16A1, the M16A2 and the M-4 carbine). During the Civil War, however, at least eighty-five different sorts of small arms were used in all of the Union military services, and an uncertain but similarly unwieldy number was employed by the Confederacy. These ranged from Revolutionary War-era flintlock muskets to the most modern repeating, metallic cartridge rifles, and included both domestic and European weapons.

Despite the great variety of weapons in use, however, the primary rifles used on both sides were the M1842 .69-caliber Harpers Ferry Rifle and the M1861 .58-caliber Springfield rifle, both muzzle loaders. Most other rifles made in either part of the country were little different than these two basic types. One of the most notable foreign rifles was the English Enfield rifle, some 700,000 of which were purchased by the Confederacy (many were also purchased by the U.S. government).

Pistols of many sorts were used during the war, but the most common were Colt **revolvers**, notably the M1851 .32-caliber navy model and the M1860 .44-caliber army model.

Carbines were generally breach loaders loaded with either metallic or combustible linen cartridges. These included the M1865 .56-caliber Spencer carbine (which held seven metallic rounds in an internal magazine), the .44-caliber lever-action Henry repeating rifle (which held fifteen rounds and was released in 1860), and the M1855 .577-caliber Sharps carbine, which was a single-shot breach loader that accepted a linen cartridge. Such weapons had much better rates of fire than single-shot muzzle loaders. However, because

Pistols like this Colt revolver, typically in .32 or .44 caliber, were used in the various military services of each side. Beyond the war, such reliable, powerful sidearms found a place in the frontier culture of the Far West.

ammunition was perpetually in short supply during the war, many commanders disliked such modern weapons, believing that they were overly expensive, unreliable and would induce soldiers to squander ammunition.

Hand grenades were also used during the Civil War. Hanes' Excelsior was a metal sphere about the size of a softball that was armed by opening it, attaching **percussion caps** to several nipples on an inner core filled with gunpowder, then reassembling it. Hanes' grenade could then be thrown. It was expected that upon impact at least one of the caps would bang against the inside of the outer shell, causing the weapon to explode. Because it was hazardous even to its user, however, it did not see wide use. Ketcham's grenade was used more extensively, especially in siege and trench warfare. It was a percussion explosive that consisted of a fin-stabilized body armed with an egg-shaped explosive head.

Costs of small arms varied widely, but represented a large expenditure for both governments. Sharps carbines, when purchased in bulk, cost the government $30 each. Colt revolvers cost around $10 each, price varying by model (in the 1850s on the West Coast, however, when such weapons were considerably newer and had to be shipped, Colt revolvers were selling for $250 to $500 apiece).

Small-Arms Ammunition

Ammunition in a wide variety of types and calibers was used during the Civil War, reflecting the many sorts of weapons in use on both sides. Logistically, this presented all kinds of difficulties to commanders on both sides, who often had to ensure their troops were supplied with many different sorts of ammunition.

Powerful, rifled longarms like this .57 caliber Enfield, firing bone-shattering, high-velocity minié balls, were carried by most soldiers during the Civil War. Elevated sights like those shown here were disliked by many troops, and, when provided, they were often removed.

Smoothbore muskets, little different from those used during the Revolutionary War, were carried by some regiments at the beginning of the war. Most of these had the antiquated flintlock (shown above) replaced by a modern percussion lock.

Minié balls were the most common sort of ammunition for rifles, and ranged in size from .44 to .69 caliber. Smoothbore weapons could fire either a round musket ball or the somewhat more lethal **buck-and-ball**. Pistols, whether single-shot or revolvers, generally fired a simple round ball.

Both rifle and pistol ammunition was usually issued to soldiers in cartridge form, a lead slug and the amount of powder needed to fire it wrapped in paper. Cartridges were usually issued in paper packages and transferred into tins that would hold twenty rounds each. In combat, a rifleman would tear open the cartridge, pour the powder down the muzzle of the weapon, put the slug into the rifle muzzle and discard the paper, and ram the slug down to the bottom of the barrel. To fire the weapon, he would place a **percussion cap** on the hollow nipple of the weapon's lock, cock it and squeeze the trigger.

Cartridges were often unavailable to Confederate soldiers early in the war. When this was the case they would carry their musket or minié balls loose in a pouch or pocket and their powder in a flask or horn.

Ammunition was usually stored and shipped in pinewood boxes. A standard box had a wooden handle on each end, was sixteen inches wide, eleven inches long, eight inches deep and was packed with one thousand rounds (cartridges) of ammunition. Boxes were sometimes color coded to indicate the kind of ammunition within; the specific type of ammunition, its caliber and its quantity was usually marked on the side of the box; and the date and place of manufacture was usually stencilled on the lid.

Curved slashing swords like this M1860 U.S. Cavalry saber were favored by cavalry soldiers on both sides. Infantry officers and NCOs typically carried straight swords, while Union heavy artillery troops carried heavy, leaf-shaped short swords.

M1833 Heavy artillery sword.

MELEE WEAPONS

Swords, bayonets, knives, daggers, pikes, axes and other hand-to-hand combat weapons inflicted a relatively small, some might even say negligible, number of fatal injuries during the Civil War. However, it is impossible to say how many soldiers were not mortally wounded by such weaponry, or how many enemy positions were routed by the spirited charge of infantrymen wielding bayonet-mounted rifles. Such weapons are also colorful and can inspire a wealth of description.

Civil War bayonets came in many shapes and sizes. The most common were more spikelike than knifelike and were typically triangular in cross section, inflicting wounds that would not heal properly. Other types included **sword bayonets** and saber bayonets. Curved sword bayonets were often issued to Zouave regiments. Prices for hand-to-hand combat weapons increased dramatically after the outbreak of the war. For example, Ames cutlasses cost $2.25 each in 1860 and doubled to $4.50 apiece in 1861. Sword or saber bayonets cost the Union government from $5 to $7 each in 1864.

HEAVY WEAPONS AND AMMUNITION

Almost as large a variety of heavy weapons as of small arms were used during the Civil War by the armies and navies of each side. These could be broadly divided into **cannons, mortars** and **howitzers**, and further divided into weapons that were either smoothbore or rifled.

Cannons and howitzers, with their long bronze, iron or steel barrels, looked much the same, although howitzers were slightly shorter. Lighter ones were mounted on wheeled carriages drawn by teams of horses. Heavier ones were mounted upon large, stationary frames that could be rotated within an arc of fire; such guns were set up either within fortifications for defense, outside of them for siege and even on the battlefield. Heavy cannons and howitzers could also be mounted on ships, barges and gunboats and used for shelling coastal positions, such as fortifications.

Mortars had thick, stubby-looking barrels and were aimed upward at a steep angle. Such weapons were almost always mounted on flat, sturdy wooden platforms and used against fortified areas or cities. Like other artillery pieces, mortars were also mounted on watercraft, notably mortar boats, and were also sometimes mounted on railroad flatcars, allowing them to be used as mobile artillery.

Especially large or powerful siege guns were sometimes given proper names. For example, a large Union mortar mounted on a railway car and used during the siege of Petersburg, Virginia, was dubbed "The Dictator," while a 180-pounder, 8-inch Parrott gun that had to be transported over marsh to bombard Charleston, South Carolina, was nicknamed the "Swamp Angel" (this weapon is traditionally misidentified as a 200-pounder).

Even light artillery pieces required six or more men to operate optimally, and the larger siege or seacoast weapons needed even larger crews as well as special equipment, such as small cranes, to help move and load the shot and shells.

Regardless of caliber, light smoothbore artillery pieces had a range of about 1,500 yards (i.e., about a mile), while light rifled artillery pieces had a range of about 2,500 yards (i.e., well over a mile and a half), depending on the type of ammunition being fired. Heavy and seacoast artillery pieces, which fired much heavier ammunition, had a range of about 2,000 yards.

The most basic type of ammunition for artillery pieces was solid shot, or cannon balls. Various other forms of ammunition were also used, including explosive shells, **canister** or **case shot**, **bar shot**, **chain shot** and **grapeshot**.

Beyond the standard types of artillery weapons used during the war, more exotic and deadly weapons were also used by the artillery, largely on an experimental basis. Such weapons included the Gatling gun, a forerunner of the machine gun, a six-barreled .45-, .50-, or 1.0-caliber weapon that was fired by turning a crank. More amazing than that such weapons existed during the Civil War is that they were used on such a limited basis, despite their evident lethality.

During the war, bronze cannon typically cost 46¢ per pound; e.g., a 1,000-pound barrel for a 6-pounder bronze gun would have cost $460 each. Rifling cost an additional $50 and sighting an additional $20. Iron weapons cost 8¢ to 10¢ per pound; additional cost for rifling and sighting varied with the size of the gun in question.

Cost of ammunition was based on the size of the gun for which it was manufactured. In 1861, the Ames Manufacturing Company charged $2.25 each for solid shot, explosive shell and canister shot for a 6-pounder gun, and $32.12 each for solid shot or explosive shells for a 400-pounder gun (in quantities of 580 rounds). Powder charges for shot over six pounds cost extra.

INFANTRY WEAPONS AND EQUIPMENT

Infantrymen had to be able to carry all of the weapons, ammunition and equipment they would need, which frequently amounted to more than fifty pounds of gear. As a result, experienced soldiers threw away whatever was not absolutely essential. Often, however, something that was a hindrance at one point could be deeply desired at another; overcoats tossed away in the heat of the summer, for example, had to be replaced when the weather cooled.

An enlisted infantryman or noncommissioned officer was generally armed with a single-shot, muzzle-loading rifled musket (typically of .58 caliber), forty rounds of ammunition and a bayonet. Officers and sometimes noncommissioned officers typically carried six-shot revolvers and swords.

Other infantry equipment included a canteen and tin cup, a **knapsack** or blanket roll, a **cartridge box**, a **haversack**, a **cap box** and possibly a rubber blanket. Some of the Union equipment was shoddily made by government contractors and fell apart quickly. Confederate troops, on the other hand, especially later in the war, often used copies of the equipment used by Northern troops, captured Union equipment or none at all.

Bulky equipment that soldiers tended to leave behind the lines when going into battle, such as knapsacks, soldiers sometimes marked with their regiment, company and state (e.g., Co. A, 54th Massachusetts Regiment, or, if light artillery, 5th Rhode Island Battery). Occasionally, haversacks, canteens and other equipment were also marked in this way.

Many period photographs and etchings also that show private soldiers posing with pistols and bowie knives or other large fighting knives, and there are numerous references in letters from soldiers requesting their families send them items like pistols, derringers and daggers. There is also evidence that soldiers carried various other weapons to augment their rifles or muskets, such as knuckledusters. In the Confederate army, such nonregulation weapons would have been more common. However, as indicated by court martial proceedings, such weapons were far more likely to be used while on furlough or against fellow soldiers in camp than in combat.

Some soldiers also purchased armored vests for about $12 each. However, the owners of these bullet-proof vests were generally ridiculed by their comrades, and, as such items were also heavy and bulky, they were generally abandoned before long. Greaves, armored shin guards, were also purchased by some soldiers, although less frequently than vests.

CAVALRY WEAPONS AND EQUIPMENT

Cavalry soldiers on both sides were among the best equipped of the war. Typical cavalry weapons included breech-loading carbines, six-shooter revolvers and sabers; some Southern cavalrymen also favored shotguns.

Equipment included saddles, spurs, bits and bridles, blanket rolls and saddle bags (used instead of the infantryman's haversack and knapsack).

The most important piece of equipment for a cavalryman was his horse. Union troops had their mounts issued to them by the government. Unfortunately, early in the war these were acquired through an inefficient and sometimes corrupt procurement system that often secured substandard mounts for the Union cavalrymen.

Confederate soldiers, on the other hand, personally owned their horses, and as a result the horses tended to be much higher in quality. However, a cavalryman who lost his horse in combat had to replace the horse at personal expense. If he was unable to purchase or otherwise procure a remount within thirty days, he became a foot soldier and was sent to the ranks of an infantry regiment.

When the war ended, these soldiers were generally allowed to keep their horses, which were treated by the victors as personal property rather than public Confederate war materiel subject to confiscation. This was a veritable lifesaver in many cases, as it provided the deactivated soldiers with the means for plowing their fields when they returned to their farms.

ARTILLERY WEAPONS AND EQUIPMENT

Light, horse and heavy artillery units on either side used markedly different equipment, in keeping with their different missions and responsibilities. While the weapons used by Northern and Southern gunners varied to some extent, for the most part they were the same, and new artillery weapons developed by the Union were often copied by the Confederacy.

Light artillery batteries on both sides fired about 90 percent of their rounds from about ten basic sorts of cannon, including a 3″ rifled **cannon**; 6- and 12-pound cannons; 12-, 24-, and 32-pound **howitzers**; a mobile 12-pound mountain howitzer; and 10- and 20-pound **Parrott rifles**. In all cases, ''pound'' refers to the weight of a piece of solid shot, or ball, fired by the weapon, not to the weight of the gun itself, and ''inch'' refers to the caliber, or width of shell, not to the weapon's barrel length. More projectiles were fired from the quintessential

Twenty-pound Parrott rifle—a heavy field artillery cannon.

model 1857 smoothbore **Napoleon 12-pound** howitzer than from all other types of artillery piece combined. Virtually all of the Union's Napoleons were of bronze, but Confederate knockoffs were made of bronze, brass or even cast iron.

Horse artillery tended to use the lightest, most mobile guns available to the light artillery, such as 6- and 12-pound cannons, 12-pound howitzers, the 12-pound mountain howitzer and the 10-pound Parrott rifle.

Heavy artillery batteries manned the heaviest, most unwieldy and destructive artillery pieces. These included huge cannon mounted on massive wooden barbette carriages, which allowed them to be rotated in a semicircle and cover an arc of fire in front of a fortification; 13″ seacoast mortars; 24-pound guns mounted on heavy siege carriages; and the largest sorts of heavy rifled cannon, such as 100- and 300-pound Parrott guns.

Additional Artillery Equipment

Ideally, a single 12-pound light artillery piece was supplemented by a limber and a caisson, drawn by a total of twelve horses and serviced by a crew of eight gunners and six drivers. However, artillerymen were trained to work with smaller crews in the case of casualties, and limbers and caissons could be drawn at a slower rate of speed by few horses. Heavier guns required proportionately more horses for transportation and larger crews to operate them. As with their cavalrymen, Confederate artillerymen typically owned the horses they used.

Accessories included the thumbstall, a leather guard used to protect the

Third Ordinance Rifle—a light artillery cannon.

thumb from a hot gun barrel while ramming powder and shot down the **bore**; a quadrant, used to measure a gun barrel's angle of elevation; a rammer, for shoving a bag of powder and shot into the bore of the cannon; a sponge mounted on the end of a haft, used to swab out the bore in between shots and extinguish sparks that could prematurely ignite the powder; and a worm, a double corkscrew mounted on a haft and used to remove obstacles from the bore (such as damp powder bags that would not ignite).

Light artillerymen were also equipped with brass shoulder boards, which theoretically helped protect against downward-cutting saber blows from enemy cavalrymen. However, it is not likely that these accoutrements ever served the desired effect; veteran soldiers had usually lost or discarded them early on, and new recruits threw them away so as to look less green.

NAVY WEAPONS AND EQUIPMENT

Sailors did not generally carry weapons (marines were responsible for security on board ships), but when it was necessary they were issued revolvers (if available), cutlasses, sabers, pikes and axes. In boarding actions, sailors might also wield makeshift weapons, such as **belaying pins** or **gaffs**.

The 1857 model Napoleon, a brass, smoothbore, muzzle-loading howitzer that fired 12-pound solid shot, was the basic artillery piece used by both the Union and the Confederacy. An experienced crew could fire three rounds a minute with this gun.

MARINE CORPS WEAPONS AND EQUIPMENT

Marines on both sides tended to use the same weapons, equipment and accoutrements as did army infantrymen. When on board ship, weapons and equipment were generally stored in an arms room and issued when needed.

REVENUE CUTTER SERVICE WEAPONS AND EQUIPMENT

In the decade prior to the Civil War, weapons issued to Revenue Cutter crews were typically requested from the War Department. Most of these were

Coastal artillery piece, mounted on a wooden barbette.

Mortar.

weapons none of the other services wanted, and a great many of them were substandard.

For example, in 1853 the service purchased single-shot, muzzle-loading pistols and carbines from the Perry Arms Company of Newark, New Jersey, the primary criteria apparently being that the muskets were short enough to fit within a cutter's four-and-a-half foot long arms chest. One Revenue Cutter officer, 1st Lt. Edgar O. Murden of the USS *Washington*, proclaimed the weapons "unfit for sea use." However, requests by cutter officers for Jenks or Sharps carbines, Colt revolvers and law enforcement equipment like handcuffs and leg irons were repeatedly denied. Heavy weapons tended to be similarly antiquated or substandard and included 9-pounder cannons dating to the War of 1812.

By 1861, some cutters had been equipped with more modern weapons, including Sharps rifles, Maynard carbines, Colt 1858 revolvers (in the hands of officers) and new 12-pounder cannons. However, most of these were Southern cutters, many of which defected to the Confederacy at the outbreak of war.

Other equipment included bayonets for the muskets, rifles and carbines; pikes, cutlasses and axes; and belts designed to hold a cutlass or a cutlass and pistol.

OTHER ITEMS

Soldiers, sailors and marines lived in the field or on shipboard for extended periods of time, and were often away from home for a year or more. Thus, in addition to their weapons, equipment, uniforms and other items prescribed by regulation, they often had other things, subject to the limitations of what they had room for in their knapsacks or sea chests.

Such personal items included razors, shaving brushes, soap, towels and other toiletry items; pocket knives; eating utensils or folding knife-fork-and-spoon combinations; pipes and tobacco pouches; writing kits; sewing kits, called "housewives"; musical instruments, such as banjos or harmonicas; dice or decks of cards; and *cartes de visite*.

UNIFORMS

At the beginning of the war, troops wore a staggering array of different uniforms, from the Algerian-style outfits of the Zouaves, to tartan kilts in the largely Scottish Seventy-ninth New York Regiment, to the regulation blue of the North and gray of the South. Nonetheless, blue uniforms did appear in the Confederate ranks, and gray uniforms amongst some regiments of the Union, and soldiers on both sides were dressed in uniforms that included many other colors.

One reason for this startling variety of uniforms is that most of the units that fought were volunteer or state regiments that were initially uniformed and equipped locally, rather than by the Federal or Confederate governments. As the war progressed, however, uniforms became more and more standardized and alike, and, ideally, were issued by the appropriate quartermaster department. By the end of hostilities, a preponderance of men in the North were wearing regulation blue, while those in the South were wearing gray, butternut (a yellowish-gray made from a readily available dye) or anything they could obtain, from civilian clothes to Union uniforms.

A forage cap, often called a kepi, was the regulation headgear for soldiers on both sides. Even in the North, however, some other sort of headgear was substituted, either because a regiment desired a distinctive look, because regulation caps were not available or because individual soldiers preferred different sorts of hats.

Footwear included a low-heeled black shoe called a brogan for infantrymen and knee-high black boots for cavalrymen. In Southern units especially, soldiers were often poorly equipped with shoes and boots, and wore whatever they could find, going barefoot if necessary. This was also sometimes true of Northern units.

In the border regions of the West and Midwest, a preponderance of troops in any given locally raised unit might have no uniforms at all, and at times troops of either side in any theater of the war might be wearing only what their families were able to send them. Captured stores of enemy uniforms were typically distributed to (or looted by) victorious soldiers. For example, when

Union Major General Sherman's men marched into Atlanta, many of them were wearing captured Rebel uniforms. Understandably, commanders did not want their men wearing uniforms that looked like those of the enemy and usually put out an order stating that uniforms had to be dyed and that they would be confiscated if they were not.

Uniforms, shoes, belts and other equipment, especially those mass-produced in Northern workshops by war profiteers, were frequently cheaply made and of substandard quality, contributing even more to the suffering of soldiers in the field.

Union Uniforms

Army officers were to wear, according to regulation, "a frock coat of dark blue cloth, the skirt to extend from two-thirds to three-fourths of the distance from the top of the hip to the bend of the knee; single-breasted for captains and lieutenants; double-breasted for all other grades." The number and placement of buttons was dictated by rank. Trousers were to be dark blue (except for light artillery men, who were supposed to wear light blue trousers), with a gold cord along the outer seam for staff officer, a colored cord along the outer seam for regimental officers and plain for general officers.

Enlisted foot soldiers in the U.S. Army were to wear "a single-breasted frock, of dark blue cloth, made without plaits, with a skirt extending one-half the distance from the top of the hip to the bend of the knee; one row of nine buttons on the breast, placed at equal distances; stand-up collar, to rise no higher than to permit the chin to turn freely over it, to hook in front at the bottom, and then to slope up and backward at an angle of 30 degrees on each side; cuffs pointed according to the pattern, and to button with two small buttons at the under seam; collar and cuffs edged with a cord or welt of cloth" in a color appropriate to the corps. Infantrymen also wore a four-button fatigue jacket designed for field wear (worn in every branch of the service, it was possibly the most frequently seen garment worn by Federal troops).

Enlisted cavalry soldiers were to wear a jacket rather than a coat, with twelve buttons in a single row. Musicians were to wear a coat or jacket the same as that of the other soldiers in their corps, with the addition of lace in line with each button, forming a herring-bone pattern on the chest, in appropriate colors, as above.

Regulations called for trousers to be of plain dark blue cloth for all except light artillery, who were to wear sky blue, with the addition of a stripe of a color appropriate to the corps for sergeants and corporals. In practice, however, light blue trousers predominated in all branches of the army.

Cuff edgings, musician's lace and trouser stripes and cords were colored according to the corps of their wearer—sky blue for infantry, yellow for cavalry and red for artillery.

Regulation headgear for all ranks included broad-brimmed black felt hats and smaller, dark blue forage caps ("kepi"). Union soldiers generally embellished their caps with their regimental number and/or company letter and the emblem appropriate to their combat arm—a bugle for the infantry, two crossed cannons for the artillery and two crossed sabers for the cavalry.

Navy uniforms included navy blue, double-breasted frock coats for officers' dress or undress uniform, and jackets. Officers also wore **epaulets**, cocked hats and sword knots in full dress, but dispensed with them otherwise. Petty officers, seamen and other enlisted sailors wore navy blue jackets or blue wool frocks and blue trousers in cold weather (substituting white frocks and trousers in warm weather), dark blue hats, black silk neckerchiefs and black shoes or boots.

Marine Corps officers and enlisted men wore uniforms similar to those worn by soldiers in the army, distinguished by scarlet stripes and edging appropriate to the rank of the wearer and U.S.M.C. buttons and insignia.

Revenue Cutter Service uniforms were similar to those of the navy. Officers wore a double-breasted blue frock coat; a buff, blue or white vest; white or blue pantaloons; a black silk cravat; and a regulation blue Navy cap emblazoned with a gold Treasury shield. Officers wore gold epaulets in full dress and blue shoulder straps embroidered with gold in undress (a pair of foul anchors for a cutter's captain, a single foul anchor and two bars for its first lieutenant, a single foul anchor and one bar for its second lieutenant, and a single foul anchor alone for its third lieutenant). Captains were distinguished by two strips of gold lace around their cuffs, first lieutenants by a single strip of gold lace.

Revenue Cutter Service petty officers wore blue jackets and white or blue pantaloons. Seamen, firemen, coal-passers, stewards, cooks and boys wore either a white frock with blue facings and collar or an all-blue frock, white or blue trousers, and a blue mustering cap or sennet hat. The season determined whether white or blue pantaloons or other items were appropriate.

Confederate Uniforms

At the outbreak of the war, many Confederate troops and officers wore civilian clothes or U.S. military uniforms until C.S.A. uniforms could be issued to them by the quartermaster. In early 1861, the Confederate Congress did issue descriptions of what the uniforms in the various services were supposed to look like. For example, infantrymen were supposed to wear a "Cadet Gray" double-breasted frock coat with sky blue facings, sky blue pants and a sky blue kepi with a dark blue band. It is unlikely, however, that any such uniform was actually issued to or worn by Confederate troops.

In practice, Confederate soldiers were issued uniforms similar to those worn by their Union counterparts, the main difference being the color—usually gray or butternut. Regulations prescribed a midlength frock coat, but these were always in short supply, and infantry and cavalry soldiers alike tended to wear a shell jacket.

As in the North, regulation headgear for soldiers was the kepi, or forage cap. Naturally, however, the shortage of regulation equipment in the South meant the forage caps were often the exception to the rule, which was toward a broad assortment of military and civilian headgear.

C.S. Navy regulation uniform consisted of either a gray jacket, similar to that worn in the U.S. Navy, or a gray wool shirt with white duck cuffs and collar, along with the traditional wide-bottomed trousers. Accessories, such as shoes, boots, silk neckerchiefs and hats, were all supposed to be black. Early in the war, Confederate sailors tended to wear their old U.S. Navy uniforms, but regulations eventually called for all of their items to be gray, a measure that proved to be quite unpopular. It was a difficult order to fulfill in any case, and throughout the war sailors and officers alike wore blue, gray and even black uniforms, and, regulations notwithstanding, Confederate seamen often adopted a casual attitude toward their garb. There were some notable exceptions to this rule, however, among them the case of Capt. Raphael Simmes of the CSS *Alabama*, who was adamant that his sailors be in proper, Confederate gray uniforms. Confederate marines usually dressed like their infantry counterparts, and revenue service personnel looked much like any other Southern sailors.

RANK AND INSIGNIA

When referring to ranks in text, capitalize ranks when they appear directly before a name; otherwise, leave them lowercase, as with all other nonproper nouns. For example, "Captain Morris drew his saber as he began clambering over the ramparts, followed by his troops. It was the first time the captain and his men had been so close to the enemy."

The following descriptions of rank and insignia apply mostly to field uniforms. The color and appearance of some accessories varied for dress uniforms.

Branch Insignia

Each branch of the opposing armies had its own distinctive insignia. Some also had distinctive colors associated with them that might be incorporated into uniform components, such as jacket facings or trouser stripes. Branch symbols are described below.

Artillery Corps: Two crossed field guns, of gold color metal. In continuous use since 1834, when they were placed on regimental colors, knapsacks and as part of the cap insignia for artillery officers. Color: Scarlet.

Cavalry Corps: Two crossed sabers in scabbards, cutting edge up, of gold color metal. Color: Yellow.

Infantry Corps: A bugle. Color: Sky or light blue.

Engineer Corps: A gold color triple-turreted castle. Selection of the turreted castle as the engineer insignia followed the first major construction undertaken by the Corps of Engineers—the building of a system of castle-like fortifications for the protection of harbors along the Atlantic Coast. These fortifications, many of which are still standing, were called "castles."

Medical Department: A caduceus embroidered in yellow silk on a half chevron of emerald green silk (worn by hospital stewards).

Ordnance Corps: Flaming bomb, of gold metal. The use of the "shell and flame" by the Ordnance Corps dates back to 1832. It is considered to be the oldest branch insignia of the army. Color: Crimson.

Union Rank and Insignia

Union army and marine rank for both enlisted men and officers was similar in appearance to that worn in the U.S. Army today.

Enlisted men's rank was designated by chevrons, a device shaped like a V, and worn on their coat sleeves. Color of U.S. Army chevrons, as for other uniform embellishments, was appropriate to the corps of the wearer—sky blue for infantry, yellow for cavalry and red for artillery. U.S. Marine Corps chevrons were of yellow silk on a scarlet background.

Union army and marine enlisted men wore the following rank insignia:

Private: none

Corporal: two chevrons

Sergeant: three chevrons

1st Sergeant: a hollow diamond above three chevrons

Ordnance Sergeant: a hollow star above three chevrons

Quartermaster Sergeant: three stripes above and connecting three chevrons

Sergeant-Major: three rainbow-shaped stripes above and connecting three chevrons

In addition to rank insignia, enlisted men wore service stripes, diagonal bands

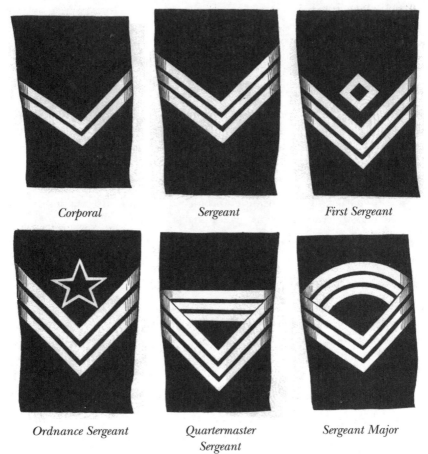

Corporal   *Sergeant*   *First Sergeant*

Ordnance Sergeant   *Quartermaster Sergeant*   *Sergeant Major*

Rank of non-commissioned officers (NCOs) was shown with chevrons, worn on the uniform sleeve; corporals wore two chevrons, sergeants three, first sergeants three with a diamond, ordnance sergeants three with a star, quartermaster sergeants three with three straight stripes, and sergeants major three with three rockers. Color of the chevron was determined by branch, blue for infantry, red for artillery and yellow for cavalry. Marine Corps chevrons looked like upside down Army chevrons, and were yellow on a red background.

just above the jacket cuff; they were entitled to one stripe for every enlistment or three years of service. Such insignia were not frequently seen in state regiments, however.

Officers wore their rank insignia on their epaulets. Union officers wore the following rank insignia:

Second Lieutenant: none (i.e., empty rectangular shoulder boards)

First Lieutenant: one bar on each shoulder

Captain: two bars on each shoulder

Major: a gold oak leaf on each shoulder

Lieutenant Colonel: a silver oak leaf on each shoulder

Colonel: a silver eagle on each shoulder

Brigadier General: one silver star on each shoulder

Major General: two silver stars on each shoulder

Lieutenant General: three silver stars on each shoulder

General: four silver stars on each shoulder

Union Army Corps Badges

From 1863 onward, Union soldiers wore badges designating which army corps they were members of, following a tradition begun in the First Corps by Gen. Philip Kearney in 1862. Such badges were intended build esprit de corps and make soldiers, whether straggling or on the battlefield, recognizable to their officers.

These badges were generally of cloth, but soldiers could purchase and wear ones made of colored metal. Corps badges were typically 1½" to 2" wide and were generally worn on the front or top of the cap, or on the breast. Eventually, the corps insignias appeared in other places, such as on wagons and ambulances. Officers were sometimes expected to wear the badges in conjunction with colored ribbon or other backgrounds, something that varied widely by corps.

Each corps was generally divided into three divisions, and the color of the badges was in most cases determined by the division, red for the first division, white for the second division and blue for the third division. For example, soldiers in the Third Division, Fifth Army Corps would have worn a blue Maltese cross. If a corps contained a Fourth division, an additional color was selected, yellow and green being two examples.

Union army corps wore the following badges. Contemporary terms used to describe them are defined where necessary. Most badges were adopted in 1863, but if an exact date for the order of issue is available, it is listed. In some cases, part of the order is quoted.

First Army Corps: a sphere (circle; March 21, 1863)

Second Army Corps: a trefoil (three-leaf clover; March 21, 1863)

Third Army Corps: a lozenge (equilateral diamond; March 21, 1863)

Fourth Army Corps: an equilateral triangle (March 26, 1864)

Fifth Army Corps: a Maltese cross (March 21, 1863)

Sixth Army Corps: a Greek cross (cross with equal arms; March 21, 1863)

Seventh Army Corps: a crescent nearly encircling a star (June 1, 1865)

Eighth Army Corps: a six-pointed star (date uncertain)

Ninth Army Corps: "a shield with the figure nine in the center crossed with a foul anchor and cannon" (April 10, 1864)

Tenth Army Corps: no badge

Eleventh Army Corps: a crescent (March 21, 1863)

Twelfth Army Corps: a five-pointed star (March 21, 1863)

Thirteenth Army Corps: no badge

Fourteenth Army Corps: an acorn (April 26, 1864)

Fifteenth Army Corps: a miniature cartridge box with the words "Forty Rounds" above it (February 14, 1865)

Sixteenth Army Corps: "a circle with four minié balls, the points toward the center, cut out of it" (no orders issued)

Seventeenth Army Corps: an arrow (March 25, 1865)

Eighteenth Army Corps: a cross, worn on the left breast (June 7, 1864)

Nineteenth Army Corps: "a fan-leaved cross, with an octagonal center" (November 17, 1864)

Twentieth Army Corps: "a star, as heretofore worn by the Twelfth Corps," which, along with the Eleventh, was absorbed into the Twentieth (April 26, 1964)

Twenty-first Army Corps: no badge

Twenty-second Army Corps: "quinquefarious in form, that is, opening into five parts, and having a circle in the center" (no orders)

Twenty-third Army Corps: a plain shield (no orders)

Twenty-fourth Army Corps: a heart (March 18, 1865)

Twenty-fifth Army Corps: a square (February 20, 1865)

Confederate Rank and Insignia

Rank worn by Confederate enlisted men was very similar to that worn by Union soldiers, i.e., none for privates, chevrons for corporals and sergeants, chevrons and a diamond for first sergeants, etc. Color for Confederate army chevrons was supposed to be appropriate to the corps, as in the U.S. army, but when colored cloth was unavailable chevrons were typically black.

Rank worn by Confederate officers deviated to a great extent from that worn by their Union counterparts, the most immediately noticeable difference being that it was worn on the collars and sleeves, rather than on shoulder boards. Such rank would have been more important for ceremonial occasions rather than for day-to-day wear; in practice, company-level Confederate officers (second and first lieutenants and captains) were often indistinguishable from their enlisted men.

Confederate officers wore the following rank insignia:

Second Lieutenant: one bar on each collar

First Lieutenant: two bars on each collar

Captain: three bars on each collar

Major: one star on each collar

Lieutenant Colonel: two stars on each collar

Colonel: three stars on each collar

General officers: a cluster of three stars inside a wreath on each collar

FLAGS

As novelists, poets and other writers have long done, those writing about the Civil War may find it useful to describe the appearance of the flags borne and rallied around by the soldiers and civilians of the opposing sides. In addition to the sorts of flags described below, regiments carried regimental flags and state units carried state flags.

United States Flags

In 1860, on the eve of the rebellion, the U.S. national flag looked much the same as it does today, the only exception being that it had thirty-four, rather than fifty stars—one for each state.

With the formation of the Confederacy in early 1861, the number of states loyal to the Union had been depleted by eleven. Nonetheless, to remove that many stars from the flag would have been a flagrant admission that the Union

First national flag of the Confederate States of America, at a distance or in the confusion of battle the 'Stars and Bars' was often mistaken for the U.S. national flag.

had failed and could not be restored (indeed, had this been done there might not have been a war at all, nor a United States as we know it today). So, not only were thirty-four stars retained for the nation's flag, additional stars were added in 1863 and 1864, when West Virginia and Nevada, respectively, were admitted to the Union as states.

Confederate Flags

The flag most generally associated with the Rebel cause—a square red field bearing two crossed diagonal blue bands bordered with white, inside of which are thirteen white stars—was not a Confederate national flag at all. Designed by Gen. P.G.T. Beauregard mainly as battle colors for cavalry, infantry and artillery units, this flag was often given a blue, yellow, orange or white border. Eventually, the battle flag, did become the canton (upper inside corner) of the second and third Confederate national flags.

In March 1861, the Confederate States of America adopted its first national flag, the "Stars and Bars," which consisted of a blue canton holding seven stars and a broad white bar in between two broad red bars. Each of the seven stars represents one of the original Confederate states. This flag, however, was often hard to distinguish from the United States flag, especially during battle, something that led to unintended fratricides and the accidental capture of prisoners of war by both sides.

In March 1863, the Confederacy adopted its second national flag, which

As in all other wars, soldiers of both sides took part in looting. This ranged from seizing food at farms in enemy territory to taking clothes, money, or other goods from dead or wounded soldiers.

was intended to bear no resemblance either to the first national flag or the Union's Stars and Stripes. It was a solid white field that used for its canton the familiar Rebel battle flag. Unfortunately, in the haze of combat this flag's long white field often made it appear to be a surrender flag. It was this flag that draped Gen. Stonewall Jackson's casket in 1864 and flew over Fort Sumter until the Confederate evacuation of Charleston in February 1865.

On March 4, 1863, the Confederacy adopted its third national flag, but did not have the opportunity to use it much. It was essentially a modification of the second national flag, with a red stripe added to its fly (outer) end to reduce the chances of it being mistaken for a surrender flag.

LOOTING

Looting was an inevitable event in the aftermath of battle. In its most innocuous form, it involved the victors helping themselves to needed stores of enemy food, clothing and equipment. Beyond this, however, looting was extended to dead and wounded soldiers, civilian farmsteads, whether abandoned or not, and other easy targets.

In the aftermath of a battle, poorly equipped troops, particularly Rebels, would often strip bodies for shoes, uniforms and anything else of use. Sometimes the looting took on an even more brutal aspect, as in the looting of dead or wounded soldiers for valuables rather than necessities. This phenomena is most characteristic of the second half of the war, when people were becoming brutalized by the conflict.

One of the most striking examples of this was the case of Col. Ulric Dahlgren, a Union cavalry officer who led a raid against Richmond, deep into enemy territory, on March 2, 1864. Killed in an ambush by Confederate militia, Dahlgren was stripped of his personal papers, gauntlets, sash and even his wooden leg, and his mutilated body was publicly displayed in Richmond (while this is sometimes explained by referring to rumors that Dahlgren was intending to assassinate Confederate President Jefferson Davis, it really points to how brutalized many people on both sides had become by 1864).

More disturbing than the looting of dead enemy soldiers was the looting of friendly soldiers. Many accounts exist of this being done by hospital orderlies, who were often assigned to such duty because they had shown themselves to be otherwise useless to their regiments. Observers of field hospitals have noted that every dead man and almost every wounded man had his pockets cut open and his personal possessions looted by such ruffians.

TERMS

accoutrements, accouterments: Equipment other than clothes or weapons carried by a soldier, including his belt, blanket roll, cap, cartridge box, canteen, mess kit (i.e., cup, plate, knife, fork and spoon), haversack and knapsack or backpack.

aiguillette: An ornamental tasseled cord worn on dress uniforms after the war. Different colors were often used to distinguish various army corps (e.g., red for Union light infantry, scarlet for artillery, yellow for cavalry, etc.).

armes blanche: A French term that literally means "white weapons" and traditionally referred to swords. In the American armies of the Civil War, its meaning was also extended to the bayonet.

bar shot: A type of artillery shot used primarily against enemy ships. Bar shot consisted of two oval-shaped iron pieces, connected like a pair of paper clips. When fired, the two pieces would extend and whirl through the air like a dull blade, making it effective against sails and rigging.

Beecher's Bibles: Term used for the 1848 model .50-caliber Sharps' hunting rifles that Rev. Henry Ward Beecher purchased and sent to antislavery forces in Kansas, using money he had raised to buy Bibles.

belaying pin: A short, clublike wooden pin that can fit into a hole on the rail of a ship to secure running gear.

bootee: An ankle-high boot or shoe.

bore: The open part of a cannon gun barrel into which powder and shot were rammed.

bricole: A leather harness, about eighteen feet in length, used by artillerymen for dragging guns when horses were unavailable.

bridoon: The rein and snaffle of a military bridle, which acted independently of a bit.

brogans: Ankle-high black boots that laced in front. Standard for Union soldiers.

buck-and-ball: One large and three smaller balls used as ammunition for smoothbore muskets. Such ammunition had terrible range, but when fired in volley could be devastating at close ranges.

bull's-eye canteen: The M-1858 canteen, which sometimes had nine concentric rings stamped into each side to give it extra strength.

caliber: The width of a round of small-arms ammunition or artillery ammunition as expressed in inches. For example, a .60-caliber musket ball would be six-tenths of an inch across, and a 10″ howitzer fired a shell 10″ wide.

caltrops: Jacklike metal obstacles with four or more points forged from pieces of iron or nails. Caltrops were scattered across an area to impede enemy cavalry.

camp colors: Flags 18″ square, white for infantry and red for artillery, with the number of the regiment on them. Mounted on eight-foot-long poles, they were used to identify the occupants of a camp.

camp gear: Equipment that armies took to the field with them, including camp cots, field desks, etc.

chapeau de bras: A type of hat.

canister, canister shot, case shot: Tin containers or bags of shot that could be fired up to two hundred yards, turning a cannon or howitzer into a giant shotgun that was extremely lethal at close ranges. Canister was usually the last thing artillerymen fired at infantry advancing on their positions, often crippling the assault or being overrun immediately thereafter.

cannon: An artillery piece that fires a projectile in a straight line toward its target (compare with howitzer and mortar).

carbine: A short rifle easier to use by cavalry troops than a full-length rifle would have been.

cap box: A small belt pouch intended to hold rifle percussion caps. Cap boxes were manufactured in both the North and South and imported from England by the Confederacy.

carte de visite: Used since the end of the eighteenth century, a small card displaying the name and sometimes the address of the bearer and presented when visiting. During the Civil War, this term was applied to the porno-graphic cards imported from Europe depicting photographs of nude or scantily clad women.

cartridge box: A rectangular leather box closed with a wide flap and some-times equipped with a shoulder strap. It could carry up to forty cartridges (usually in a pair of twenty-round tin containers) with a small pocket near the front to hold cleaning supplies. The black .69-caliber and .58-caliber models were standard on either side. Confederate troops sometimes carried copies made from undyed leather.

chain shot: A type of artillery projectile used primarily at sea and consisting of two balls connected by a short length of chain. When fired, chain shot would open up in flight and was much more likely to cut through the rigging of enemy ships than regular solid shot. Other versions consisted of a hollow sphere that would break into four pieces when fired, each piece connected by a chain to a round metal plate inside the sphere.

Coehorn mortar: A relatively light, twenty-four-pound mortar, used for indi-rect fire especially against troops hiding in trenches.

colors: A battle flag carried by an infantry or other unmounted unit.

crooked shoes: Term used by rustic soldiers to refer to shoes made for left and right feet, as opposed to the straight shoes that could be worn on either feet that were more familiar to them.

crow's feet: An alternative name for **caltrops**.

Dahlgren gun: A large artillery piece used mainly by the Union navy. Invented by U.S. Naval officer John A. Dahlgren.

Coehorn mortars, the lightest sort employed during the war, were largely used to harry troops in fortified positions and trenchworks who could not be effectively attacked with direct-fire weapons.

ditty-box: Originally intended as collar boxes, but used during the war to carry all sorts of small items. Typically made of sandalwood with hinged gutta-percha covers.

epaulets: A shoulder decoration made of stiff gold braid worn on officers' uniforms, with a strap that displayed the regimental number and rank insignia of the wearer.

fez: A cap of Turkish or North African design, usually red with a round, flat-topped, brimless crown from which hung a tassel. Such headgear was worn in action by Zouave units and around camp by some other soldiers.

foul anchor: An anchor that has become entwined with its own line.

frog: A leather accessory used to attach a sword or bayonet scabbard to a belt.

gaff: A piece of shipboard equipment consisting of a metal hook at the end of a pole.

gaiters: Shin-high leather or cloth leg coverings worn in conjunction with low boots.

garrison flag: A national flag flown in a military fort, thirty-six feet in fly (length) by twenty feet in hoist (height).

guidon: A small silk flag carried by military units that was often used to signal the execution of commands in battle (when vocal commands alone might go unheard).

grapeshot: Shot that consisted of about a dozen small balls of perhaps a pound each, sandwiched together between round pieces of wood.

havelock: A cap cover made of white linen that included a short "cape" that covered the wearer's neck. Named for a British general who had designed the items for use in India during the 1850s, these accessories were worn by some regiments early in the war.

haversack: A leather, cloth or canvas duck bag about one foot square with a shoulder strap. Soldiers used haversacks to carry their food and eating utensils. Early in the war, some soldiers purchased nonregulation patent-leather haversacks but were often subsequently ordered to discard them. U.S. Army haversacks tended to be coated with tar, making them more impervious to water than most Confederate models.

Regardless of construction, haversacks quickly became soiled from use. "By the time one of these haversacks had been in use for a few weeks as a receptacle for chunks of bacon fat and fresh meat, damp sugar tied up in a rag, potatoes and other vegetables that might be picked up along the route, it took on the color of a printing-office towel," one soldier wrote.

hot shot: Solid artillery shot that was heated to set fire to buildings or ships.

howitzer: An artillery piece that fires a projectile in a low arc toward its target (compare with **cannon** and **mortar**).

identification disks: Such devices were not issued to troops, but many individuals carried handmade metal or wood disks, or even scraps of paper, that could be used to identify them should they die in battle. Some were stamped with slogans like "Against Slavery" or "War of 1861." The widespread carnage of the Civil War, in which an entire company might be wiped out in one battle, made such identification a new necessity of war.

Jefferson boots: A type of ankle-high boot or shoe.

kit, kit bag: Informal term for a soldier's knapsack and its contents.

knapsack: A leather or waterproof canvas backpack, sometimes mounted on a wooden frame, with a single pocket that was intended to carry a wool blanket, rubber blanket or tent half. Most soldiers discarded the previous contents to make room for extra food, clothing, ammunition and personal possessions, and for a variety of reasons many soldiers on both sides carried blanket rolls, or mule collars, rather than the knapsack itself. Most knapsacks were 14″ or 15″ wide, 15″ to 17 ″ high and 4″ or 5″ deep.

minié ball, minnie ball: A conical lead ball that was standard ammunition for Civil War-era rifles and took its name from French army officer Claude F. Minié, who invented it in 1848. The minié ball was designed to be rammed down the bore of a weapon quickly and easily (although this was not always the case). It would expand when fired, catching the rifling of the weapon and spinning out of the barrel with much greater velocity than a standard musket ball. A preponderance of wounds during the war, especially those that required amputation, were inflicted by minié balls.

mortar: An artillery piece that fired a projectile in a high, indirect arc toward its target, which was often unseen by the gunners. Such weapons were not nearly as accurate as other artillery pieces and were generally fired into large areas rather than at specific targets (compare with **cannon** and **howitzer**).

mule collar, horse collar: The rolled blanket or quilt worn diagonally over one shoulder by soldiers used to carry their belongings. Confederate troops often used this arrangement because of a lack of backpacks, while toward the end of the war many Union troops adopted it instead of their own heavy backpacks. Regulations called for it to be worn over the left shoulder, but photographs of the period indicate soldiers often wore it over the right shoulder as well.

Napoleon 12-pounder: The 1857 model Napoleon, a brass, smoothbore, muzzle-loading howitzer, was the basic artillery piece manufactured and used by both the Union and the Confederacy; its name derived from the fact that it was the gun France adopted in 1856 while under Napoleon III. An experienced crew could fire three rounds a minute with this gun, which was also referred to as "the gun howitzer" and "the light 12-pounder."

ostrich feathers, black: Often used by cavalrymen to adorn the left side of their hats—one feather for enlisted men, two for company-grade officers and three for field-grade officers.

Parrott gun, Parrott rifle: Introduced in 1862, this was America's first rifled cannon; its name derived from that of its inventor, Robert Parker Parrott, a West Point physics instructor who spent a decade developing the gun after learning that a German artillery firm had manufactured a similar weapon. This weapon played a significant role in the Union victory.

percussion caps: A small brass or copper cap filled with fulminate of mercury that fit over a nipple on the lock of a rifle or musket. When the hammer of a cocked weapon snapped down and hit the cap, it would explode, sending a spark into the breach of the weapon, igniting the powder and discharging the ball.

pistol: Either a single-shot handgun or a revolver. Single-shot pistols were used mostly by the navy and Revenue Cutter Service or as civilian weapons. They could be either muzzle-loaded with powder and ball, like a musket (as with most regulation weapons), or, more rarely, breach-loaded with a metallic cartridge (as with several civilian models). Revolvers included a metal cylinder that had five or six chambers into which could be loaded either black powder and lead balls or paper cartridges containing powder and a lead bullet. Percussion caps placed on hollow nipples at the rear of each chamber would discharge the ammunition. A revolver's metal cylinder would rotate when the weapon was cocked. Such weapons had greater rates of fire than single-shot weapons (but also took five or six times longer to reload).

pup tent: A slang term used from about 1863 to refer to the army's two-man tents. See **shelter tent**.

rifling: Spiral grooves cut into the inside of a weapon barrel that cause the ammunition being fired to spin, imparting upon it greater velocity and more stability in flight. Smoothbore muskets were inaccurate at ranges over 100 yards, whereas rifled weapons could be lethal at 250 yards or more.

round shot: The round iron balls that made up the majority of ammunition fired from artillery pieces. The weight of each piece of ammunition was identified by the sort of gun it was fired from; e.g., a twelve-pound Napoleon fired twelve-pound iron round shot.

shelter tent: From about 1863, this term referred to a small, two-man tent that hung from a ridge rope supported by two poles.

slouch hat: A British style of soft, brimmed hat introduced to Americans in the 1830s and worn widely by soldiers of both sides, especially Southerners, during the Civil War.

Stars and Stripes: The primary nickname for the United States flag.

sword bayonet: A bayonet, usually with a single-edged blade, long enough to be either mounted on a rifle or used as a short sword. Such weapons were typically 18″ to 24″ in length.

Wellingtons: Ankle-high boots without laces in the front.

APPENDIX ONE

CIVIL WAR TIME LINE

Major events of the Civil War and the period preceding and following it are listed on the following time line.

While the Civil War was the result of decades of increasing tensions, the time line begins in 1859 with John Brown's raid on Harpers Ferry, Virginia—a relevant, if arbitrarily chosen, event. The time line continues through 1877 and the end of Reconstruction. As with the years leading up to the Civil War, the legacy of the war continued long past Reconstruction, but its end represents the reunification of the country.

The 1861 dates that the various Southern states seceded from the Union are listed. Note that seceding from the Union and joining the Confederacy were not, technically, synonymous acts. However, all states that seceded did join the Confederacy shortly thereafter.

Battles were sometimes known by different names in the North and South (e.g., Northerners referred to the Battle of Antietam, while Southerners knew it as the Battle of Sharpsburg). Thus, in many cases the Southern name for the battle is given in brackets. One reason for the differences in names is that Union generals tended to name battles for nearby streams, while Confederate leaders generally named them for towns.

Initially, the Confederacy bested the Union on the battlefield. These early victories ultimately prolonged the war; had the Federal government been able to deliver enough crushing defeats to the rebellion early on, the war might have ended in its first year. Three battles, Antietam in September 1862 and Gettysburg and Vicksburg in July 1863, heralded the shifting of the war in favor of the Union and represented major setbacks for the Confederacy. In the casualty listings for major battles, numbers are given for troops missing; soldiers might be so classified because of desertion, capture or death from which their bodies were not recovered (e.g., from drowning, crawling into a ravine to die, etc.).

Events for which a specific date is not important (e.g., the invention of some item or creation of a work of art) are listed under the year they occurred.

Technically, the rank of general refers to a full, or "four star," general. In the following listings, this title is used broadly to refer to a general of any level, whether it be brigadier general (one star), major general (two star), lieutenant general (three star) or full general.

To help make it easier to follow the major events of the time line, many are labeled with symbols. This key is for ease of reference and is not intended to make value judgments (i.e., by labeling an event military rather than political).

E = military events in the eastern theater

W = military events in the western theater (i.e., the Mississippi River valley)

P = political, rather than military, events (such as secessions)

C = civil unrest

1859

Alexandre Edmond Becquerel invents the fluorescent lightbulb (which is not perfected for another eighty years). The Great Atlantic and Pacific Tea Company (A&P) is founded. A "bellows-and-box" hand-powered vacuum cleaner is patented. Edwin Drake discovers and begins drilling for oil in Titusville, Pennsylvania. The first paper clothing patterns are sold under the name "Mme. Domoreset's Mirror of Fashions." Darwin's *Origin of Species* is published.

(C) Oct. 16, 1859: Fanatical abolitionist John Brown leads a force of twenty-one armed men into Harpers Ferry, Virginia (now West Virginia), seizing the town and the Federal arsenal. A unit of marines commanded by Col. Robert E. Lee arrives the next day and battles Brown's followers, killing ten of them; Brown himself was wounded. Charged with treason, Brown aroused sympathy amongst Northerners, many of whom considered him a martyr, and outrage amongst Southern whites, who considered him a dangerous fanatic.

(P) Dec. 2, 1859: John Brown is hanged. His death eventually comes to symbolize the coming violence of the Civil War.

1860

Louis Pasteur demonstrates the process of killing germs with heat (i.e., pasteurization). Hamilton Smith patents an early washing machine (by 1873, more than two thousand additional patents for washing machines were issued). English inventor and industrialist Sir Henry Bessemer patents the tilting converter for steel manufacture.

(P) November 6, 1860: Abraham Lincoln is elected president of the United States.

(P) Dec. 20, 1860: South Carolina's legislature, perceiving a threat to the state's autonomy from the presidential election of Abraham Lincoln, a known opponent of slavery, votes to secede from the United States of America. It is the first Southern state to secede.

1861

Kansas admitted to the Union as the thirty-fourth state. Van Camp introduces canned pork and beans. Julius Sturgis begins commercially baking pretzels in Lititz, Pennsylvania. Linus Yale patents the pin-tumbler lock. An early form of the bicycle dubbed a "bone shaker" is developed.

(P) January-February 1861: Six more Southern states (Mississippi, Florida, Alabama, Georgia, Louisiana and Texas), driven by a perception of Abraham Lincoln as an especially strong opponent of slavery, declare their secession from the Union and form the Confederate States of America.

(P) Jan. 9, 1861: Mississippi secedes from the Union, the second state to do so.

(P) Jan. 10, 1861: Florida secedes from the Union.

(P) Jan. 11, 1861: Alabama secedes from the Union.

(P) Jan. 19, 1861: Georgia secedes from the Union.

(P) Jan. 26, 1861: Louisiana secedes from the Union.

(P) Feb. 4, 1861: Delegates from the six seceding Southern states convene in Montgomery, Alabama. They begin to draft a constitution for the Confederate States of America, similar to the U.S. Constitution but with greater emphasis on the autonomy of each state and protection of the institution of slavery.

(P) Feb. 8, 1861: The seceding Southern states form the Confederate States of America.

(P) Feb. 9, 1861: Pending elections, the delegates select Jefferson Davis as provisional president of the Confederacy.

(P) Feb. 18, 1861: Jefferson Davis is inaugurated president of the Confederate States of America.

(P) Feb. 23, 1861: Texas secedes from the Union.

February 1861: U.S. President James Buchanan (Lincoln's predecessor) refuses to surrender Federal forts in the South to the seceding states. Confederate troops respond by seizing them. At Fort Sumter, South Carolina, Southern troops repulse a supply ship trying to reach Union forces stationed in the fort.

(P) March 4, 1861: Lincoln is inaugurated president of the United States of America. At the ceremony, the new president says he has no plans to end slavery in states where it already exists. He also declares that secession is unacceptable and expresses hope that the national crisis can be resolved without warfare.

March 6, 1861: Jefferson Davis, with the authorization of the C.S. Congress, calls for 100,000 one-year volunteers for the Confederate military.

(P) March 1861: About equally divided between secessionists and Unionists, an Arkansas state convention votes against secession.

(E) April 1861: President Lincoln informs South Carolina that he is planning to send supplies to Fort Sumter. Although the president's goal is to avoid conflict, South Carolina fears trickery and demands the immediate surrender of the fort. Maj. Robert Anderson offers to surrender once his supplies are exhausted, but this offer is rejected.

(E) April 12-13, 1861: Confederate artillery batteries under Gen. P.G.T. Beauregard fire on Union-held Fort Sumter in the harbor of Charleston, South Carolina. After a heavy bombardment, Fort Sumter surrenders to South Carolina. Armed rebellion has begun.

April 15, 1861: Abraham Lincoln calls for 75,000 volunteers for the Federal forces.

(P) April-June 1861: Encouraged by the attack on Fort Sumter, four more states—Virginia, Arkansas, Tennessee and North Carolina—join the Confederacy.

(P) April 17, 1861: Virginia secedes from the Union and joins the Confederacy. Soon after, in May, the capital of the Confederacy is moved from Montgomery, Alabama, to Richmond, Virginia.

(C) April 19, 1861: A mob of Southern sympathizers attacks the Sixth Massachusetts Regiment as it marches through the streets of Baltimore, Maryland, on its way to Washington, DC. Four soldiers and 20 rioters are killed.

(P) May 6, 1861: Reversing a vote of just two months earlier, an Arkansas state convention votes to secede from the Union and join the Confederate States of America. Also, the Confederacy recognizes a state of war with the United States.

(P) May 20, 1861: North Carolina opts to secede and join the Confederacy.

(E) May 1861: Forces under Union Gen. George B. McClellan drive the rebels out of western Virginia as far as the Alleghenies, bringing this antisecessionist portion of the state under U.S. control. For his success, McClellan earns the nickname "Young Napoleon."

(P) June 8, 1861: Tennessee votes to secede from the Union, the last Southern state to do so. The state is torn between almost unanimous support for the Union in its eastern third and equally strong support of the Confederacy in the middle and west.

(P) June 1861: Although they are slave states and have divided loyalties, Delaware, Kentucky, Maryland and Missouri remain within the Union, largely through a combination of military pressure from the Federal government and political maneuvering by Lincoln and other politicians.

(E) July 21, 1861: First Battle of Bull Run (First Manassas). Bowing to public demand, Union General-in-Chief Winfield Scott orders Gen. Irvin McDowell to advance on Confederate troops stationed at Manassas Junction, Virginia, even though the Union troops are inadequately trained and untried. McDowell's attack is initially successful, but the arrival of Confederate reinforcements results in a Southern victory and the rout of the Federal forces back to Washington. Fearing a protracted war and mindful of the army's need for training and organization, Lincoln replaces McDowell with McClellan, the "Young Napoleon."

(P) July 1861: Union naval blockade of Southern ports begins to take effect, largely because of improvements in the Federal navy. The Confederacy responds by building small, fast ships that can outmaneuver the heavier Union vessels.

(E) November 7, 1861: A naval bombardment by warships under Union Capt.

Samuel F. Dupont drives the defenders from Confederate forts Walker and Beauregard, South Carolina. This allows soldiers under Union Gen. Thomas W. Sherman to occupy Port Royal, Beaufort and all the Sea Islands of South Carolina.

(P) November 8, 1861: **The Trent Affair**. USS *San Jacinto*, under Capt. Charles Wilkes, stops the British ship *Trent* in international waters and seizes Confederate Commissioner to England J.M. Mason and Confederate Commissioner to France John Slidell (because the Confederacy was not recognized as a sovereign state, it had to send commissioners, rather than ambassadors, to appeal for aid and recognition). The two are transported to Boston, where they are imprisoned. Britain reacts strongly, and President Lincoln and Secretary of State Seward disavow the action and release the two commissioners.

1862

Ebenezer Butterick creates the pattern for the Garibaldi blouse.

(E) January 27, 1862: Lincoln issues General War Order No. 1, authorizing Union forces to launch a unified assault against the Confederacy. Union Gen. McClellan, overall commander of the Federal armies, ignores this order.

(W) February 16, 1862: Confederate Gen. Simon Bolivar Buckner surrenders Fort Donelson, Tennessee, to Union Gen. Ulysses S. Grant. This was the Union's first major victory of the war, and it destroyed the Rebel base of power in Tennessee and Kentucky.

(P) February 25, 1862: For the first time, the U.S. Congress authorizes the issue of legal tender banknotes. Union forces occupy Nashville, Tennessee.

(E) March 1862: Confederate Gen. Thomas J. "Stonewall" Jackson, commanding troops in the Shenandoah Valley, attacks Union forces and causes them to retreat across the Potomac. This results in Union troops being rushed to protect Washington, DC, from possible Confederate attack.

(W) March 7-8, 1862: Battle of Pea Ridge (Elkhorn Tavern). Union forces defeat Confederate troops in an especially bloody battle at Pea Ridge, Arkansas. Over a two-day period, Confederate Gen. Earl Van Dorn sends his 16,000-man force, which includes some Texas cavalrymen and two regiments of Cherokee Indians, against a dug-in force of 10,250 Union soldiers under Gen. Samuel R. Curtis. Union casualties include 203 killed, 980 wounded and 201 missing, while Confederate casualties include about 1,000 killed or wounded and 300 captured.

(E) March 9, 1862: CSS *Virginia,* an ironclad warship, attacks and destroys two wooden Union warships off of Norfolk, Virginia. Steaming down the coast from New York, USS *Monitor* arrives on the scene before the Confederate ship can wreak any more havoc. The two ironclad warships engage in a five-hour battle in Hampton Roads, Virginia, the first such battle between armored vessels. The Confederate vessel had originally been the scuttled Union frigate USS *Merrimac,* which the Confederacy retrieved, renovated, and outfitted with iron plate and a ram.

(W) April 6-7, 1862: Battle of Shiloh. In the first great bloodbath of the war, some forty thousand Confederate troops under Gen. Albert Sydney Johnston launch an attack against Federal forces under Gen. Ulysses S. Grant at Shiloh, Tennessee. Nearly defeated, the Union forces receive reinforcements during the night, bringing their total strength up to about sixty-three thousand; by morning, Grant regains control of the battlefield. Nonetheless, the Union troops are too exhausted to pursue the retreating rebels. Casualties of the battle include 1,754 killed, 8,408 wounded and 2,885 missing Union soldiers, and 1,723 killed, 8,012 wounded and 959 missing Confederate soldiers.

(E) April 10-11, 1862: Union Gen. Quincy A. Gillmore batters into submission Fort Pulaski, which guarded entry to the Savannah River. This action highlights the vulnerability of even such an imposing masonry fortification when faced with modern rifled artillery.

(W) April 25, 1862: Flag Officer David Farragut leads an assault up the Mississippi River and captures New Orleans.

(E-P) April 1862: Union troops of General McClellan's Army of the Potomac leave northern Virginia and begin to march toward Richmond, initiating the Peninsular Campaign.

(E) May 4, 1862: Union troops under McClellan occupy Yorktown, Virginia.

(E) May-August 1862: The Peninsular Campaign. McClellan's army manages to advance as far as Fair Oaks, a mere five miles from Richmond. At this point, however, his advance is checked by Robert E. Lee, and he orders a retreat to Harrison's Landing on the James River.

(E) May 25, 1862: Battle of Winchester (Virginia). Gen. Stonewall Jackson's sixteen thousand Confederate troops defeat the eight thousand men under Union Maj. Gen. Nathaniel Prentiss Banks, forcing the Federal troops to withdraw toward Harpers Ferry, Virginia.

(E) May 31-June 1, 1862: Battle of Fair Oaks (Seven Pines). Confederate troops attack Union forces at Seven Pines, Virginia, and nearly defeat them.

However, Union reinforcements arrive at the last minute and prevent the victory from being complete. Gen. Joseph E. Johnston, commander of the Confederate army, is severely wounded, and leadership of the Army of Northern Virginia passes to Gen. Robert E. Lee.

(E) June 25-July 1, 1862: Seven Days' Battles. Over a period of a week, Union and Confederate forces fight a series of especially savage battles (June 26-27, Mechanicsville; June 27, Gaines's Mill; June 29, SavageStation; June 30, Frayser's Farm; and July 1, Malvern Hill). The Confederates withdraw to Richmond on July 2, ending the Peninsular Campaign. During the course of the battles casualties include 1,734 dead, 8,062 wounded and 6,075 missing Union soldiers, and 3,478 dead, 16,261 wounded, and 875 missing Confederate soldiers. With more than 36,000 casualties, the Seven Days are second only to Gettysburg in terms of total bloodshed.

(E) July 11, 1862: Annoyed by McClellan's failure in Virginia and his plodding pace, Lincoln issues an order relieving him as general-in-chief of the Union armies, naming Maj. Gen. Henry Halleck general-in-chief of the Union army and Gen. John Pope commander of all the armies north and west of Virginia. McClellan is given command of a single army, the Army of the Potomac, under Pope.

(E) July-August 1862: Pope's Campaign.

(E) August 28-30, 1862: Second Battle of Bull Run (Second Manassas). Confederate forces under Generals James Longstreet and Stonewall Jackson decisively defeat Union troops under Gen. John Pope near Manassas, Virginia. Union Gen. Fitz-John Porter, who allegedly failed to send his troops into the battle quickly enough, was held responsible for the defeat and was forced out of the army by the beginning of the next year. More than twenty-six thousand soldiers are among the casualties of the battle (1,724 killed, 8,372 wounded and 5,958 missing Union soldiers, and 1,481 killed, 7,627 wounded and 89 missing Confederate soldiers). Following this defeat, Lincoln replaces Pope with McClellan.

(E) September 1862: Union General McClellan defeats Confederate General Lee at the battles of South Mountain and Crampton's Gap.

(E) September 15, 1862: Confederate Gen. Stonewall Jackson captures Harpers Ferry, Virginia, along with thousands of Union prisoners and a great quantity of supplies. Despite his proximity to Harpers Ferry, plodding General McClellan does not move quickly enough to prevent its capture.

(E) September 17, 1862: Battle of Antietam (Sharpsburg). McClellan intercepts a Confederate force on the banks of Antietam Creek, near Sharpsburg, Maryland, leading to the single bloodiest day of the entire war. Casualties include 9,549 Union soldiers wounded and 2,108 killed, and 9,029 Confederate soldiers wounded and 2,700 killed (more soldiers are slain in a handful of other battles, but never so many in a single day).

Tactically, the battle is a draw, but strategically it is a decided loss for the Confederacy. Lee is forced to retreat back to Virginia and McClellan claims a victory. In light of the Confederate defeat, Britain and France, both of which had been contemplating official recognition of the Confederacy, decide against it.

(P) September 22, 1862. Lincoln announces in his Preliminary Emancipation Proclamation that all slaves in rebelling areas will be free as of January 1, 1863. However, slaves in Union and "neutral" states are not covered by this proclamation.

October 8, 1862: Battle of Perryville. Kentucky's only major battle of the war is fought because of a chance encounter between Union foragers and Confederate troops. Union Gen. Don Carlos Buell's army defeats Confederate Gen. Braxton Bragg's force, despite being deployed piecemeal. Casualties include four thousand Union soldiers killed, wounded or missing (about one-tenth their force), vs. about sixteen thousand Confederate casualties (nearly a quarter of their force). In the aftermath of the battle, Lincoln relieves Buell of command for failing to destroy the Confederate army.

(E) November 7, 1862: Annoyed by the escape of the Confederate forces from Antietam, continuous raiding by Rebel cavalry and inactivity of McClellan's armies for more than a month, Lincoln relieves "the Young Napoleon" of all command for the last time and replaces him with Maj. Gen. Ambrose E. Burnside.

(E) December 13, 1862: Battle of Fredericksburg. Burnside's forces are defeated in a series of attacks against entrenched Confederate forces at Fredericksburg, Virginia. As a result, Burnside is replaced with Gen. Joseph Hooker. Among the casualties are 1,284 killed, 9,600 wounded and 1,769 missing Union soldiers, and 595 killed, 4,061 wounded and 653 missing Confederate soldiers.

(W) December 31, 1862 to January 2, 1863: Battle of Stone's River (Murfreesboro). This sporadic, bloody and pointless battle was fought between Union and Confederate forces struggling for control of Tennessee, resulting in 12,906 Union soldiers killed, wounded or missing, and 11,795 Confederate killed, wounded or missing. After three days of fighting, Confederate Gen.

Braxton Bragg inexplicably withdraws from the field, leaving Murfreesboro in control of Union forces under Gen. William S. Rosecrans.

1863

West Virginia admitted to the Union as the thirty-fifth state. Ebenezer and Eleanor Butterick sell their dress patterns throughout the world. James Plimpton invents steerable roller skates.

(P) January 1, 1863: Lincoln issues the Emancipation Proclamation declaring free all slaves in areas under Confederate control. This act comes amid growing public sentiment in favor of abolition, favored by radical Republicans but resisted by Lincoln, who wishes to placate slave-holding border states and keep them loyal to the Union.

This proclamation follows a series of measures that had been moving in the direction of abolition. Some Union generals had decreed that in areas under their control, slaves belonging to men bearing arms against the Union were to be considered free. Congress had also taken steps toward abolition—in 1861 passing an act stating all slaves being used against the Union were to be considered free, and in 1862 passing an act stating that slaves owned by men supporting the Confederacy were to be considered free.

(P) March 1863: The Federal government responds to recruiting difficulties by passing the First Conscription Act. This makes all men between twenty and forty-five liable for military service, but service can be avoided by providing a substitute or by paying a fine. Because of this, the act is seen as unfair to the poor, and leads to riots in some cities. Facing similar recruitment problems, the Confederacy also passes a conscription act, which provokes similar reactions.

(E) April 27, 1863. Union Gen. John Hooker crosses the Rappahannock River in Virginia, intending to attack General Lee's army.

(E) May 1-4, 1863: Battle of Chancellorsville. Lee responds to Hooker's foray across the Rappahannock by splitting his forces and attacking the Union army in three places. He defeats it nearly completely and forces Hooker to withdraw back across the river. Although a clear Southern victory, it is the Confederacy's most costly in terms of casualties, with 9,081 wounded, 1,665 killed and 2,018 missing; among the dead is invaluable Gen. Thomas J. "Stonewall" Jackson. Union casualties are 1,575 dead, 9,594 wounded and 5,676 missing.

(W) May 1863: Vicksburg Campaign. Union Gen. Ulysses S. Grant wins a number of victories near Vicksburg, Mississippi, a fortified city deemed essential to Union plans to regain complete control of the Mississippi River.

(W) May 22, 1863: Union General Grant assaults Vicksburg, Mississippi.

(P) June 20, 1863: The western sections of Virginia are admitted to the Union as the new state of West Virginia. A preponderance of citizens in this area have been opposed to secession since the beginning of the war.

(E) June-July 1863: Gettysburg Campaign.

(E) June 13, 1863: Confederate General Lee defeats Union forces at Winchester, Virginia, and continues north toward Pennsylvania. Union General Hooker is forced to alter his plans to attack Richmond and must instead pursue Lee.

(E) June 28, 1863: Hooker resigns as commander of the Army of the Potomac, and Halleck replaces him with Gen. George G. Meade.

(E) July 1-3, 1863: Battle of Gettysburg. Union and Confederate forces clash near the town of Gettysburg, Pennsylvania. Northern troops under Meade outnumber the Southerners and are eventually able to occupy superior defensive positions. The Federal army is victorious but fails to pursue Lee during his retreat to Virginia. More soldiers die than in any other battle of the war—3,155 from Northern units and 3,903 from Southern units (more died in a single day of fighting at Antietam, but the most died during the entire three days of Gettysburg). Other casualties include 14,529 wounded and 5,365 missing Union soldiers, and 18,735 wounded and 5,425 missing Confederate soldiers.

After its defeat at Gettysburg, the Confederacy has its hopes of formal recognition by foreign governments forever dashed.

(W) July 4, 1863: Siege of Vicksburg Ends. Succumbing to Grant's siege after six weeks, Confederate Gen. John Pemberton surrenders Vicksburg and thirty thousand troops. Soon thereafter, Union troops capture Port Hudson, Louisiana, bringing the entire Mississippi River under Union control and splitting the Confederacy in half.

(C) July 13-16, 1863: Draft Riots. Sparked by Irish workers angry at being conscripted and unable to afford to pay substitutes, and encouraged by Southern sympathizers, the worst draft riots of the war erupt in working-class sections of New York City. During three days of violence, rioters loot ships, burn buildings (including an orphanage for black children) and attack and kill blacks in the streets. Federal troops have to be called in from the battlefield at Gettysburg to restore order. Antidraft violence on a smaller scale also erupts in other Northern cities, including Boston.

(E) August-November 1863: After Gettysburg, Union General Meade engages in a series of cautious and inconclusive military operations.

(W) September 19-20, 1863: Battle of Chickamauga. Union and Confederate forces meet near Chickamauga Creek on the Tennessee-Georgia border. Confederate troops led by Gen. Braxton Bragg come close to completely destroying the Union army under Gen. William Rosecrans, forcing it to retreat to Chattanooga. Casualties include 1,657 dead, 9,756 wounded and 4,757 missing Union soldiers and 2,312 dead, 14,674 wounded and 1,468 missing Confederate soldiers (34,624 total).

(W) September-November 1863: Chattanooga. After nearly crushing the Union army at Chickamauga (September 19-20, 1863), troops under Confederate General Bragg occupy the mountains surrounding Union-held Chattanooga, Tennessee, critical rail center.

(P) November 19, 1863: President Lincoln dedicates part of the battlefield at Gettysburg as a national cemetery and delivers his famous Gettysburg Address.

(W) November 23-25, 1863: Battle of Chattanooga. Union troops drive Confederate forces away from Chattanooga, setting the stage for Union General Sherman's Atlanta Campaign. Grant, called in to break the Confederate ring around Chattanooga, directs a series of brilliantly executed attacks that destroy the blockade.

(W) November 24: Battle of Lookout Mountain. In this sideline to the Battle of Chattanooga, troops under Union General "Fighting Joe" Hooker storm Confederate positions on Lookout Mountain.

(W) November-December 1863: Siege of Knoxville. Taking advantage of the compromised position of the Federal forces following Chickamauga, Confederate General Bragg sends a force under Lieutenant General Longstreet to drive Burnside's army out of eastern Tennessee. Burnside holes up in Knoxville, which he successfully defends.

(W) December 3, 1863: Unable to penetrate the Union defenses of Knoxville, Longstreet ends his siege and withdraws.

1864

Louis Pasteur develops his germ theory that correctly states bacteria can cause disease.

(E) May-June 1864: Grant's Wilderness Campaign. Now commander of the

Union armies, General Grant plans to fight Lee's forces in Virginia until they are destroyed.

(E) May 5-6, 1864: Battle of the Wilderness. The Union and Confederate armies battle inconclusively for two days. Grant's forces suffer 17,666 casualties. Lee's casualties, while uncertain, were less than this; unlike Grant, however, Lee receives no replacements for his losses.

(E) May 8-12, 1864: Battle of Spotsylvania. Grant's forces continue to attack Lee's, fighting for five days at Spotsylvania Court House, Virginia. Grant vows to fight all summer if necessary. Nearly eleven thousand Union casualties and an uncertain but similar number of Confederate casualties are the price of the battle.

(E) May 12-16, 1864: Battle of Drewry's Bluff. Grant's troops continue to battle Lee's. Casualties include 4,160 Union soldiers who are killed, wounded or missing, along with an unknown number of Confederate soldiers.

(E) June 1-3, 1864: Battle of Cold Harbor. Grant attacks Confederate positions at Cold Harbor, and his forces are savagely repelled. More than seven thousand men on both sides are killed in the worst twenty minutes of the holocaust; total Union casualties are twelve thousand. Although the last clear victory for Lee during the war, his army never recovers from the unrelenting attacks of Grant's troops.

(E) June 15-30, 1864 to April 2, 1865: Siege of Petersburg. Grant hopes to quickly capture Petersburg, Virginia, a vital rail center south of Richmond, then advance on the Confederate capital from the south. This attempt fails, costing him 16,569 casualties, and bogs down into a ten-month siege in which thousands more soldiers on each side are killed and wounded.

(E) June 27, 1864: Battle of Kennesaw Mountain (Georgia). After several days of maneuvering and skirmishing in the rain, Union troops under Maj. Gen. William T. Sherman make three uphill assaults against well-entrenched Confederate forces under Gen. Joseph E. Johnston. The Union forces are driven back each time with heavy losses, resulting in embarrassment for Sherman and a victory for Johnston.

(E) July 1864: Confederate Gen. Jubal Early leads his troops into Maryland in a raid-in-force in an attempt to relieve pressure on General Lee's army. Early gets within five miles of Washington, DC, causing some fear and consternation.

(E) July 13, 1864: Union forces drive Confederate Gen. Jubal Early's forces back into Virginia.

(W) August 1864: Atlanta Campaign. Union Maj. Gen. William Tecumseh Sherman leaves Chattanooga, Tennessee, and soon encounters Confederate Gen. Joseph Johnston, who skillfully holds off the Union force, almost twice the size of his own. Nonetheless, Johnston's superiors decide to replace him with Gen. John Bell Hood, who is soon defeated.

(W) September 1, 1864: Sherman forces Hood to relinquish Atlanta, Georgia, and occupies it the next day. The capture of this vital city greatly boosts morale in the North.

(W) September-November 1864: Sherman's troops occupy Atlanta for two and a half months, resting and accumulating supplies.

(W) November 15, 1864: Before Sherman departs the city, he orders his troops to demolish military facilities and set fire to the rest of the city. Much of the city is destroyed in the conflagration.

(W-E) November 15-December 13, 1864: Sherman's March to the Sea. Sherman continues his march through Georgia and to the sea, cutting himself off from his lines of supply and forcing his men to live off what they can forage or pillage. Sherman's force cuts a path sixty miles wide and three hundred miles long during their march through Georgia, destroying bridges, factories, railroads and public buildings as they went.

(P) November 1864: Abraham Lincoln Reelected. The Republican party nominates incumbent President Abraham Lincoln as its candidate for president and Andrew Johnson for vice president. The Democratic party chooses Gen. George B. McClellan for president and George Pendleton for vice president. Widespread war-weariness among Northerners makes victory for Lincoln seem doubtful at times, and Lincoln's veto of the Wade-Davis Bill (which called for the majority of each Confederate state's electorate to swear past and future loyalty to the Union before the state could be officially restored) loses him the support of radical Republicans who think he is too lenient. However, Sherman's victories in Georgia boost Lincoln's popularity and help him win the election by a broad margin.

(E) December 13, 1864: Sherman storms Fort McAllister, Georgia, and orders the fortifications dismantled before continuing northward.

(W) December 15-16, 1864: Confederate Gen. John B. Hood, true to his policy of taking the offensive whenever possible, attacks the Union defenses at Nashville, Tennessee. Union Gen. George H. Thomas repulses the attack completely, winning the war's most complete victory.

(E) December 21, 1864: Sherman captures Savannah, Georgia.

1865

Civil War ends. Reconstruction begins in the Southern states. Nevada admitted to the Union as the thirty-sixth state. Results of Mendel's first genetic experiments are published. Lewis Carroll's *Alice in Wonderland* is published. Louis Pasteur publishes his germ theory. Joseph Lister revolutionizes antiseptic surgery with the introduction of carbolic dressing. Celluloid is developed. *The Nation* is published for the first time. Mark Twain's "The Celebrated Jumping Frog of Calaveras County" is published.

(E) January 1865: Union Rear Adm. David D. Porter's squadron of warships subjects Fort Fisher, North Carolina, to a massive artillery bombardment.

(E) January 15, 1865: Soldiers, sailors and marines storm weakened Fort Fisher and capture it. With the loss of this strategic bastion, Wilmington, North Carolina, critical to Southern attempts to circumvent the Union blockade, is cut off.

January 1865: The South suffers acute shortages of food and supplies, caused by disruption of rail traffic and supply lines and the tightened Union blockade. Starving soldiers begin to desert the Confederate army in large numbers. In a desperate move, Confederate President Jefferson Davis approves arming slaves to reinforce the collapsing army, but this measure is never actually carried out.

(E) February 1865: Sherman's army marches north through Georgia, into South Carolina and then North Carolina, destroying almost everything in its path.

(P) February 1865: Confederate President Jefferson Davis agrees to send delegates to a peace conference with President Lincoln and Secretary of State William Seward, but insists upon recognition of the South's independence. Lincoln refuses and the conference does not occur.

(E) March 25, 1865: General Lee attacks General Grant's forces at Fort Stedman, near Petersburg, Virginia, but is defeated.

(E) April 1, 1865: Union Gen. Philip Sheridan defeats Confederate Gen. George Pickett at Five Forks, necessitating the evacuation of Richmond.

(E) April 2: Lee evacuates Richmond, abandoning the Confederate capital to the Union army, and then heads west to join forces with remnants of the Army of Tennessee.

(E) April 3, 1865: A smoldering Richmond, set on fire the previous evening by retreating Confederate troops, is captured by Union forces.

(E) April 7, 1865: Grant sends a message to Lee, calling upon him to surrender and end the war.

(E) April 9, 1865: Surrender at Appomattox Courthouse. Grant and Lee meet at Appomattox Courthouse, Virginia, and agree upon terms of surrender. Lee's command at this point consists of a mere 26,765 men who are sent home on parole after agreeing not to take up arms against the Union. Enlisted cavalry and artillery men are permitted to keep their horses, and officers their swords and pistols. All other equipment is surrendered to the Union army.

April-May, 1865: The last remnants of the Confederate army surrender or are defeated.

(P) April 14, 1865: Pro-Confederate actor John Wilkes Booth, obsessed with avenging the defeat of the Confederacy, shoots President Lincoln at Ford's Theatre in Washington, DC, during a performance of "Our American Cousin," and then flees through Maryland to Virginia.

(P) April 15, 1865: Lincoln dies from his wounds.

(P) April 25, 1865: Trapped in a burning barn in Virginia, Booth is fatally shot by a Union soldier. Nine other people are determined to have been involved in the assassination, and of these four are hanged, four are imprisoned and one is acquitted.

(E) April 26, 1865: Confederate Gen. Joseph Johnston surrenders to Union General Sherman at the Bennett House near Durham Station, North Carolina, bringing the war to an end.

(P) May 2, 1865: U.S. President Johnson offers a $100,000 reward for the capture of Jefferson Davis.

(P) May 10, 1865: Jefferson Davis is captured in southern Georgia.

May 12-13: Battle of Palmito Ranch. This battle between 80 Union soldiers and 350 Confederate cavalrymen is a victory for the former and the last battle of any size fought during the war.

May 19, 1865: Johnson declares that armed insurrection against the Federal government has come to an end.

(E) May 23-24, 1865: Grand Review. A total of 150,000 men from the armies of Union generals Meade (Army of the Potomac) and Sherman (Army of Georgia) march through Washington, DC, to the wild cheers of thousands of spectators.

June 1865: Congress declares that pay, arms, equipment and medical services for black troops should be equal to that of whites.

(P) August 23-October 24, 1865: A Union military commission led by Gen. Lew Wallace (future author of *Ben Hur*) tries Confederate Capt. Henry Wirz, commandant of the notorious Confederate prison at Andersonville, Georgia. The commission finds Wirz guilty of war crimes and sentences him to death.

(P) September 1865: Congressman Thaddeus Stephens urges that estates belonging to former Confederate leaders be confiscated and divided up into forty-acre parcels for freed blacks.

November 10, 1865: Wirz is hanged in the yard of the Old Capitol Prison, the only person to be tried and executed for war crimes in the wake of the Civil War.

December 24, 1865: Six former Confederate officers meet in Pulaski, Tennessee, and form a secret society that eventually becomes the Ku Klux Klan.

1866

Laying of transatlantic cable, started in 1858, is completed. A key-opened can is patented. The first-known milk bottle is produced. Machine-made sewing needles are produced.

1867

Nebraska is admitted to the Union as the thirty-seventh state. Arkansas is placed under Federal military rule. United States purchases Alaska from Russia. Nobel invents dynamite. Dostoyevsky's *Crime and Punishment* is published. Great Britain grants dominion status to Canada. Joseph Lister performs the first antiseptic operation through the use of carbolic acid. Part one of Karl Marx's three-volume *Das Kapital* is published in German.

1868

Dr. Elizabeth Blackwell founds the Women's Medical College of New York Infirmary and runs it with an all-female staff. Commercially produced yeast cakes are sold for the first time. Edmund McIlhenny introduces Tabasco Sauce. A.J. Fellows patents a measuring tape enclosed within a circular case. Machines are developed to cut coal. Shoes made of rubber and canvas are introduced as "croquet sandals" for the affluent in New Haven, Connecticut (these are referred to as "sneakers" and "sneaks" by 1873). Carlos Glidden and Christopher Latham Sholes patent the typewriter. The Fourteenth Amendment, preventing states from infringing upon the Constitutional rights of citizens (i.e., freed blacks), is ratified. Reconstruction ends in Arkansas.

November 1868: Ulysses S. Grant, former general-in-chief of all the armies of the United States, is elected president of the United States.

1869

Suez Canal opens in Egypt. Susan B. Anthony and Elizabeth Cady Stanton organize the National Woman Suffrage Association. A gyrator clothes washer, consisting of a tub with rotating blades and a hand crank, is developed. Hippolyte Mege-Mouries patents margarine, made from skim milk and beef tallow. H.J. Heinz markets horseradish in glass jars. Russian Count Leo Tolstoy's *War and Peace*, begun in 1864, is completed.

May 10, 1869: First U.S. transcontinental railroad is completed with the meeting in Promontory, Utah of the Union Pacific Railroad line from the east and the Central Pacific line from the west.

1870

Franco-Prussian War begins with French declaration of war; the Germans employ strategies and tactics influenced by their observations of the U.S. Civil War. Robert Chesebrough patents Vaseline. Benjamin Babbitt introduces baking powder, sold under the brand name Star Yeast Powder. Margaret Knight invents the brown paper bag. The Fifteenth Amendment to the Constitution is ratified.

March 30, 1870: Texas is readmitted to the Union after ratifying the Thirteenth, Fourteenth, and Fifteenth Amendments to the Constitution.

October 12, 1870: Robert E. Lee, the general formerly in overall command of the Confederate armies, dies at his home in Lexington, Virginia.

1871

War ends between France and Prussia with defeat of the French. The Third Republic is established in France. Bismarck becomes the first chancellor of the German empire. Thomas Adams introduces the first chewing gum, unflavored and made from chicle, and called Adam's New York Gum—Snapping and Stretching. A.L. Jones patents corrugated paper.

1872

Elijah McCoy invents an automatic machine lubricator. Amanda Jones develops a vacuum pressure process for preserving food. Jane Wells invents the baby jumper. Montgomery Ward publishes its first mail-order catalog.

1873

Maxwell's *Electricity and Magnetism* is published. Joseph Glidden develops barbed wire. The Dover egg beater is patented.

1874

Benjamin Disraeli becomes prime minister of Great Britain (until 1880). Paul Verlaine's *Romances sans paroles* is published. Robert Green of Philadelphia introduces the ice-cream soda. The St. Louis Stamping Company introduces Graniteware, a lightweight cookware made from enameled steel.

1875

R.J. Reynolds Tobacco Company is founded and begins to produce chewing tobacco, including Brown's Mule, Golden Rain, Dixie's Delight, Yellow Rose and Purity brands.

1876

The United States celebrates its Centennial. Alexander Graham Bell patents the telephone. Mark Twain's *Tom Sawyer* is published. Heinz begins to sell ketchup. Melville Bissell invents the carpet sweeper. Most Sioux are expelled from the Black Hills of South Dakota by the end of the year.

June 25, 1876: Battle of Little Big Horn. Lt. Col. George Armstrong Custer (a former Union army general) is slain in the battle against Sioux forces at Little Bighorn, Montana, the last major Indian victory in the West. Other casualties of "Custer's Last Stand" include his entire command, a regiment of about 225 Seventh Cavalry soldiers.

1877

Reconstruction ends in the Southern states. Colorado is admitted to the Union as the Thirty-eighth state. Thomas Edison invents the phonograph. Great Britain's Queen Victoria becomes empress of India. Chester Greenwood invents earmuffs.

RECOMMENDED BOOKS/ BIBLIOGRAPHY

Material for this book was drawn from a great many sources, all of which are included here. To help readers identify those that would be most useful to them, they are divided into five sections. Subtitles have been provided when available to further help identify the most helpful resources. Books used in the compilation of this work have "*" preceding them.

PART ONE is a list of general sources for writers who will only read one or two other books on the Civil War and need books that are packed with a broad variety of information.

PART TWO is a list of recommended books more specialized than those on the first list, but which are excellent sources of information about specific aspects of life during the Civil War.

PART THREE is a list that includes books not as comprehensive or specialized as those on the first or second lists, but which could still be useful resources.

PART FOUR is a discussion and list of Civil War literature and novels. No recommendations are implied here, as a preference for one work of fiction over another is largely a matter of taste and opinion. Also, many of the titles, especially classics like *The Red Badge of Courage* and *The Killer Angels*, speak for themselves.

PART FIVE is a discussion of Civil War films, documentaries, and other programs.

A NOTE ON SOURCES

Secondary sources—nonfiction books written by scholars—comprise the majority of what most writers will use for background information about the Civil War. By and large, nothing is wrong with this, especially as there are so many excellent secondary sources available (e.g., most of the items on the following lists).

However, don't neglect the value of primary sources, which include regimental histories and the diaries and memoirs of combatants and civilians who witnessed the events of the war.

Several other sorts of primary sources are also available (e.g., ships' logs, which can serve as excellent sources of information). Such records typically provide straightforward, accurate accounts of day-to-day ships' activities, battles and incidents unlikely to be reported in other sources. In a story where a ship and its crew play a central or even an important role, a ship's log could be used for anything from planning a story line featuring a specific ship to a source of details about maritime life in general.

Primary sources are not necessarily difficult to work with or hard to find, either. Every year several Civil War diaries and regimental histories are printed or reprinted, and official documents, such as ships' logs, can often be obtained through the National Archives or historians' offices of the various branches of the armed forces.

PART ONE: GENERAL SOURCES

The Civil War Day by Day: An Almanac, 1861–1865. E. B. Long, Barbara Long, photographer. Da Capo Press, 1985.

The Civil War Dictionary. Mark Mayo Boatner, J. Laslocky, ed. Vintage Books, 1991.

* *The Civil War Society's Encyclopedia of the Civil War.* The Civil War Society. Portland House, 1997.

* *The Civil War: Strange and Fascinating Facts.* Burke Davis. The Fairfax Press, 1982.

The Coming Fury (The Centennial History of the Civil War, Volume 1). Bruce Catton. Doubleday and Company, 1961.

Days of Defiance: Sumter, Secession, and the Coming of the Civil War. Maury Klein. Alfred A. Knopf, 1997.

* *Don't Know Much About the Civil War.* Kenneth C. Davis. Bantam Books, 1998.

* *Never Call Retreat* (The Centennial History of the Civil War, Volume 3). Bruce Catton. Amereon, 1976.

* *A Short History of the Civil War: Ordeal by Fire*. Fletcher Pratt. Dover Publications, 1997.
* *Soldier Life in the Union and Confederate Armies*. Philip Van Doren Stern, ed. Indiana University Press, 1961.
* *Sword Over Richmond: An Eyewitness History of McClellan's Peninsula Campaign*. Richard Wheeler. Harper and Row, 1986.
* *Terrible Swift Sword* (The Centennial History of the Civil War, Volume 2). Bruce Catton. Doubleday and Company, 1963.

PART TWO: SPECIALIZED SOURCES

* *American Country Building Design: Rediscovered Plans for 19th Century Farmhouses, Cottages, Landscapes, Barns, Carriage Houses & Outbuildings*. Donald J. Berg. Sterling Publishing Company, 1997.

Arms and Equipment of the Confederacy (Echoes of Glory series, vol. 2). Time Life, 1992.

Arms and Equipment of the Union (Echoes of Glory series, vol. 1). Time Life, 1991.

Bloody Bill Anderson: The Short, Savage Life of a Civil War Guerrilla. Albert Castel and Thomas Goodrich. Stackpole Books, 1998.

The Capture of New Orleans, 1862. Chester G. Hearn. Louisiana State University Press, 1995.

* *City People: The Rise of Modern City Culture in Nineteenth-Century America*. Gunther Barth. Oxford University Press, 1980.

Civil War Battlefields and Landmarks: A Guide to the National Park Sites. Frank E. Vandiver, ed. Random House, 1996.

* *Civil War Medicine, 1861–1865*. C. Keith Wilbur. The Globe Pequot Press, 1998.

Civil War Poetry: An Anthology. Paul Negri, ed. Dover Publications, 1997.

* *Civil War Williamsburg*. Carson O. Hudson, Jr. Stackpole Books, 1997.

* *Confederate Infantryman, 1861–1865* (Warrior Series, No. 6). Ian Drury. Osprey Publishing, 1993.

* *Confederate Receipt Book: A Compilation of Over One Hundred Receipts, Adapted to the Times*. E. Merton Coulter, ed. University of Georgia Press, 1981.

* *Destroyer of the Iron Horse: General Joseph E. Johnston and Confederate Rail Transport, 1861–1865*. Jeffrey N. Lash. The Kent State University Press, 1991.

* *Don Troiani's Soldiers in America, 1754–1865*. Don Troiani, Earl J. Coates, James L. Kochan and Brian C. Pohanka. Stackpole Books, 1998.

* *Fort Macon: A History*. Paul Branch. Nautical and Aviation Publishing Company of America, 1999.

From Winchester to Cedar Creek: The Shenandoah Campaign of 1864. Jeffry D. Wert. Stackpole Books, 1997.

Glory at a Gallop: Tales of the Confederate Cavalry. William R. Brooksher and David K. Snider. Brassey's, 1995.

Glory Road (Army of the Potomac Trilogy, Volume 2). Bruce Catton. Anchor Books, 1952.

* *I Hear America Talking: An Illustrated History of American Words and Phrases.* Stuart Berg Flexner. Simon and Schuster, 1976.

Illustrated Atlas of the Civil War (Echoes of Glory series, vol. 3). Time Life, 1992.

* *Illustrated Catalog of Civil War Military Goods: Union Weapons, Insignia, Uniform Accessories and Other Equipment.* Schuyler, Hartley and Graham. Dover Publications, 1985.

* *Mr. Lincoln's Army* (Army of the Potomac Trilogy, Volume 1). Bruce Catton. Anchor, 1951.

The Official Military Atlas of the Civil War. George B. Davis, Leslie J. Perry, Joseph W. Kirkley and Calvin D. Cowles, ed. Government Printing Office, 1891; Gramercy Books, 1983.

* *Raiders and Blockaders: The American Civil War Afloat.* John M. Taylor, Norman C. Delaney and William N. Still, Jr. Brassey's, 1998.

* *Reliving the Civil War: A Reenactor's Handbook.* (2nd edition). R. Lee Hadden. Stackpole Books, 1999.

* *Resources of the Southern Fields and Forests.* Francis Peyre Porcher. Ayer Publishing Company, 1970.

Seasons of War: The Ordeal of a Confederate Community, 1861–1865. Daniel E. Sutherland. Free Press, 1995.

* *Seven Months in the Rebel States During the North American War, 1863.* Justus Scheibert. Confederate Publishing Company, 1958.

* *A Shield and Hiding Place: The Religious Life of the Civil War Armies.* Gardiner H. Shattuck, Jr. Mercer University Press, 1987.

* *Speaking Freely: A Guided Tour of American English From Plymouth Rock to Silicon Valley.* Stuart Berg Flexner and Anne H. Soukhanov. Oxford University Press, 1997.

* *A Stillness at Appomattox* (The Army of the Potomac Trilogy, Vol. 3). Bruce Catton. Doubleday, 1953.

* *The Story the Soldiers Wouldn't Tell: Sex in the Civil War.* Thomas P. Lowry. Stackpole Books, 1994.

* *Union Cavalryman, 1861–1865* (Warrior Series, No. 13). Philip Katcher. Osprey Publishing, 1995.

* *The United States Revenue Cutters in the Civil War.* Florence Kern. U.S. Coast Guard Historian's Office, 1989.

When the Devil Came Down to Dixie: Ben Butler in New Orleans. Chester G. Hearn. Louisiana State University Press, 1997.

PART THREE: OTHER SOURCES

Battle Cry of Freedom: The Civil War Era (Oxford History of the United States). James M. McPherson. Oxford University Press, 1988.

A Blockaded Family: Life in Southern Alabama During the Civil War. Parthenia Antoinette Hague. Reprint edition (July 1995) Applewood Books.

* *The Chronological Tracking of the American Civil War; Per the Official Records of the War of the Rebellion.* Ronald A. Mosocco, Arthur W. Bergeron, designer. James River Publications, 1995.

The Civil War: A Narrative (three volumes). Shelby Foote. Random House, 1974.

* *Civil War Etchings.* William Forrest Dawson, ed. Oxford University Press, 1957; Dover Publications, 1994.

* *The Civil War Supply Catalogue: A Comprehensive Sourcebook of Products From the Civil War Era Available Today.* Alan Wellikoff. Crown Publishers, 1996.

Confederates in the Attic: Dispatches From the Unfinished Civil War. Tony Horwitz. Pantheon Books, 1998.

* *Diary of a Southern Refugee During the War: By a Lady of Virginia.* Judith W. McGuire, Jean V. Berlin (introduction). University of Nebraska Press, 1995 (reprint edition).

Echoes From the Battlefield: First-Person Accounts of Civil War Past Lives. Barbara Lane. A.R.E. Press, 1996.

* *Ersatz in the Confederacy: Shortages and Substitutes on the Southern Homefront.* (Southern Classics Series). Mary Elizabeth Massey, Barbara L. Bellows (introduction). University of South Carolina Press, 1993 (reprint edition).

* *The Expansion of Everyday Life, 1860–1876.* Daniel E. Sutherland. Harper and Row, 1989.

* *Fighting Men of the Civil War.* William C. Davis. Salamander Books, 1989; University of Oklahoma Press, 1998.

Heroines of Dixie: Spring of High Hopes. Katharine M. Jones, ed. Mockingbird Books, 1955.

Heroines of Dixie: Winter of Desperation. Katharine M. Jones, ed. Mockingbird Books, 1987.

* *How the Other Half Lives: Studies Among the Tenements of New York.* Jacob August Riis, 1890. Dover Publications, 1971.

Lee. Douglas Southall Freeman. Collier Books, 1997 (reprint edition).

Lee's Lieutenants: A Study in Command. Douglas Southall Freeman. Scribner, 1997 (reprint edition).

* *Letters of a Civil War Soldier.* George W. Stilwell. Dorrance Publishing Company, 1997.

* *The North Fights the Civil War: The Home Front.* J. Matthew Gallman. I. R. Dee, 1994.

* *The Official Price Guide to Civil War Collectibles.* Richard Friz. House of Collectibles, 1995.

* *The Price of Union.* Herbert Agar. Houghton Mifflin Company, 1950.

* *Queen Victoria's Enemies (4): Asia, Australasia and the Americas.* Ian Knight. Osprey Publishing, 1990.

* *A Rebel War Clerk's Diary.* John B. Jones, Earl Schenck Miers, ed., and Earl Schenck, ed. Louisiana State University Press, 1993 (reprint edition).

* *Redlegs: The U.S. Artillery From the Civil War to the Spanish-American War, 1861–1898.* John P. Langellier. Stackpole Books, 1998.

* *Shots That Hit: A Study of U.S. Coast Guard Marksmanship, 1790–1985.* William R. Wells, II. U.S. Coast Guard, Historian's Office, 1993.

Sojourns of a Patriot: The Field and Prison Papers of an Unreconstructed Confederate. Richard Bender Abell and Fay Adamson Gecik. Southern Heritage Press, 1998.

* *Three Years With the 92d Illinois: The Civil War Diary of John M. King.* Claire E. Swedberg, ed. Stackpole Books, 1999.

* *U.S. Fighting Forces: A Complete History of the U.S. Army, Marine Corps, Navy, Air Force.* Mark Lloyd, Robin Cross, Richard Humble, Bernard Fitzsimons, and Derek Avery, ed. Chevprime, 1989.

* *Weapons: An International Encyclopedia From 5000 B.C. to 2000 A.D.* The Diagram Group. St. Martin's Press, 1990.

* *What People Wore: 1,800 Illustrations From Ancient Times to the Early Twentieth Century.* Douglas Gorsline. Dover Publications, 1994.

PART FOUR: NOVELS AND LITERATURE

A great body of literature has been inspired by the Civil War and includes everything from works by witnesses to the Civil War, like Ambrose Bierce, to history in the form of literature, like the novels of Michael and Jeff Shaara, to the alternative histories of Harry Turtledove and Peter Tsouras. Such works can show writers the directions others have taken and serve as models to be emulated, improved upon or even avoided.

As far as using works of fiction as source material, it is the works of fiction that came out in the years following the war, often written by former soldiers, that are most likely to be useful. Of these, the first to really convey a sense of realism was *Miss Ravenel's Conversion From Secession to Loyalty*, by former Union soldier John William DeForest. Many better known works of fiction can also shed light on period attitudes and details of life. Among these are the works of Stephen Crane (e.g., *The Red Badge of Courage*) and Ambrose Bierce (who also produced a body of valuable nonfiction).

One unfortunate product of Civil War literature is the inflexible, predictable way Civil War leaders are depicted. This phenomena is perhaps more profound in Civil War novels than in any other genre except for mythology or religion, and is subject to the same sort of rigid canon. Just as Jesus or Zeus are only depicted or described in certain ways by the pious, so too are figures from the Civil War. While these dogmatized depictions may ultimately be based upon the actual characteristics of these people, their traits have become exaggerated and their characteristics and motivations are rarely examined critically.

For example, was Robert E. Lee really so very humble, so excruciatingly quiet and cordial, so crushed by bearing the weight of the Confederacy upon his noble shoulders, as virtually every Civil War novelist would have us believe? Did Ulysses S. Grant really chain smoke cigars, as is so often described? Was Joshua Chamberlain really good-naturedly boyish and perpetually bewildered by his own successes, as Jeff Shaara asserts? Well, perhaps. However, I would check a few primary sources before depicting any of them these ways in my work. Maybe these characterizations are accurate; maybe they are not. But, as a reader, you will certainly not reveal any complete truths by reading only fictionalized, liturgical descriptions of these leaders, and as a writer you will not produce anything original if these characterizations serve as your only models. Do a bit of research and do not rely on novels as major sources of information.

An uncanny number of the following books are subtitled "A Novel of the Civil War" or something similar. Because this is evident from their presence on this list, I've omitted such subtitles.

Across Five Aprils. Irene Hunt. Berkley Publishing Group, 1991 (reissue edition).

Ambrose Bierce's Civil War. Ambrose Bierce. William McCann, ed. Wings Books, 1996.

Andersonville. MacKinlay Kantor. Harper and Row, 1955; Plume 1993.

Banished Children of Eve. Peter Quinn. Viking Penguin, 1994; Penguin, 1995.

Bring the Jubilee. Ward Moore. Ballantine Books, 1981.

Chickamauga, and Other Civil War Stories. Shelby Foote, ed. Delta Publishing, 1993.

Civil War Women. Frank McSherry Jr., Charles G. Waugh and Martin Greenberg, eds. August House, 1988.

Civil War Women II. Frank McSherry Jr., Charles G. Waugh and Martin Greenberg, eds. August House, 1997.

Cold Mountain. Charles Frazier. Atlantic Monthly Press, 1997.

The Confessions of Nat Turner. William Styron. Random House, 1967; Vintage, 1993.

Freedom. William Safire. Doubleday, 1987; Avon, 1988.

Gettysburg: An Alternate History. Peter G. Tsouras. Greenhill Books, 1997.

Gods and Generals. Jeff Shaara. Ballantine Books, 1996.

Gone With the Wind. Margaret Mitchell. Macmillan, 1936; Scribner, 1996.

The Guns of the South. Harry Turtledove. Del Rey, 1997.

How Few Remain. Harry Turtledove. Del Rey, 1997.

The Killer Angels. Michael Shaara. David McKay, 1974; Ballantine Books, 1993.

The Last Full Measure. Jeff Shaara. Ballantine Books, 1998.

Lincoln. Gore Vidal. Random House, 1984; Modern Library 1998.

Oldest Living Confederate Widow Tells All. Allan Gurganus. Knopf, 1984; Ballantine Books, 1990.

The Red Badge of Courage. Stephen Crane. Tor Books. 1895.

Shiloh. Shelby Foote. Dial Press, 1952; Vintage Books, 1991.

PART FIVE: TELEVISION AND FILM

To a large extent, people's perceptions of the Civil War are driven by movies, television programs and documentaries. Such films and television programs have helped popularize the Civil War and educate people about it. Unfortunately, they have also contributed to some skewed perceptions about the Civil War.

For example, most Civil War movies include scenes of Union and Confederate troops lined up against each other, opposing lines of well-fed, immaculately uniformed blue and gray soldiers, a few of the Southerners wearing straw hats or plaid shirts to reflect that faction's difficulties in fully clothing its men. While there were certainly battles that looked like this, such scenes tend to leave an inadequate impression of how these armies really appeared, as neither were really uniformed or equipped to a high enough cinematic standard (the chapter on uniforms and equipment describes what soldiers really looked like). And while many battles were fought in straight lines in open country, many more were fought by broken formations in forests, swamps and from within earthworks and other fortifications.

So why do filmmakers show these armies looking so much better than they really did and fighting differently than they did in actuality? One reason is that historical reenactors frequently fill the ranks of military units in films, and reenactors don't like to run around in homespun rags. Naturally, reenactors are also much better fed than typical Civil War soldiers, especially those of the Confederacy late in the war. So, even the best movies, like *Gettysburg, Glory* or *Andersonville,* or the most popular documentaries, like those aired on the History Channel, tend to show men who are better dressed, equipped and fed than those who really fought in the battles of the Civil War.

Also, to depict the soldiers of either side clothed in rags also begs a lot of questions that many directors clearly are not comfortable addressing. It is far easier to sell an audience on a scene of plump reenactors charging into battle in pristine uniforms and falling dramatically in an open field to an anthem of stirring music than it is to show men, ragged as scarecrows, struggling across broken ground, being shot to pieces with no background music but artillery fire and the groans of the dead and dying.

All of that said, there are many films and documentaries about the Civil War that are more or less accurate. Writers who wish to draw upon such media for inspiration, however, should hone a critical ability to separate fact from fiction.

Resources

Writers, students and historians have available to them an incredible array of information about the Civil War. A researcher's main challenge is not so much finding information as it is sorting through what is available and identifying what is most valuable.

· BOOKS

Dozens of books about the Civil War have come out since the war ended; many years, more books are published about the Civil War than about any other aspect of history, regardless of what is happening in the world or what historic anniversaries are then being celebrated.

A number of useful books are listed in Appendix Two, which includes a number of classics that have stood the test of time and some specialized sources that can hardly be improved upon. For example, some of the best sources of information about uniforms, equipment and other goods are catalogs (both those published in the nineteenth century and some published by modern manufacturers of reproduction clothing and dry goods).

Nonetheless, writers are encouraged to seek other sources as well. New books continue to be published, too, and writers have many ways of keeping up with what has been released, including best-seller lists and reviews in newspapers and other periodicals (especially Civil War and history publications). Various on-line booksellers also provide information services and will notify people by E-mail of new releases in subjects in which they have expressed interest.

PERIODICALS

In the United States today, dozens of nationally distributed magazines and other periodicals deal directly with the Civil War. Some of these have been around for several years, while others come and go; what is currently available can be easily determined by a quick perusal of a newsstand or bookstore magazine section. Readers unfamiliar with such magazines should try several to see which have the most enjoyable and useful style of writing and editing, and then, if desired, subscribe to one of them. Those who regularly buy several different genre magazines or subscribe to more than one or two quickly begin to see the same sorts of material, again and again.

Beyond publications directly concerned with the Civil War, there are many that deal with reenacting, history or geography that regularly or periodically run stories related to the conflict.

Reprints of a number of nineteenth-century publications are also available from time to time. For example, *Godey's Lady's Book*, a publication popular with homemakers during the Civil War, can provide writers with information about diet, recipes and women's day-to-day concerns. Reprints of it and other period publications are sometimes available, and copies can be found in some libraries.

WEB RESOURCES

At the threshold of the twenty-first century, writers have a vast array of resources available to them through the World Wide Web. Unfortunately, anything can end up on the Web, and some of what is available is poorly written, badly edited or just plain inaccurate. Thus, be very careful and discriminating when using the Web as a conduit for information.

Nonetheless, many good sources of information are on the Web, and the best can do things that conventional books cannot. For example, many Civil War sites include period music, giving researchers a taste of the songs Civil War soldiers played, sang and listened to.

Official U.S. government departmental and military Web sites are among the best sites available and contain background information on history, uniforms, ranks and other subjects of use to writers. Some of these, such as the U.S. Coast Guard Service and National Park Service sites, are packed with very useful information.

University and college sites also tend to be well written and edited and have fairly extensive, useful content; diaries and other historic texts, often accompanied by period art and illustrations, can often be found on such sites.

Many commercial and private organizations or individuals also maintain useful Civil War sites, many of them run by reenactment groups. It is amongst such sites, however, that researchers should exert the most caution. A few that have been around for some time and have extensive, reliable and useful content are listed next.

Everyday Life During the Civil War companion site:

http://www.LivingHistoryOnline.com/civilwar.htm

An on-line companion to the book that contains articles, additional resources, events, book reviews, texts of historical speeches and updated links to some of the best Civil War sites.

Archeology at Andersonville:

http://www.cr.nps.gov/seac/andearch.htm

Explores the site of the Civil War's most notorious prison camp.

The Carroll College Institute for Civil War Studies:

http://www.cc.edu/~civilwar/

Affiliated with Carroll College in Waukesha, Wisconsin, the Institute is a useful resource for students and scholars, especially with regard to the role of midwestern states in the Civil War.

The Civil War in Miniature:

http://www.civilwarmini.com

Contains articles, facts, maps, photographs, folklore, quizzes and a Civil War roundtable for discussions.

Civil War "ReEnact" Home Page:

http://www.reenact.org

Provides information about the war with particular attention to organizations that regularly reenact various aspects of the conflict.

Civil War Reenactors Home Page:

http://www.cwreenactors.com

Dedicated to the brave souls of the North and South who fought and died in the Civil War.

Department of the Navy Naval Historical Center:

http://www.history.navy.mil

Preserves, analyzes and interprets naval history.

Iron Guard:

http://www.skirmisher.com/SWORDS.htm

This retailer of Civil War-era swords often features articles, pictures and useful information on its site.

The Music of the American Civil War:
> http://www.geocities.com/Nashville/9958/civilwar.html
>> Contains sound files based on *The Civil War Songbook* by Richard Crawford and published by Dover Publications.

Reenactors of the American Civil War:
> http://www.home.inreach.com/mavgw/racw.htm
>> A nonprofit, living history organization based in northern California that is dedicated to both preserving and teaching about the Civil War.

Southeast Archeological Center's "The War Between the States (American Civil War) 1861–1865":
> http://www.cr.nps.gov/seac/civilwar.htm
>> A variety of useful information about the war in the southeastern states.

U.S. Army Institute of Heraldry:
> http://www.perscom.army.mil/tagd/tioh/page2~1.htm
>> Provides information about official government and military symbolic items, such as rank and unit insignia.

U.S. Army Center of Military History:
> http://www.army.mil/cmh-pg/default.htm

U.S. Coast Guard Historians' Office:
> http://www.uscg.mil/hq/g-cp/history/collect.html

U.S. Marine Corps:
> http://www.usmc.mil/

MAPS

Many sorts of maps are readily available today, from reprints of Civil War-era battle maps to modern maps that convey demographic or political information. Such tools can be an excellent resource for writers. For example, a period map that shows the placement of units on a battlefield and the subsequent movements can be invaluable in helping an author describe a battle sequence, including what characters saw and did. Or, a modern map that shows which Southern states seceded from the Union and when can reveal that none of those that actually bordered Union states joined the Confederacy until after the attack upon Fort Sumter.

HEIRLOOM SEEDS

Over the past several years, heirloom plants have become increasingly popular, and several seed companies now offer heirlooms varieties. With this ease of access, there is no reason not to give heirlooms a try. Writers with the inclination can grow Civil War-era fruits and vegetables for a historically accurate taste of the era. A listing of heirloom seed sources is available at the *Everyday Life During the Civil War* companion site, at http://www.LivingHistoryOnline.com/ civilwar.htm.

HISTORICAL SITES

Walking across Civil War battlefields and through nineteenth-century build-ings, and viewing the objects and clothes carried and worn by the people of the age, can be invaluable to an understanding of the war and its participants. Literally thousands of sites throughout the United States are associated with the Civil War, from major battlefields to the homes of generals and politicians. Several are listed next, many of them National Park Service sites.

Abraham Lincoln Birthplace National Historic Site

2995 Lincoln Farm Rd., Hodgenville, KY 42748, (502) 358-3137
http://www.nps.gov/abli/

In 1808, Thomas and Nancy Lincoln moved into a one-room log cabin near Sinking Spring and two months later, on Feb. 12, 1809, Abraham Lincoln was born. On July 17, 1916, Congress declared the area was a National Historic Site. Today, the 116.5 acre site (about one-third the size of the original farm) includes an early nineteenth-century Kentucky cabin.

Andersonville National Historic Site

Route 1, Box 800, Andersonville, GA 31711, (912) 924-0343
http://www.nps.gov/ande/

This is the only park in the National Park System that serves as a memorial to all American prisoners of war throughout the nation's history and in-cludes the historic prison site and a national cemetery. In authorizing this park, Congress stated that its purpose is "to provide an understanding of the overall prisoner of war story of the Civil War, to interpret the role of prisoner of war camps in history, to commemorate the sacrifice of Ameri-cans who lost their lives in such camps, and to preserve the monuments located within the site." Includes the National Prisoner of War Museum opened at Andersonville.

Andrew Johnson National Historic Site

P.O. Box 1088, Greenville, TN 37743, (423) 638-3551, (423) 638-9194 (fax)
http://www.nps.gov/anjo/

This site honors the life and work of the nation's seventeenth president (from 1865 to 1869), who led the country in the years following Lincoln's assassination and during the beginning of Reconstruction. Features of the site include Johnson's two homes, tailor shop and grave site.

Antietam National Battlefield

P.O. Box 158, Sharpsburg, MD 21782-0158, Programs and Information:

(301) 432-5124 Superintendent and Administration: (301) 432-7672
http://www.nps.gov/anti/

Established on August 30, 1890, this Civil War site marks the end of Gen. Robert E. Lee's first invasion of the North at the Battle of Antietam on Sept. 17, 1862, during which more men were killed than on any other single day of the war.

Appomattox Court House National Historical Park

P.O. Box 218, Appomattox, VA 24522, (804) 352-8987
http://www.nps.gov/apco/

The site of Robert E. Lee's April 9, 1865, surrender to Ulysses Grant. Authorized as a battlefield site June 18, 1930, and designated a national historical park on April 15, 1954.

Arlington House: The Robert E. Lee Memorial

% National Capital Parks-West, 1100 Ohio Dr., SW, Washington, DC 20242, (703) 557-0613, http://www.nps.gov/arho/index.htm

Today, the house that Robert E. Lee lived in for thirty years, which is also associated with the family of George Washington, is a memorial to Lee, who gained the respect of Northerners and Southerners through his service in the Civil War.

Brices Cross Roads National Battlefield Site (Baldwin, Mississippi)

Superintendent, Natchez Trace Parkway, RR 1, NT-143, Tupelo, MS 38801, (601) 680-4025, http://www.nps.gov/brcr/

Confederate cavalry was employed with extraordinary skill here during the June 10, 1864 battle at this site, during which Union forces attempted to prevent Southern troops from disrupting Federal supply routes.

Chickamauga and Chattanooga National Military Park (Fort Oglethorpe, Georgia, and Chattanooga, Tennessee)

P.O. Box 2128, 3370 LaFayette Rd., Fort Oglethorpe, GA 30742, (706) 866-9241, http://www.nps.gov/chch/

America's first National Military Park, established in 1890, honors the Civil War soldiers who fought for control of Chattanooga at the Battle of Chickamauga in September 1863 and the Battles for Chattanooga in November 1863. The park includes two visitors centers and more than 8,200 acres in both Georgia and Tennessee. Chickamauga was considered the last major Confederate victory in the West, but it was hollow, as Union forces gained control of Chattanooga just two months later.

Clara Barton National Historic Site

5801 Oxford Rd., Glen Echo, MD 20812, (301) 492-6245
http://www.nps.gov/clba/

This site commemorates the life of the founder of the American Red

Cross. From her house in Glen Echo, she organized and directed relief efforts for victims of natural disasters and war.

Fairfax Station Railroad Museum

11200 Fairfax Station Rd., Fairfax Station, VA 22039, (703) 425-9225, http://www.fairfax-station.org

Houses Civil War, Red Cross and historic railroading memorabilia along with a variety of artifacts found in and around the Civil War-era station.

Ford's Theatre National Historic Site

511 Tenth St. NW, Washington, DC 20004, (202)426-6924 http://www.nps.gov/foth/

On April 14, 1865, John Wilkes Booth shot President Abraham Lincoln, who had been attending a play at this theater. Lincoln was carried to a small bedroom in the back of the Petersen House, a boarding house across the street from the theater, where he died early the next morning. Today, both the theater and house are preserved as national historic sites.

Fort Donelson National Battlefield

P.O. Box 434, Dover, TN 37058-0434, (931) 232-5348 http://www.nps.gov/fodo/

On February 16, 1862, the Union army in Tennessee, under the command of Ulysses S. Grant, won its first major victory of the Civil War. Capture of Fort Donelson and approximately thirteen thousand Confederate soldiers delivered a devastating blow to the Rebel cause, set the stage for the Union's invasion of the deep South and catapulted Grant into national prominence.

Dry Tortugas National Park

P.O. Box 6208, Key West, FL 33041, (305) 242-7700 http://www.nps.gov/drto/

Built 1846–1866 to help protect the Florida Straits, this is the largest all-masonry fortification in the Western Hemisphere. It served as a prison during and after the Civil War.

Fort Pulaski National Monument

P.O. Box 30757, U.S. Highway 80 East, Savannah, GA 31410-0757, (912) 786-5787, http://www.nps.gov/fopu

On April 11, 1862, defensive strategy changed forever when Union rifled cannon first overcame a masonry fortification after only thirty hours of bombardment. Named for Revolutionary War hero Count Casimir Pulaski, Fort Pulaski took some eighteen years to build and was the first military assignment for a young second lieutenant fresh from West Point, Robert E. Lee. This remarkably intact example of nineteenth-century military architecture contains an estimated 25 million bricks and 7½ foot-thick walls.

Fort Sumter National Monument

1214 Middle St., Sullivan's Island, SC 29482, (843) 883-3123

http://www.nps.gov/fosu

On April 12 and 13, 1861, the first engagement of the Civil War took place here. After thirty-four hours of fighting, the Union garrison of the fort surrendered it to the Confederacy. From 1863 to 1865, the Confederates at Fort Sumter withstood a twenty-two-month siege by Union forces, during which most of the fort was reduced to brick rubble. It was declared a national monument in 1948.

Fredericksburg and Spotsylvania National Military Park

120 Chatham Lane, Fredericksburg, VA 22405, (540) 373-6122

http://www.nps.gov/frsp

About 110,000 men were killed, wounded or captured during the four major battles fought in the vicinity of Fredericksburg, Virginia, making it the bloodiest ground on the North American continent. In 1927 the Congress established the site to commemorate the heroic deeds of the men engaged at the battles of Fredericksburg, Chancellorsville, Wilderness and Spotsylvania Court House. Today, the park encompasses nearly nine thousand acres, making it the largest military park in the world, and includes the historic structures of Chatham, Ellwood, Salem Church and the "Stonewall" Jackson Shrine.

General Grant National Memorial

Riverside Drive and 122nd Street, New York, NY 10003, (212) 666-1640

http://www.nps.gov/gegr/

Popularly known as Grant's Tomb, this is the final resting place of Ulysses S. Grant and his wife, Julia Dent Grant. Designed by architect John Duncan, the granite-and-marble tomb was completed in 1897 and is the largest mausoleum in North America.

Gettysburg National Military Park

97 Taneytown Rd., Gettysburg, PA 17325, (717) 334-1124

http://www.nps.gov/gett/

Gettysburg was the site of the largest and bloodiest battle ever waged in the Western Hemisphere. It raged from July 1-3, 1863. More than fifty-one thousand soldiers were slain in a Union victory that successfully repulsed Robert E. Lee's second invasion of the North. It was Lee's last major effort to take the fighting out of Virginia and into Northern states.

Harpers Ferry National Historical Park

P.O. Box 65, Harpers Ferry, WV 25425, (304) 535-6298

http://www.nps.gov/hafe/

John Brown and the Civil War are major themes of this park, which became part of the National Park System in 1944 and covers more than

2,300 acres in the states of West Virginia, Maryland and Virginia.

Kennesaw Mountain National Battlefield Park

900 Kennesaw Mountain Dr., Kennesaw, GA 30144, (770) 427-4686 (770) 427-1760 (fax), http://www.nps.gov/kemo/

This 2,884 acre park preserves a battleground of the Atlanta Campaign.

Lincoln Boyhood National Memorial

P.O. Box 1816, Lincoln City, IN 47552, (812) 937-4541

http://www.nps.gov/libo/

Abraham Lincoln spent fourteen of the most formative years of his life and grew from youth into manhood on this southern Indiana farm. His mother, Nancy Hanks Lincoln, is buried here.

Lincoln Home National Historic Site

413 S. Eighth St., Springfield, IL 62701-1905, (217) 492-4241, ext. 221 for the Visitor Center, http://www.nps.gov/liho/

Abraham Lincoln's two-story home, the only one he ever owned, stands at the center of this park. The home, which has been restored to its 1860s appearance, was constructed in 1839 as a one-story cottage. The Lincolns lived in the house from 1844 until his election to the presidency in 1861. It stands in the midst of a four-block historic neighborhood that is being restored so the surroundings will appear much as Lincoln would have remembered them.

Manassas National Battlefield Park

12521 Lee Highway, Manassas, VA 20109-2005, (703) 361-1339

http://www.nps.gov/mana/

The battles of First and Second Manassas (Bull Run) were fought here July 21, 1861, and August 28-30, 1862. The 1861 battle, in which Confederate Gen. Thomas J. Jackson acquired his nickname "Stonewall," was the first test of Northern and Southern military prowess.

The Museum and White House of the Confederacy

1201 E. Clay St., Richmond, VA 23219, (804) 649-1861, http://www.moc.org

A great resource for anyone needing information about the South during the Civil War.

Pamplin Historical Park

6125 Boydton Plank Rd., Petersburg, VA 23803, 1(877)PAMPLIN, (804) 861-2408, (804) 861-2820, http://www.pamplinpark.org/

Includes a plantation house restored to its 1865 appearance, walking trails, and the National Museum of the Civil War Soldier.

Pea Ridge National Military Park

P.O. Box 700, Pea Ridge, AR 72751, (501) 451-8122, (501) 451-8635 (fax), (501) 451-0344 (TDD), http://www.nps.gov/peri/

This 4,300 acre park preserves the site of the March 7-8, 1862, battle that saved Missouri for the Union. Elkhorn Tavern, site of bitter fighting on both days, has been reconstructed on the site of the original. This is possibly the best preserved Civil War battlefield in the country.

Petersburg National Battlefield

1539 Hickory Hill Rd. Petersburg, VA 23803, (804) 732-3531

http://www.nps.gov/pete/

Petersburg became the site of the longest siege in U.S. history when Gen. Ulysses S. Grant failed to capture Richmond in early 1864. He settled in to subdue the Confederacy by surrounding Petersburg and cutting off Gen. Robert E. Lee's supply lines into Petersburg and Richmond. On April 2, 1865, 9½ months after the siege began, Lee evacuated Petersburg.

Richmond National Battlefield Park

3215 E. Broad St., Richmond, VA 23223, (804) 226-1981

http://www.nps.gov/rich/

From 1861 to 1865, Federal armies repeatedly attempted to capture Richmond, capital of the Confederacy, and end the Civil War. Three of those campaigns came within a few miles of the city. This park commemorates eleven different sites associated with those campaigns, including the battlefields of Gaines's Mill, Malvern Hill and Cold Harbor. Established in 1936, the park includes 763 acres of historic ground.

Shiloh National Military Park

1055 Pittsburg Landing, Shiloh, TN 38376, (901) 689-5696

http://www.nps.gov/shil/

Established in 1894 to preserve the scene of the first major battle in the West, fought April 6-7, 1862. This battle was a decisive victory for the Union forces when they advanced on and seized control of the Confederate railway system at Corinth, Mississippi. This park contains about four thousand acres and has within its boundaries the Shiloh National Cemetery.

Stones River National Battlefield and Cemetery

3501 Old Nashville Highway, Murfreesboro, TN 37129, (615) 893-9501, http://www.nps.gov/stri/

A fierce battle took place at Stones River from December 31, 1862, to January 2, 1863, and resulted in Union control of central Tennessee. Although the battle was tactically indecisive, it provided a much-needed boost to the North after the defeat at Fredericksburg. This 450 acre site includes Stones River National Cemetery, established in 1865, with more than six thousand Union graves; and the Hazen Monument, believed to be the oldest to the Civil War. Parts of Fortress Rosecrans, a large series of earthworks built after the battle, still stand.

Tupelo National Battlefield

% Natchez Trace Parkway, R.R. 1, NT-143, Tupelo, MS 38801, (601) 680-4025, http://www.nps.gov/tupe/

At this site on July 13-14, 1864, Confederate Gen. Nathan Bedford Forrest attempted to cut the railroad supplying the Union march on Atlanta.

Vicksburg National Military Park

3201 Clay St., Vicksburg, MS 39183-3495, (601) 636-0583

http://www.nps.gov/vick/

This park was established on February 21, 1899, to commemorate one of the most decisive battles of the American Civil War—the campaign, siege and defense of Vicksburg, waged from March 29 to July 4, 1863. Located high on the bluffs overlooking the Mississippi, Vicksburg was a fortress guarding the river and was known as "The Gibraltar of the Confederacy." Its surrender on July 4, 1863, coupled with the fall of Port Hudson, Louisiana, divided the South, and gave the North undisputed control of the Mississippi River. The battlefield is well preserved and includes more than 1,300 monuments and markers, reconstructed trenches and earthworks, one antebellum structure, more than 125 emplaced cannon, a restored Union gunboat (the USS *Cairo*) and the Vicksburg National Cemetery.

Wilson's Creek National Battlefield

6424 W. Farm Rd. 182, Republic, MO 65738, (417) 732-2662

http://www.nps.gov/wicr/

On August 10, 1861, the battle fought here was the first major Civil War engagement west of the Mississippi River and involved some five thousand Union and ten thousand Confederate troops, and was a nondecisive Confederate victory. With few exceptions, the 1,750 acre battlefield has changed little.

SONGS AND POETRY

The Civil War produced a large body of songs that reflected the attitudes of the period. Writers can go a long way toward understanding the people of the era by knowing the words to the songs they sang. Lyrics can also can add authenticity or flavor to stories when placed in the mouths of characters, penned by period songwriters or sung by regiments of soldiers.

Period songs reflect a wide range of sentiments and emotions, from patriotism and love of country, to derision of the enemy, to the melancholy and suffering that attended life in camp, on the march and in battle.

Songs that became popular during the Civil War included "John Brown's Body" (whose author is disputed, but which became popular with Northern soldiers upon the outbreak of war), "The Battle Cry of Freedom" (George Frederich Root, 1861) and "Marching Through Georgia" (Henry Clay Work, 1865).

Much poetry was also written about the war, and this tended to be a bit more critical than the songs. For example, "The Picket Guard" (Ethel Lynn Beers, 1861) is a sarcastic response to stories in Union papers about Gen. George McClellan's inability to advance against the Confederacy in the weeks (and ultimately months) after his defeat at Bull Run.

Poet Walt Whitman was one of the many people to tend wounded soldiers during the Civil War. He served as a volunteer assistant in a military hospital in Washington, DC. In his 1865 book of poems *Drum-Taps*, he incorporated scenes of battle described to him by convalescing soldiers.

SONG LYRICS

Dixie's Land

In the early years of the war, many popular songs were common to both sides. "Dixie's Land," written by Daniel Decatur Emmett, a Northerner, and now associated entirely with the South, was in 1861 widely sung on both sides. As the war progressed, however, and the opposing cultures became more and more separated from each other, songs became more partisan in nature.

I wish I was in the land of cotton,
Old times there are not forgotten;
   Look away! Look away! Look away, Dixie's Land!
In Dixie's Land where I was born in,
Early on one frosty morning,
   Look away! Look away! Look away, Dixie's Land!

CHORUS: *Then I wish I was in Dixie! Hooray! Hooray!*
In Dixie's Land I'll take my stand, to live and die in Dixie!
Away! Away! Away down South in Dixie!
Away! Away! Away down South in Dixie!

Old Missus married "Will the Weaver";
William was a gay deceiver!
   Look away! Look away! Look away, Dixie's Land!
But when he put his arm around her,
Smiled as fierce as a forty-pounder!
   Look away! Look away! Look away, Dixie's Land!

CHORUS

His face was sharp as a butcher's cleaver;
But that did not seem to grieve her!
   Look away! Look away! Look away, Dixie's Land!
Old Missus acted the foolish part
And died for a man that broke her heart!
   Look away! Look away! Look away, Dixie's Land!

CHORUS

Now here's a health to the next old missus
And all the gals that want to kiss us!

Look away! Look away! Look away, Dixie's Land!
But if you want to drive away sorrow,
Come and hear this song tomorrow!
 Look away! Look away! Look away, Dixie's Land!

CHORUS

There's buckwheat cakes and Injin batter,
Makes you fat or a little fatter!
 Look away! Look away! Look away, Dixie's Land!
Then hoe it down and scratch your gravel,
To Dixie's Land I'm bound to travel!
 Look away! Look away! Look away, Dixie's Land!

CHORUS

The Battle Hymn of the Republic

One of the most characteristic and stirring songs of the war, "The Battle Hymn of the Republic" was set to a popular drinking tune usually adapted to far more bawdy lyrics (e.g., one popular version of the time includes the line, "John Brown's body lies a moldering in his grave"). Its stirring words reflect some of the fervent beliefs and attitudes that prevailed during the war. Julia Ward Howe wrote it in November 1861 after being inspired by a review of Union troops and deciding the popular tune needed more redeeming words. It was first published in *The Atlantic Monthly* in 1862.

Mine eyes have seen the glory of the coming of the lord,
He is trampling out the vintage
Where the grapes of wrath are stored
He hath lossed his fateful lightning of his terrible swift sword,
His truth is marching on.

CHORUS: *Glory! Glory! Hallelujah!*
Glory! Glory! Hallelujah!
Glory! Glory! Hallelujah!
His truth is marching on.
I have seem him in the watchfires of a hundred circling camps,
they have builded Him an altar in the evening dews and damps.
I can read his righteous sentence by the dim and flaring lamps;
His day is marching on.

CHORUS

I have read a firey gospel Writ in burnished rows of steel

As ye deal with my condemners,
So with you my grace will deal;
Let the hero born of woman
Crush the serpent with his heel;
Since God is marching on.

CHORUS

He has sounded forth the trumpet that shall never sound retreat;
He is sifting out the hearts of men beneath his Judgement Seat.
Oh! Be swift, my soul to answer him, be jubilant, my feet!
Our God is marching on.

CHORUS

In the beauty of the lilies Christ was born across the sea
With a glory in his bosom
That transfigures you and me;
As he died to make men holy let us die to make men free,
While God is marching on.

CHORUS

Victory's Band

The following 1861 song by Dan Emmett reflects some of the vindictiveness that crept into songs as the war progressed. Sung to the tune of "Dixie's Land," its lyrics seem coarse and jingoistic when compared to those of the original.

We're marching under the Flag of Union,
Keeping step in brave communion!
March away! march away! away! Victory's band!
Right down upon the ranks of rebels,
Tramp them underfoot like pebbles,
March away! march away! away! Victory's band

CHORUS: *Oh! we're marching on to Victory!*
Hurrah! hurrah!
In Victory's band we'll sweep the land,
And fight or die for Victory!
Away! away!
We'll fight or die for victory!

The rebels want a mongrel nation,
Union and Confederation!
March away! march away! away! Victory's band!

But we don't trust in things two-sided,
And go for Union undivided,
March away! march away! away! Victory's band

CHORUS

We're marching down on Dixie's regions,
With freedom's flag and Freedom's legions.
March away! march away! away! Victory's band!
We're rolling down, a "Pending Crisis,"
With cannon-balls for Compromises,
March away! march away! away! Victory's band

CHORUS

Tenting on the Old Camp Ground

Written in 1864 by Walter Kittredge, this song, and many like it, is a striking counterpoint to the earlier patriotic songs.

Many commanders prohibited their soldiers from singing such songs based on the rationale that they lowered morale. However, these moves were misguided, as soldiers were still thinking the things expressed in the songs, even if they were deprived of an outlet for expressing them. Such prohibitions tended to be ineffective and short lived, in any case.

We're tenting tonight on the old Camp ground.
Give us a song to cheer
Our weary hearts, a song of home,
And friends we love so dear.

CHORUS: *Many are the hearts that are weary tonight,*
Wishing for the war to cease;
Many are the hearts looking for the right
To see the dawn of peace.
Tenting tonight,
Tenting tonight,
Tenting on the old Camp ground.

We're been tenting tonight on the old Camp ground,
Thinking of days gone by,
Of the lov'd ones at home that gave us the hand,
And the tear that said, "Good bye!"

CHORUS

We are tired of war on the old Camp ground,

Many are dead and gone,
Of the brave and true who've left their homes,
Others been wounded long.

CHORUS

We've been fighting today on the old Camp ground,
Many are lying near;
Some are dead and some are dying,
Many are in tears.

CHORUS: *Many are the hearts that are weary tonight,*
Wishing for the war to cease;
Many are the hearts looking for the right
To see the dawn of peace.
Dying tonight,
Dying tonight,
Dying on the old Camp ground.

INDEX